WANDERLUST

A Love Affair
with Five Continents

ELISABETH EAVES

SEAL PRESS

WANDERLUST
A Love Affair with Five Continents

Copyright © 2011 by Elisabeth Eaves

Published by
Seal Press
A Member of the Perseus Books Group
1700 Fourth Street
Berkeley, California

Library of Congress Cataloging-in-Publication Data

Eaves, Elisabeth, 1971-
Wanderlust : a love affair with five continents / by Elisabeth Eaves.
p. cm.
ISBN 978-1-58005-311-2
1. Voyages and travels. 2. Eaves, Elisabeth, 1971—Travel. 3. Women—Identity—Case studies. I. Title.
G465.E22 2011
910.4—dc22
2010039812

9 8 7 6

Cover design by Kimberly Glyder
Interior design by Domini Dragoone
Printed in the United States of America
Distributed by Publishers Group West

The author has changed some names and personal details to protect the privacy of those mentioned in the book.

PRAISE FOR *WANDERLUST* AND ELISABETH EAVES

"Whether the journey is emotional or geographic, Eaves again and again captures the exhilarating moment when the safe place is left behind and the new place is not yet arrived at—that 'in between' moment that contains the thrill of the journey."

—Andrew McCarthy, actor, director, and writer

"Even those of us who have read Elisabeth Eaves before and know what a poised writer she is will marvel at the elegance and embracing reach of *Wanderlust*. She conveys the nomadic romance of an adventurous soul traversing the vivid world and yet retains the intimacy of a voice confiding its secrets, taking you with her, smuggling you along. Once *Wanderlust* embarks, there'll be no place else you'd rather be."

—James Wolcott, cultural critic, *Vanity Fair*

"*Wanderlust* isn't as much a desire to travel as it is a force of nature that can course through a person's veins with such blinding power that there is nothing else in life more important. Elisabeth journeys into her self, and around the world, as she heeds the call of the open road—and her heart."

—Jen Leo, editor, *Sand in My Bra* series;
   and co-host of "This Week in Travel"

"Eaves tells a provocative story that explores the question of why we travel, and how the allure of far-flung places can turn into an obsession. Smart, soulful, and startlingly honest, *Wanderlust* takes the reader on a wild ride from Paris to Pakistan—and many points in between."

—Rolf Potts, author of *Vagabonding* and
   Marco Polo Didn't Go There

CONTENTS

part two: LUCK

part three: MOMENTUM

"Don't seek the water; get thirst."

—Rumi

PROLOGUE

*O*n an early December morning in 2005, as the Christmas lights faded and festive dark turned to gray daylight, I loaded four suitcases into a taxi on Avenue Montaigne. I went back upstairs and stepped into the parquet hall to take one last look at what was now my ex-apartment. The living room was too perfect, with its balconies, its marble fireplace, its fashionable but uninviting white sofa. I surveyed the emptiness, then locked the door from the outside and slipped the key back underneath, for my now ex-boyfriend to find. Another life was over, and I couldn't get back inside if I wanted to.

I flew back to Vancouver, where my parents met me at the luggage carousel. My four suitcases represented the household I'd acquired thus far in life. The most overstuffed among them had split open between Toronto and Vancouver. The handlers strung it up in red and white tape, but when it arrived on the carousel, the rip still gaped ominously, contents poised to escape, the whole bundle looking dangerously close to explosion. We took the suitcase to the Air Canada counter, where they provided us with an enormous clear plastic sack, into which I dumped the remaining physical artifacts of my existence: clothing, bags, boots, books. We gave the airline the broken suitcase, and four days later a new one, larger and sturdier than its predecessor, turned up on my parents' porch.

My life wouldn't be so easy to fix. I'd woken up at the age of thirty-four to realize that I wanted to go home, only to discover that I had no idea where that was.

Wanderlust, the very strong or irresistible impulse to travel, is adopted untouched from the German, presumably because it couldn't be improved upon. Workarounds like the French *passion du voyage* don't quite capture the same meaning. Wanderlust is not a passion for travel exactly; it's something more animal and more fickle— something more like lust. We don't lust after very many things in life. We don't need words like *worklust* or *homemakinglust.* But travel? Anatole Broyard put it perfectly in his essay "Being There": "Travel is like adultery: one is always tempted to be unfaithful to one's own country. To have imagination is inevitably to be dissatisfied with where you live . . . in our wanderlust, we are lovers looking for consummation." I spent a long time looking for the consummation Broyard describes, and the search was tied up with love itself. I traveled for love, and loved to travel, making it hard to disentangle cause from effect.

The American president Thomas Jefferson once cautioned his nephew against roaming. "Traveling makes men wiser, but less happy," he wrote in a letter. "When men of sober age travel, they gather knowledge, which they may apply usefully for their country, but they are subject ever after to recollections mixed with regret— their affections are weakened by being extended over more objects, and they learn new habits which cannot be gratified when they return home."

Had that happened to me? Would I never be gratified?

I wasn't so sure. It was true that I'd extended my affections far and wide. But I didn't think I would have sent home a warning like Jefferson's. I doubted that even he, who wrote to his nephew from Paris, would have traded in his own rambling.

As my taxi merged onto the Périphérique, I wondered what had propelled me. I wondered what wanderlust had done to me, and whether I'd followed it for too long.

LIBERATION

"It would be good to live in a
perpetual state of leave-taking,
never to go nor to stay, but to
remain suspended in that golden
emotion of love and longing; to be
missed without being gone, to be
loved without satiety. How
beautiful one is and how desirable;
for in a few moments one will
have ceased to exist."

—John Steinbeck,
The Log from the Sea of Cortez

PART ONE

ON INSPIRATION
chapter one

I met Graham on an airplane. He was seventeen and off to England with his rugby team, a posse of blond boys in blue-striped jerseys sitting near the back of our jet. I was sixteen, on a school trip to Paris and London, the first time I'd be abroad without my parents. We both came from suburbs east of Vancouver, which was where we embarked. After takeoff we talked sitting on the floor of the jet, amid our respective classmates, pretending a more sophisticated knowledge of our upcoming itineraries than we actually possessed. By the time we landed in London, where our paths diverged, it was clear to me that travel without parental supervision led directly to the exchange of phone numbers with cute boys. But I was quickly caught up in my two-week trip, then exams on my return home, and didn't expect to hear from the guy on the plane. I was surprised the first time he called and asked me to go to a movie, all the more so when a month later he asked me to his graduation ball. Graham hadn't yet become unique in my mind. He was athletic and had a car and listened to heavy metal; his misbehaviors were run-of-the-mill, like cutting class and smoking cigarettes or pot. We kissed passionately on the couch in my TV room. He teased me about the big words I used ("insatiable"), and I made fun of the names of his bands ("Anthrax").

I'd never been to a formal dance and was flattered to be asked; I immediately said yes. My mother altered a blue and black satin prom dress that had belonged to my cousin, and I was granted special dispensation to stay out as late as I liked. When three in the morning rolled around, and we found ourselves at an after party at someone's house, Graham volunteered to have his dad chauffeur us to our respective homes. Part of me wanted to stay out even though I could barely stay awake. I wanted to use my new freedom to its maximum, to exploit it as outrageously as I could, but I wasn't sure what that would mean. The part of me falling asleep accepted the ride and went home.

We didn't become boyfriend and girlfriend; we didn't go all the way. But we stayed in touch over the summer, while I worked at a clothing store in a Burnaby shopping mall. Graham became different in my mind from other boys, as I learned about his singular ambition: He wanted to go away and travel. Sometimes we talked on the phone about his desire, which over those first months I knew him, progressed from a hazy idea to a concrete plan. Neither of us knew anyone else who aimed to do the same thing. Many of our classmates seemed to have no plans at all, and those who did expected to go straight to university. As I entered my senior year, he scrimped and saved, working two jobs and living with his dad, so that he could buy himself a ticket to see the world. I heard less and less from Graham, until finally he called one day in the winter to tell me that he was leaving. I admired the way he'd made his own wish come true.

It wasn't until after he left, and began sending me notes from afar, that I began to really fall for him. First from Hawaii, then from Fiji, then from Australia, he mailed regular light-as-dust aerograms, those pale blue, prestamped sheets from the post office that are both stationery and envelope combined. He wrote in a dense ballpoint scrawl about palm trees, which he'd never before seen; about scuba diving, which he'd never before done; and about his evolving plans. Once he mailed a photograph of himself, now with longer hair and darker skin, accompanied by a letter saying he was living in a trailer and picking fruit. From my circumscribed life of homework and curfews and college applications, I became so captivated by Graham's voyage—by the fact that you could just *do* that, go off into the world and let it carry you along—that after a while I couldn't be sure where wanting him stopped and wanting to be him began.

I was admitted to some Canadian universities, but chose instead to go to the University of Washington, across the border and a few hours' drive south. Going to Seattle, and the United States, represented a bigger, broader world. I immediately started taking an 8:00 AM Arabic class, during which I often fell asleep. Part of my desire to take Arabic was that it was the more distant, exotic thing. I already spoke French and Spanish, and had traveled in Europe with my family. We'd also been to Turkey when I was fourteen, and that had stoked an appetite to see what was farther East. The architecture in Istanbul had left an indelible impression. I was so awestruck after visiting the Topkapi Palace that as I gazed back at the Golden Horn from our ferry, skimming the strait where sultans had drowned their predecessors' concubines, I shushed my mother when she tried to talk to me.

If buildings could look so radically different, with their Ottoman minarets, Byzantine domes, and serpentine blue-tiled halls, then it stood to reason that much more could be different too. Seattle was disappointingly unexotic; its palette was gray and green like Vancouver's. Since I was raised to regard college as obligatory, it didn't occur to me that I could leave and do something else instead, even as I envied Graham his freedom. But I could take Arabic, and a language was another kind of new world. Through study I hoped to quench that urge that he was satisfying through actual travel.

I joined a sorority and gravitated to new friends: to Kim, whose goal in life, at eighteen, was to get to Germany and a boy named Sasha, who had been an exchange student at her high school; and Katerina, the daughter of Czech émigrés, who told us about the Velvet Revolution unfolding that very fall. It was 1989, and we were all hearing from our parents and teachers that the world as we knew it was changing. But we didn't really know what it had been like in the first place.

As sorority sisters we were expected to participate in the Greek system. Inside the house that meant occasional meetings and sometimes dressing up for dinner, and outside it meant an endless round of drinking parties at the neighboring fraternities. I considered all new experience good experience, and threw myself in, carousing up and down the leafy streets with Kim and Katerina, looking for the party with the biggest crowd, the best music, or the most freely flowing alcohol. Sometimes I'd meet someone funny or interesting, with a story to tell about driving his car to California or spending a semester in France. The Greek system, though, quickly came to seem like a bubble, and most of the stories in which I pretended to seem interested revolved around the last drinking party. Here we were, released from adult oversight for the first time in our lives, and our social activity of choice was to rove the same five-block radius over and over, drinking insipid beer. The novelty of moving from Vancouver to Seattle quickly wore off, and I couldn't shake the feeling that the world was elsewhere.

My sorority mail room, which also housed the telephone switchboard, was the node that connected us to the outside world. Juniors and seniors took turns staffing it, sorting the mail and announcing phone calls and visitors over a PA system that reached through the upper floors. If a "visitor" was announced, that meant a girl; "guest" was the code word for boy. I was thrilled the first time a letter from Graham found its way to my sorority mailbox, and afterward started checking my mail more often and with more eager anticipation. He'd arrived in New Zealand and was hitchhiking from town to town. His letters put me in touch with a way of living that was more spontaneous and adventurous than my own.

It was my mom who first floated the idea of Spain. Her friend Janet, a Canadian who'd married a Spaniard, worked as a preschool teacher in Valencia, and she mentioned that some parents at her school wanted English-speaking summer nannies. My mother had barely finished saying the words when the idea took visceral hold: I wanted to—I *had* to—go. I was surprised that it was she, whom I still associated with curfews and groundings, who proposed the Spanish scheme, but she was more sensitive to my restlessness than I knew. And my parents trusted Spain; they trusted Janet and her husband, Manolo.

For me, Spain was a happy childhood memory. It was the place that had showed me, for the first time, that when you were somewhere else, you could be someone else.

❋ ❋ ❋

I was nine and my brother Gregory was five when my parents moved us to Rocafort, just outside of Valencia, where my father would work during his academic sabbatical. We lived in a white stucco villa, and other than a handful of houses on our dirt lane, were surrounded for miles by orange groves. The scent of oranges mingled with diesel fumes to this day makes me think of Spain.

My parents enrolled me at a three-room public school in Roca-fort. I spoke no Spanish, and at first spent my lunch hours sitting on the banister of the stairs leading down to the concrete school yard, surveying my running, shrieking classmates from on high. When they tried to talk to me, I gave them blank stares, but they were persistent. One day a ringleader named Maria Teresa approached me again and started talking. This time, to my surprise, I understood what she was saying: She wanted me to come play hopscotch. After weeks of incubation, my Spanish had sprung to life fully formed, and it operated like a reflex, subliminal and involuntary. I hadn't heard Maria Teresa's words and translated them into English; I'd just understood.

At home my father brought my brother and me Tintin, Asterix, and Smurf comic books in Spanish, as well as *Guerreros del Anti-faz,* a clash-of-civilizations-themed comic in which a Christian hero battles the Moors. At first he read to us from them, in part to prac-tice his own Spanish, but I complained and rolled my eyes when he stopped to explain grammatical points. Soon Gregory and I were reading the books ourselves.

Tintin, with his wild foreign adventures, was one of my first literary heroes. With his sidekick Captain Haddock, an irascible drunk, Tintin went to America, Egypt, Congo, Tibet, China, a South Pacific island, the ocean floor, and the moon. He also solved scientific mysteries and ancient archaeological riddles. In my favorite book, *Tintin en el Pais del Oro Negro,* the intrepid boy-explorer dis-covers oil in Arabia. I reread books like *Vuelo 714 Para Sydney* and *Tintín y el Lago de los Tiburones* dozens of times, looking for some hint of how I might make my life more like his.

A few months after my language breakthrough on the hopscotch grid, I was playing in the yard of my friend Amparo's apartment, in the next village over from Rocafort. Her friends asked me where I was from. I told them Canada, and tried to explain about it being a foreign country, near the United States, but they howled in disbelief. "You're from Rocafort!" they screeched. When I absorbed the meaning of this turn of events, I was electrified. I still stood out as a white-blond, self-dressed ragamuffin among my groomed and cologned classmates, but I sounded just like them. I could pass as something I wasn't. I could be two people. It could be that all my subsequent travel has been an attempt to recapture the feeling of that first time.

When the school year ended, we spent the summer touring Europe and Morocco in our Volkswagen van. My parents made us feel like we were helping direct the expedition. I'd study maps and go through lists of campgrounds, urging them to take us to one with a swimming pool. Gregory collected bottle caps from everywhere we went, and I begged to have my picture taken with a cobra. By day we traipsed around cathedrals or Roman ruins. At night my brother and I took the top bunk and my parents took the one below, and as it got hotter, we slept with the door open to the night. Every day we were in our home, and every day we were somewhere new.

I had a game I liked to play in the campgrounds, many of which were set up as vast grids, echoing the Roman fortresses that once dotted the region. (I learned my Roman history from *Asterix*.) Once I was permitted to walk to the bathhouse by myself, I made getting lost a deliberate goal. For example, if I knew I should go right to get back to our van, I'd go left instead, and take a series of wrong turns with the aim of becoming disoriented. I'd wander amid the maze of tricked-out campers and families grilling their dinners, admiring accessories I thought we should have, like a tent that attached to a parked trailer to create a covered front porch. When I knew I was really lost, not just pretend lost, I'd try to find my way back. The best moments in this manufactured joy were when I confidently believed I was on the right trail back to our van—then discovered that I was lost again. Really lost.

We returned to Canada the next school year, and to the house we'd rented out. My mother cried: She couldn't find some of her things, while others had broken. I entered the fifth grade, where I took an immediate dislike to my teacher. Getting home was an all-around disappointment. I was outgrowing comic books, but Gregory carefully collected and organized all of our Spanish literature on his shelf. I'd sometimes go and pick one of the *Tintin*s, and mull where to someday go.

✼ ✼ ✼

In February of my freshman year of college, Graham returned from his twelve-month trip. Our relationship had been mostly chaste before he left, no more intimate than kisses. As it became purely epistolary, though, my longing to see him had built up. My desire was inextricable from his having gone away. When he called and told me he'd returned, I made a plan to see him on my next trip to Vancouver.

He had no car, so I borrowed my parents' Taurus and picked him up on the road outside his father and stepmother's wooded trailer park. It was a typical Vancouver winter day; a granite sky pressed down. He looked very different from when I'd first met him, now deeply tanned and with curly blond hair past his shoulders. It was pulled back into a ponytail, and he wore a heavy dark overcoat against the chill—an oilskin, souvenir of Australia. I thought he looked great on a superficial level, and his transformation was also reassuring deeper down. It told me you could go and invent yourself. Our parents and schools, these wooded roads, this city, didn't have to be the whole story.

I felt skittish and excited as he got into the car, and we spent a long few moments staring at each other and nervously laughing. He'd brought a mix tape with no heavy metal whatsoever, and envelopes full of photographs to show me, but we had no idea where to go. Around us the cold damp forest of Anmore tapered into suburban sprawl. The idea of a mall was abhorrent. We decided to drive all the way across Port Moody, Burnaby, and Vancouver to one of the beaches of Stanley Park, for no reason, really, other than our need to have a destination.

As he told me his stories, images lodged in my mind as surely as if they had been my own memories: Graham waiting on a table in a long white apron; Graham jumping off a bridge over a gorge; Graham driving a Volkswagen van—which he called a "combi"—at sunrise, with two English girls asleep in the back and Roxy Music playing on the tape deck. He'd gone until he had no more money, worked, then gone on again.

Around the time of Graham's return, my summer plans were falling into place, and so I had exciting news to share. I'd spend the months between my freshman and sophomore years working for a Valencia couple with a two-year-old girl and a four-year-old boy. They had a summer home in a beach town called Moraira, on the Costa Blanca between Valencia and Alicante. Graham beamed, taking pleasure on my behalf. He, too, was already set on going away again. At first the idea had been just an inkling. After all, he'd only flown home a few weeks before. Now, after penniless, carless winter days in an isolated trailer park, failing to connect with the friends he could rustle up, he was confirmed in his plan. He'd stay only long enough to save up money. This time he'd go in the other direction, to London. His antipodean trip had stoked his desire for more, clueing him in to how much more of the world there was to see.

A high school friend of his attended my university and lived in a fraternity house nearby. Several weeks after we first reunited, Graham borrowed a car to drive to Seattle, and arranged to stay with Paul for a couple of nights. For a few hours I was able to smuggle him upstairs in my sorority, to the living space I shared with several roommates (I slept elsewhere in the house in a dorm room), where we lolled on a quilted bunk amid an upperclassman's cushions and teddy bears. Apropos of nothing, he looked up and said, "I love you," and it dawned on me: That's what this was—this longing, this excitement, this frisson at the sound of his name, the wanting to talk about him all the time to Kim and Katerina, who always indulged me and listened. I had had boyfriends, but this was something new. I was happy but also alarmed, suddenly and for the first time realizing that I had no control—of my feelings, or of this other person with whom they were so bound up. I felt immensely vulnerable, and wondered how I could make myself feel less so. I asked him to always be honest with me. I thought we could last forever—not necessarily as lovers but as something, maybe friends, maybe in some new form of relationship I'd never heard of. Maybe this was when people starting calling one another "soul mates." Of course he couldn't promise not to hurt me, but he didn't know that at the time.

Love was immediately associated with travel, now between Seattle and Vancouver. On one of my trips I was able to stay in his room in his father's home. Now we finally went where we had known for months, or maybe years, we were headed. I was newly nervous and awkward as he removed my clothing piece by piece, and I did the same for him. We'd both imagined ourselves confident and experienced people of the world, in my case on no grounds whatsoever.

I saw him a few more times on weekends that spring, and in the weeks after my final exams. I marveled at our extraordinary privilege.

I must have, I realized, been passing in-love people all the time, without understanding their world. I didn't want to exit this place of warmth and pleasure, didn't, in fact, understand that you could. I couldn't imagine why you might have to, because to be in love felt expansive. It included the whole world, made anything possible. I was so happy about two things, the way I felt about Graham and my upcoming trip to Spain, that it didn't immediately occur to me that they might be at odds. I didn't anticipate the pain of parting ways.

The night before I was to fly, I drove Graham back to his father's place and stayed too late, feeling like a hollow was opening up in my chest every time I tried to leave. Finally I sped home, sobbing all the way. Halfway along Barnet Highway, between Burnaby Mountain and the inlet shore, sirens invaded the haze of my emotional emergency, and I pulled over. The officer asked me what was wrong. I took a moment to bring my breathing under control, then choked out, "I just said good-bye."

"Ya just said good-bye, eh?" he repeated back, not cruelly, and handed me a ticket. "Try to slow down now, okay?"

ON WANTING MORE

chapter two

Maria José taught engineering, and Toni was a dentist; they were in their forties. They spent most of the year in Valencia, but in the summer retreated to a breezy, white stucco hillside home in Moraira, where Toni also kept a practice. The children were named for their parents. Maria José Jr., at two a tottering bundle of baby fat, was sandy-haired and blue-eyed like her mother, while Antonito, at four, had his father's tawny skin and black hair. Maria José's parents would come to visit for weeks on end, as would her sister. Toni's parents had a house nearby. I was unsure about my job description, but it seemed to be: Be around most of the time, speak English to the kids, and baby-sit solo as needed.

I was given a cubby perched on the roof of the two-story home. To get there I exited the main floor of the house onto a veranda, then climbed a set of outdoor stairs. The room was just big enough for a single bed, a shelf, and a chair. Its chief attraction was the wide window, which gave me a panoramic view. Moraira sits on a south-facing bay, and the house was on a hill on the east side, so I could see the scrubby, sand-color hills that surrounded the town, a tumble of white stucco homes with red-tiled roofs, and the Mediterranean, which shifted from iridescent gray in the dawn to bright aquamarine in the late morning. When I first took in the view—mine for the next two months—I felt the charge of dumb luck. The next minute I felt lonely. Here I was, queen of my castle, with no Graham, no one to share.

The family had a summer routine with almost no daily variation. Every morning after breakfast, I loaded up on towels and water toys and walked the children down the hill to the beach, where we set up camp under an umbrella. Sometimes Maria José Sr. walked with us, and sometimes she came a little later. Sometimes the children's grandparents were there too, making me feel particularly useless, so keen were they to baby-sit. In the early afternoon we returned home and had lunch. Afterward I took the children to the swimming pool down the street.

Then the most chaotic and work-intensive portion of the day began. Both children had to be bathed, dressed, and combed in preparation for the hours ahead. Antonito was manageable, but Maria José Jr. usually chose this time of day to pitch a fit. Her mother discouraged napping during the day in hopes that she would sleep at night, so she was always exhausted, and screamed and sobbed until she ran out of steam. Toni would come home from work during this period, and by seven o'clock, somehow all five of us managed to be dressed and ready to face the evening.

Their nightly routine was as fixed as their daytime schedule, and I usually accompanied them. From the house we drove down the hill, past an enclave called El Portet and the beach I went to every day, over a rocky outcropping, and down into the center of Moraira, a village with pharmacies and ice cream parlors, a marina, a cathedral, and pedestrian plazas lined with restaurants that served whole fried fish and paella. After parking we went for a walk on the waterfront, sometimes stopping to talk to their friends. Maria José tried to introduce me to young people she thought would be simpatico, like a nanny from France, who told me she was granted a full day off every week, and an obese Californian brunette, Abby, who along with her brother was staying with a Spanish host family as part of a student exchange.

Always, we ended up at a restaurant called Casa Dorita, sitting outside on the cathedral plaza, amid a large group of Maria José and Toni's friends. At first they asked me polite questions about where I was from and what I studied, but their attention quickly returned to things that mattered, which mostly consisted of news about their children and gossip about their circle. I couldn't blame them. Common ground eluded us, and my Spanish was too creaky to bridge the gap as a sparkling conversationalist.

Casa Dorita was family-run, named for the matriarch, Dora. Three of her kids worked in the restaurant. Pepe, nineteen, and Nuria, seventeen, took turns tending bar and waiting tables, while their older sister—also Dora, in her twenties—worked in the kitchen with her fiancé. Pepe had bristly brown hair and a five o'clock shadow, and was immediately friendly, asking me about Seattle and patiently waiting out my answers. He was doing his *mili*—his military service—by day, which involved a lot of zipping around in a Zodiac on maneuvers. Sometimes they pulled in at El Portet Beach, where I took the children. He said he would look for me there.

My employers' version of family life was fascinating and strange. I couldn't imagine my parents so socially engaged, every day of the week, and I'd never lived with extended family so close: Cousins and grandparents were people I saw at most a few times a year. But observation of the Spaniard in his natural habitat could hold my interest for only so long. About a week in, it became clear that I wouldn't have any days off. Nor did I really have any freedom of movement. I could walk to the beach or swimming pool, but the center of town was too far. When I ran out of sunscreen, I couldn't even do something as simple as go buy some myself—I had to ask Maria José, or arrange to be taken to town. I wasn't sure what I'd expected of the family—sightseeing trips?—but I was boggled at the tight circle that formed their world. With a growing sense of alarm, I saw that this was going to be my summer. My days were spent talking to a four-year-old, and my evenings to adults who were older than me and alien, or reading the handful of novels I'd brought. If I stayed in I could read, but I feared running out of English books, since I had no way to get more. This wasn't the way it was meant to be at all. I wanted adventure. But as the baby-sitter, I was also baby-sat. My tower, with its glamorous and enviable view—a view to write home about, which I did, in misleadingly jaunty tones—was a jail.

I had to take emergency action. I sensed a possible loophole in my well-monitored world, and that was the nighttime. After dinner Toni and Maria José couldn't possibly need me—couldn't possibly demand me, I thought, after I'd been on tap all day—and going out at night seemed to be accepted local young-adult practice. Abby, the Californian, had told me that her brother went out all night with his Spanish hosts. All I needed was an entrée. A native guide.

One night as the extent of my prisonerlike status was sinking in, we were down in the town taking the evening *paseo*, and, unusually, Maria José and Toni accepted an invitation at a restaurant that was not Casa Dorita. Antonito began playing with a friend, and little Maria José fussed noisily and tried to climb onto her mother's lap. I saw an opportunity, possibly my only one for who knew how many more days, and I didn't want to spend another evening in my tower. "Why don't I take her for a walk?" I suggested. Her mother looked grateful, and I picked up the child and sat her astride my hip. "Now don't you start screaming," I whispered to her as we walked away.

I had maybe twenty minutes to accomplish my goal, plus the possibility of toddler mayhem at any second. I didn't think I could have the conversation I hoped to have with Pepe in full view of Maria José, Toni, and their crowd, so I had to succeed before they descended on Casa Dorita. I rounded the corner toward the restaurant rehearsing Spanish words in my head. Luckily Pepe was behind the bar, which opened onto the plaza. *"Hola,"* I said. He tickled Maria José under the chin, free from the intergenerational fear that afflicts my own culture. He asked me what I'd been up to, and seemed genuinely distressed to learn that I'd been neither to a certain beach bar nor to a particular *discoteca*. "Why don't you come out later tonight?"

Maria José and Toni accepted the idea right away. Pepe was a known quantity, son of their longtime restaurateurs, and would deliver me home. And so my tour of Costa Blanca nightlife began later that evening, on the back of Pepe's motorcycle.

❋ ❋ ❋

When I realized that Maria José Sr. and Toni didn't mind at all if I went out after the children were in bed, I started abusing the privilege. Regarding the night as the only time that was my own, I maximized it by staying out late, often until three or four in the morning. The consequence, since I had to get up when the children did, was that soon my days were passing in a sleepy haze. But that never stopped me from going out again. At 11:00 PM, all I could think about were the two or maybe five hours of freedom stretching ahead. After the children went to bed, I primped and brushed my teeth and climbed to my tower. From there I could see the road in the distance, winding over the ridge from the village center and around the beach at El Portet. One headlight meant a motorcycle: hopefully Pepe's.

He seemed to know someone everywhere: old friends from school, friends from the *mili,* foreigners he'd come to know in the restaurant over the years, and, all along the coast, bartenders and waiters who didn't charge him for drinks. I wrapped my arms around his torso and we rode on two-lane highways to towns like Dénia, where we walked on a crowded boardwalk and he explained how to mix a favorite cocktail. He told me that his friends called him *"el más moro,"* which as near as I could figure out meant either the most macho, the most sexist, or the most Moorish. The Moors had left half a millennium earlier, but up and down the coast you could see, in the words on maps, evidence of their culture. Every place that began with "Al" or "Ben" came from an Arab word: Alicante, Alcázar, Almoines; Benissa, Benigánim, Benidorm.

One day Maria José came to pick us up at the beach, and got into a yelling match with an older man about a parking space. I watched from a short distance, and realized that I had no idea what they were saying. Other than a few exclamations—*"¡huevos!"*—it wasn't Spanish. In the car, after she'd regained her calm, I asked what language she'd been speaking. *"Valenciano,"* she said. It was a local dialect similar to Catalan. The old man had accused her of not being from around here, of having the parking skills of a tourist. In her fury she'd broken into Valencian, indicating the deepest possible roots in the land. I was impressed with how deeply she was *from* here, in a way I could never imagine being from anywhere, not even my hometown. My family tree was made up entirely of people who'd moved from one place to another. The irony was that the Morairans assumed that I, though alien here, had a connection to home like their own. I was the representative of something that didn't exist, and so felt fraudulent. I also envied them.

✳ ✳ ✳

The first time I let Pepe kiss me we were parked—he had borrowed his family car—on a quiet hillside road in El Portet, somewhere up from the beach but below my house. We had gotten out of the car to gaze down at the bay, and Sinead O'Connor, singing "Nothing Compares to You," was playing on the stereo. The pining romance of the song made me think of Graham. I was annoyed at Pepe's insistence; I had thought I would probably kiss him at some point, but later. After we kissed I was still annoyed and he was mollified. He dropped me off at home.

We went one night to the summer house of a Belgian friend of his, who had a heart-shaped swimming pool in a terraced yard. It was after midnight, the air was warm, and the turquoise pool was lit up from within. I stripped down to my bra and panties and dove off the diving board, not caring about the inconvenience of wet clothes. It was the sort of thing I couldn't *not* do. A dim sort of logic was at work: If I became the kind of person who jumped into swimming pools in her underwear after midnight, in a terraced garden on the Mediterranean, then a life that presented these sorts of opportunities would accrue.

In a nightclub in Gandía, the youth of Europe danced in the strobe lights to acid house music, vocalists crying out over throbbing electronica. Every ten minutes I'd see a boy from some Nordic country, with long blond curling hair, and feel desperate for him to turn around and be Graham. I carried these feelings with me like a shadow self, always walking along beside me, riding on the motorcycle with me, swimming in a pool or the sea. I imagined him seeing me see whatever I saw.

One night we went to Casa Dorita after hours. Chairs were stacked on tables, and the glass-doored refrigerator gave off a glow.

Pepe spread seat cushions on the floor. The illicit place excited me, and we fucked in a beam of light filtered through orange soda. Afterward he fetched ice cream bars from the kitchen. As one melted, he dragged it along my collarbone, then lapped it up. It seemed like a kind of dare: What could we dream up next? Our bodies and minds were landscapes, and I could do anything at night.

When I saw Pepe during the daytime or early evening now, I wanted to touch him or be touched. But we couldn't kiss during business hours at Casa Dorita, nor when he pulled up at El Portet in the Spanish coast guard's Zodiac.

Giddy at our discoveries, we had sex with sweet ingredients from the restaurant kitchen, sex with an empty glass soda bottle, and sex on a large, flat rock that flanked the pier at the marina. It was like marking territory—both the physical terrain of Moraira and an experiential map I was forming in my own head. The night at the marina, my house key fell down between the rocks. I was appalled that I would now have to knock on the door and wake someone up, and that Maria José and Toni would now realize just how late I was coming home. I knocked with dread at about 4:00 AM. The door clicked open, and as I pushed it in I glimpsed Maria José hurrying away naked from the foyer. They had a new key made for me the next day.

I stopped monitoring the time going by. On the beach at El Portet one day I saw Abby, the girl from California I'd met my first week. She spotted me from a distance and marched in my direction, wearing enormous green shorts over a blue one-piece. She wanted to speak to a fellow-sort-of-American. "Did you hear?" she asked. "There's a war." Iraq had invaded Kuwait. I hadn't heard. I hadn't seen a television or newspaper in weeks. The whole subject seemed very far away, and I couldn't identify with the lumbering ambassador from the United States. This beach was my world now. People knew me here. I looked askance at the sunburned and top-less Brits; I was tanned and be-topped. My boyfriend came in with the coast guard, and a Spanish child held my hand. I enjoyed my sense of pseudo-belonging, even as I knew that I'd leave. The trav-eler always betrays the place.

❋ ❋ ❋

Pepe had a small apartment over Casa Dorita that he shared with a friend, and when the friend was away we sometimes went there. I found it exotically domestic to be in a bed with a man in his actual home, even if it was just a cramped bachelor pad. We'd managed to evolve a sort of banter. He was trying to explain to me why he found the English-language word *sure* so comical. It was because if you drew it out, and said "shuuuurrrre," it sounded like an engine revving.

"Pepe," I said.

"You know, it's been a long time since you've said my name like that," he said. I completely forgot what I'd been planning to say, and something else jumped to my lips, something he'd said to me recently, which I'd pretended to ignore and later checked in my dictionary: *"Te quiero mucho."* And I meant it—meant that I loved him.

How had this happened? In eighteen years I'd never fallen in love with anyone, and now, just six months after I'd fallen in love with Graham, I was in love with someone else. It was different, but it felt definitive. Did love open up your heart, so that you became more susceptible to falling in love again? I wondered at the elasticity of my own feelings. I didn't think that this second love contradicted the first. I didn't even think Graham would begrudge it. For one thing, my love for Graham was the clearest feeling I'd ever had. It didn't seem vulnerable. For another, it seemed that to love me, as Graham did, also meant wanting for me the things I wanted for myself, and what I wanted, at the moment, was to experience life, to discover its pleasures and excitements. No, Graham wouldn't withhold this from me. Graham and Pepe were not even relevant to one another. They were in different languages, and I was a different person with each one. They belonged to two separate worlds.

The thing I couldn't quite figure out was when, exactly, I'd gone from mild annoyance at Pepe's advances to genuine affection. Nor why this had happened. I understood that sex could result from love. But it hadn't occurred to me that love might result from sex. Was that what had transpired? Or was it our accumulated time together that had led me to feel this way? Or was I just grateful for what he was doing, taking me around the coast? My heart wasn't as reliable as I'd thought.

❋ ❋ ❋

I'd been dimly conscious of physical risk. One night we ran across Pepe's sister Nuria in the cathedral plaza, after everything was closed, with a male friend of hers. They'd been in a fender bender and she said she was okay, but seemed shaken as she recounted the story. Pepe touched her shoulders like she was a delicate doll, and asked over and over, *¿Estas bien?* He glared at her friend, the erstwhile driver. Yet Pepe liked a drink before he hit the road, liked to speed, liked to get high on cocaine. Twice we did wheelies. I held his back on the motorcycle as he took on the straightaway south of town. He picked up speed, then picked his front tire up clear off the ground. The pitch of the engine rose to a whine, air whipped my cheekbones, and I squeezed my arms and legs for life. Afterward, my eyes teared from the sting of the air.

There was a popular brand of clothing called Pepe Jeans, and Pepe semi-ironically wore one of their T-shirts, which bore his name in big rose-colored letters across the front. He knew I coveted the T-shirt, and near the end of the summer he gave it to me, freshly laundered and folded. I placed it reverentially in my suitcase. I was still in Spain, still able to see him. And yet I was already anticipating my own nostalgia, looking forward to the moment when I would look back. I learned the meaning of *echar de menos* and used the phrase regularly to tell Pepe that I would miss him, and ask if he would miss me.

A few nights before I was to leave I stayed with Pepe in his apartment until dawn, at which time he drove me home on his motorcycle. After I got in, Maria José came to me, infuriated. *"Oye, Eleesabet,"* she said, and I thought she was finally going to call me out for my ridiculous hours. Instead she told me that Toni had just called from the office: On his way to work, he'd passed Pepe and me on our way home, and observed that we weren't wearing our helmets. "I'm serious," she said, "you two really need to smarten up."

Physical injury, though, was the least of my concerns. My idle adventuring had become an attachment, and now the letting-go loomed. Pepe had slipped into my affections when I thought the risks lay elsewhere.

❀ ❀ ❀

One day late in the summer, my friend Kim, from my sorority, called the Moraira house. She was traveling around Europe on a Eurail Pass; could I meet her in Valencia? I couldn't, nor could she come down to Moraira. Though I'd see her in the fall, this missed connection, and consciousness of her roving freedom, tugged at me. It reminded me of my own captivity. I formed wild plans—

fantasies with no hope of success—to invite Pepe and catch a train, to the South of France or to Italy.

I took the train from Valencia back to Madrid, speeding through artichoke fields to catch my flight, with new confidence: I knew my way around here. But it was with a sense of loss, because I didn't want to go back to Seattle and school. I didn't want to stay in Moraira, either. I wanted to travel. Pepe would soon transform in my mind to a part of the Costa Blanca landscape, intrinsic to white stucco, fried fish, and the particular blue of the water. But a desire had been whetted by my summer in Spain, and left unfulfilled.

ON ROOTS
chapter three

*W*hen *I was five,* I thought I was Chinese. My mother and father were WASPs who had migrated to Vancouver from Oregon and New York, respectively. But my mother had told me that all Chinese people had black hair, and since my father had black hair, I made the natural assumption of someone who didn't yet have a strong grasp of "if-then" reasoning. My skeptical first-grade teacher was the one who figured out my logical error and set me straight.

Then I thought for a while that my father must be Jewish because he made my brother and me watch the PBS Holocaust documentary whenever it aired, with its piles of emaciated bodies. I thought this implied some sort of identification with the victims. But when I asked my father about Hanukkah—which sounded like a good opportunity for present-getting—he said that this wasn't our religion.

So I wasn't Chinese or Jewish. I knew kids who went to Croatian, Swedish, and Korean community centers, and to mosques and temples, but there didn't seem to be any such institutions for Anglo-Americans.

As I grew up I had trouble identifying with Vancouver, too. While dramatically beautiful when the clouds parted, with its backdrop of snow-topped peaks, it always felt a little transient to me, like its residents were all in the process of moving on to somewhere like Srinagar or Toronto. The whole metropolis had sprung up quickly in historical terms, beginning in the late 1800s, atop a blank slate of evergreens and a handful of native Squamish and Musqueam people. Later I'd be drawn to cities with ancient underpinnings, like London and Damascus.

Nationality wasn't much help either. I always had two: American from having been born to U.S. citizens, and Canadian from having been born in Canada. We went south to visit my mother's family, up and down the I-5, back and forth over the border. As binationalism goes, there are many more awkward combinations: the dual Iranian-American citizen, the German-Turk. Even if you're from two countries that are much alike, though, binationalism affects your perception of the world. In the back of your mind you always know there's another option.

Of course, everyone has roots. If I trolled back a few generations, I'd find Slovaks and Scots, along with Europeans who had landed in New England hundreds of years back. And like many citizens of immigrant nations, I had a smorgasbord of identities from which to pick. I could make the story up.

ON COMING AND GOING
chapter four

"*Passing like ships in the night*": That's what my mother said about Graham and me, before I knew anything about actual ships passing in the actual night. We thought we had much more to go on. When I returned from Spain, we overlapped by a couple of weeks in Vancouver and were able to spend entire evenings together. In any case, who said that time spent together was some sort of barometer of love? Love didn't demand endless hours; that only proved tolerance. It demanded respect for the self-fulfillment of the other.

He left for London. I went to Seattle. His first weeks in England, where it was damp, cold, and expensive, left him daunted and depressed. A quick epiphany, at least partly weather-related, showed him the way: He bought a ticket to Thailand with a stop in Greece. In the late fall he mailed me a bag of pebbles collected on a beach on Crete, with instructions to put them in water so that they would shine like they had when he found them. I did so, placing the jar on my dresser near a photograph of him. I exalted him above all other boys. The bond between us seemed elastic, the distance between us a testament to its strength. He told me he would come to me, wherever I went.

❋ ❋ ❋

I spent much of my sophomore year plotting to get away from Seattle again. I had to go beyond Europe, because I needed more stimulus than that. I needed something that would sear me, something that might hurt. I discovered that my university sent one or two juniors to the American University in Cairo each year, and immediately I resolved to apply. My closest college friends were also trying to get away; both Kim and Katerina hoped to study in Germany.

I marched determinedly around campus in the drizzle to solicit transcripts and recommendations. I wrote an essay. I petitioned the dean responsible for exchange programs, visiting a concrete-and-glass block called Schmitz Hall to knock on his door. I argued my case, pointing to my thick application packet. I found it in myself to be pushy and had insomnia for the first time in my life. If I'd fallen in love with someone local, I might have seen things differently. But beyond the utilitarian getting of an education, I felt no attachment to Seattle. The idea of going away sustained me like nothing else. I waited by the telephone.

Finally, he called, and after an agonizing moment of niceties, gave me the good news.

I'd by now taken a year and a half of Arabic, as well as courses on the literature and history of the Middle East. I was a student of the faraway, the alien East, like Pyle in Graham Greene's *The Quiet American*. Fowler, the old Saigon hand, foreshadowing the problems Pyle will cause, says of him, "Perhaps only ten days ago he had been walking back across the Common in Boston, his arms full of the books he had been reading in advance on the Far East and the problems of China. He didn't even hear what I said; he was absorbed already in the dilemmas of Democracy and the responsibilities of the West."

I was as ready as Pyle, which is to say not ready at all but brimming with enthusiasm.

ON OBJECTIFICATION
chapter five

*T*ahrir *Square: Liberation Square.* Michelle and I didn't
know whom had been liberated from what, any more than
we knew why the October 6th Bridge or the May 15th Bridge bore
their names. Our hotel was on one side of the square, the American University in Cairo on the other. We wanted to go see our
new campus. As we stepped out of our hotel door, three cries of
"You want taxi?" went up; since we could see our destination, this
seemed unnecessary. Ten paces on, a young mustachioed man fell
into step beside us.

"Excuse me, would you like to buy some perfume?" he asked.
"Where are you from? Ohhhhhh, Amreekan girls. George Bush," he
went on. We kept moving. "You come to my shop."

We crossed through a minibus rendezvous point and were
further queried. "You go pyramids?" Michelle was practicing saying no in Arabic—*la*—which made it sound like she was singing: "la-la-la la-la." Then we came upon multiple lanes of traffic,
a median, and many more lanes. I looked left and right; there
was no traffic light in sight. The cars, many of them black and
white taxis, were barreling, careening, disrespecting any notion
of order. Stymied, we stood on the edge of the river of traffic for a
minute. We saw some Egyptian boys cross; inspired, we decided

to go for it. We ran, zigging and zagging, and finally jumped onto the median just as a car whooshed by inches behind us, horn wailing like a siren.

We reached the far sidewalk giddy with victory, and high-fived. "Hellooo," called a newspaper vendor. We would later learn that you didn't just cross Tahrir Square like that. You went around or took a taxi. Our achievement seemed worthy of celebration, and so we bought Coca-Colas from the *shwarma* stand on the corner. In my head I proudly sounded out the Arabic lettering on the bottles, the lips of which were rough and translucent from a million uses. We toasted each other and swigged. With our backs to the wall, we paused and looked around. The square seemed to be a solar system, obeying physical rules of its own, the whining taxis sucked to and fro like comets. A hulking government building, the *mogama*, dominated the south end of the square, the Cairo Museum was far away on the north side, and opposite us, between the square and the Nile, was a row of luxury hotels. The foot traffic was dense where we stood: young men in Western clothes that seemed too shiny and loose, old men in *galabiyas* and turbans, brassy-looking women in lipstick and bright head scarves, hugging books and purses in a way that made me think of 1950s secretaries. Vast billboards rose over the far side of the square, one for a pesticide almost certainly banned in the United States, with a silhouette of a cockroach in its death throes. Smoke from Cleopatra cigarettes wafted around the *shwarma* stand, mingling with the tang of cooking meat. I'd already heard the Cairo joke: You had to smoke, because the filter on your cigarette sieved out the pollution in the air.

A minute later we tried to walk away with our drinks, which caused an eruption from the *shwarma* vendor. He wanted his bottles back.

❋ ❋ ❋

Since the university had selected Michelle and me to go, we'd made a point of meeting several times over the summer. We went through the motions of early friendship even as we groped for connection, like soldiers thrown together in war, compensating with shared interests for what we lacked in mutual attraction. I found her suspiciously cheerful and well-organized. She was twenty-one, but her determined optimism belonged to someone younger, and her love of planning to someone older. To my mystification, she seemed bent on emphasizing her own mousiness, rolling her shoulders forward and padding around in Birkenstocks.

We found the apartment advertised on a bulletin board in the student lounge. The landlady told us she'd previously rented it to a foreigner, a Christian missionary, a nice man. It was a ten-minute walk south of the university and had two bedrooms, both facing the street and sharing a long balcony where Michelle and I could hang our laundry. The street filled up with passing vendors in the early morning, each shouting his wares—bananas, water—from a donkey cart. We bought robust cockroach poison. The gas man rolled in a new tank every month, and rolled out the old one. We never found a place to buy a shower curtain—that kind of project never seemed like a priority—and so instead used an enormous cotton sheet. It did a surprisingly good job of keeping water off the floor, and dried quickly in the desiccated air.

Every mundane task was a challenge, but each one was eventually surmountable, and so most days ended in satisfaction. It felt good in the way that the body does after physical exertion. Something as simple as figuring out where and how to buy ibuprofen could be a two-hour project, of wandering Qasr al Aini Street, checking stores, asking for directions, and finally finding a pharmacy and learning that you didn't just pick things off the shelf, you waited your turn and then pointed, and the team of shopkeepers—everything was overstaffed—retrieved your items from the shelves and packaged them more than necessary, wrapping them in brown paper before placing them in a plastic bag and tying it with a flourish in a knot.

❀ ❀ ❀

There's a photograph I took during my first week in Cairo. I'm not exactly sure where it was, only that it was in a poor neighborhood somewhere west of the Nile. A group of American students, seven or eight of us, had gone walking: Aleem from Emory, Riva from Columbia, Rob from Kalamazoo, Fred, Patricia, Paul, Michelle, me. We had no ringleader, though someone occasionally consulted a guidebook for the location of a mosque or museum. Really we were just walking, and we didn't much care where we ended up. We carried bottled water and day packs and cameras, except for Fred, who said he didn't believe in taking photographs; he planned to store his memories in his head, an idea I found incomprehensibly radical. My impulse to record was almost on par with my impulse to travel.

We wandered into a dead-end alley, and as the rest of the group was turning around to leave, I stayed. Though it was lined with homes, there was no one in the alley, which ended in a slope of rubble, as though a house had once stood there and been demolished, or just fallen apart. Bathed in the hot afternoon sun, the street, the walls, and the pile of rubble were all, like much of Cairo, the color of bleached sand. A laundry line was strung from the dark window of one of the homes to a metal pole, stretching across the rubble, and bright articles of clothing, squares of rose and blue and green, hung still over the dust. That was the picture I took: the glassless window, the rubble, the vivid laundry signaling life. It wasn't a picture I would have taken after ten months in Cairo or even one; it could only have been taken in my first week, after which, as I was confronted with poverty every day, the way it looked to me would no longer be so striking.

❋ ❋ ❋

There were other things we noticed only at first, before we accepted them as a part of daily life. Then they got harder to describe, the way it's hard to describe what it feels like to breathe air.

One of the first things was the presence of men with guns. They wore the black uniforms of the Egyptian military and had automatic weapons slung around their chests—AK-47s, we thought, but mainly because that was the only automatic weapon we'd ever heard of. The soldiers were posted at the airport and outside big hotels, embassies, and government buildings, their faces usually scowling or stony, though sometimes you glimpsed one having a quick laugh with another over a cigarette, and then they seemed soft and human. Sometimes they trundled past by the truckload. Max Weber floated back to me from Poli Sci 101: A "state" is an entity with a successful monopoly on the legitimate use of violence. The soldiers were posted at the gates to our campus, where, that first time Michelle and I entered, we eyed them apprehensively, wondering if they had authority over us. But they ignored us, for where could two tall, pale, disheveled girls belong but at the university? We didn't understand our relative power yet. To me the surly, black-clad men with guns looked menacing. But they were listless cogs in a dictatorship; they wouldn't help me, but I was too rich and foreign to be worth troubling much. It would create a hassle. I quickly inferred that I was exempt from fearing them, and embraced my special status without a second thought.

❋ ❋ ❋

The government bullied the soldiers, the soldiers bullied the people, the people bullied each other and the visitors from foreign lands. I didn't understand much about it, this way of treating people, this fear that went straight to the top. I felt it immediately, though, the first day when we stepped into Tahrir Square and the tormenting began. It came mostly in the form of demanding, accusing, or insinuating words, and sometimes in the form of a stroke or a pinch. The assault on my sense of self felt violent, even when no physical contact was involved. It was a shock administered in slow motion, in tiny cuts, absorbed in phases. It never went away, not as long as I traveled in places that were Arab or Muslim or poor or oppressed. It's the way of half the world.

At first it startled. Some of the calls were staccato, like gunfire, stopping as quickly as they started but leaving me wondering when they would start again. Some were more ingratiating. Some men avoided the possibility that I might walk off by falling into step beside me at just my pace. They sped up when I sped up and slowed down when I slowed down, like comical, sinister mimes. These ones talked more softly and correctly in their handling of English.

There was begging, some by cripples, some made that way for profit. I read Naguib Mahfouz's novel *Palace Walk* that fall, where I learned that there was such a thing as a cripple maker. I couldn't have imagined this on my own. A man outside the touristed Khan al Khalili rested his legless torso on a small wheeled platform and pushed himself along with his hands; he was always there.

There were sales pitches. The vendors, like the beggars, were egalitarian in their choice of targets; money came from men as well as women. Boys of twelve at the Pyramids were wilier than

American used car salesmen, determining at a glance which member of a couple wielded influence, shifting fluidly into Japanese. Academics have spent too much time trying to explain objectification, considering that there's an easy way to make white, Western men understand: You just have to go out in public somewhere poor. You become a thing. Your conscious and unique self becomes irrelevant, as a thousand eyes try to figure out how to best tap your wealth. And objectification begets objectification. The harassers become an undifferentiated mass themselves, made up of identical things that torment.

There's a special hell reserved for foreign women. The catcalls came ineloquently in English—"I want fuck you"—and mellifluously in Arabic, where they were all food-related: Foreign women quickly learned the words for banana, strawberry, honey, and cream. My first reaction was to try to answer the calls, human to human. Someone addressed me; I owed them a reply. A "no, thank you," as I moved on. But "no, thank you" was taken as an opening, an opportunity for persuasion. And so as early as that first day I began to ignore them, or rather try to give the appearance of ignoring them, since I hadn't yet learned how to be unaware.

The guidebooks, the literature, the how-to-deal-with-Egypt memos from my university, the people who'd been here, all agreed: Female visitors should dress modestly, with arms and legs covered. This, it was suggested, would "show respect" for Muslims and their culture, and cut down on sexual harassment. I couldn't have been more game. The summer before I left, biding my time in Vancouver, I sewed two long sack dresses from the same pattern. They would have been ideal for members of the Fundamentalist Church of Jesus Christ of Latter Day Saints. They had long sleeves and fell past midcalf, and were roomy enough to fit two of me in each. One was a black-and-white check, and the other made of thick white cotton, a mistake given the ambient sand and exhaust that permeates Cairo's air, turning white to dun. My bigger mistake, though, was misunderstanding the dresses themselves. I was approaching the risk of harassment as a problem that could be solved. I thought I understood. I thought the obsession with female modesty across this whole stretch of the planet must exist because it worked. "Working," to my mind, meant something to do with my own well-being, with the well-being of women, things I supposed mattered. All the veils and dresses and covered arms might be an inconvenience, but I was willing to be inconvenienced in exchange for comfort and safety. I thought clothing could protect me the way guardrails prevent falls, or seat belts cut down on death. Problem, solution. But it didn't work that way. I could drape my body in fabric, but I remained visibly female and foreign. I couldn't eliminate my height, my light skin and blond hair, or all the little things I took so for granted that I forgot they marked me: the backpack for my books, the natural fabrics, the engineered shoes.

As it sunk in that the deluge wouldn't stop, my initial energy dissipated and panic set in. People followed me, sometimes closely and muttering, sometimes at a distance; I became paranoid and wondered if I was followed all the time. We experimented with tactics: We tried grabbing the hands of our male friends, thinking a faux boyfriend might defray it all, but American college boys were not seen as deterrents—indeed, their friendship with foreign girls increased their popularity. We tried fake wedding bands and stories of fake husbands. We tried shaming them: yelling "Hey, what are you doing," when a hand grazed our behinds. Shouting vented my building anger, but that was all it did. Nothing worked.

My reactions changed. Like in an Impressionist painting, discrete elements of the barrage came in and out of focus. Sometimes it was a wall of sound, whereas sometimes a comment caught my attention and lodged in my mind, to be mulled over at length and never forgotten. Someone shouted *"arousa"* from a passing truck; I thought the word meant "bride." I tried to decipher this; an Egyptian friend explained that the word for "bride" also meant "doll." I understood that I was a generic object, that the shouts and whispers were sprayed out on anyone of my kind, and yet I couldn't help but take them personally. This is the trauma inflicted by categorization.

A foreign woman in a public place wasn't a person in Cairo. As for other women, I knew only anecdotes. Every now and then a story spread of a groping or a rape on a public bus. Cairo's shiny new subway included an exclusive women's car, to help prevent such events. The rich women, like our classmates at AUC, had their ways of coping. They avoided public space. They rode in cars. They hung out on campus, where the gardens and courtyards were enclosed by high walls, or in their sheltered homes in Zamalek or Maadi or Heliopolis, or at the private country clubs where they could run, swim, and dine away from the prying eyes of the *fellaheen*. They didn't wear Mormon frocks. On our first day of class I realized yet another way in which my dresses were a mistake. AUC was studded with boys and girls in real designer jeans and sunglasses. The girls wore heels. They hung out on the broad platform in front of the library gossiping about holidays in France; they'd studied Sartre in high school. Mostly they smoked Marlboro Reds, distinguishing them from the *hoi polloi* outside the gates who smoked Cleopatras. One or two boys, cool enough to get away with it, went fashionably slumming and smoked the people's cigarette, held between silver-ringed fingers. I vaguely wished for entrée into their milieu but sensed I didn't have the background for it; no year-abroad student was known to have pulled this off.

I sent the Mormon dresses and the rest of my carefully planned, intentionally drab wardrobe to the back of the closet, for use on nonschool days. This left me with jeans. An American friend took me to the Benetton store in Maadi, where a sweater cost a month's food. I blended in a little more on campus; this was the best I could hope for. Michelle, to my exasperation, kept wearing her Birkenstocks to school.

The rich Egyptians could go behind high walls, but outside of campus we foreigners didn't have access to private places to do the things we thought of as public activities. Moreover we thought of the streets as both an obligation and a right. The obligation: We were here to see the place, and had some idea that the real Egypt wasn't in a country club. It would be *wrong* of us to see only the rich. We saw the extreme stratification as soon as we arrived on campus, saw that the lives of the wealthy and the poor intersected only as master and servant. We immediately abhorred this state of affairs, and resolved not to embrace it. None of us would keep that resolution. Instead we'd learn that as middle-class North Americans we were also part of a global class, and that class was stronger than any of us.

As for the right: We thought that public space belonged to us. We thought it ought to be a safe commons, where strangers were equal. We were confronted with the fact that this idea wasn't universal. I was supposed to know that, had studied the various forms of social structure. But as I was learning with religion and government and sexism, study got you only a tiny way toward understanding.

I felt the difference in the structure of things. You can guess the value a culture places on public space by the architecture. One that builds high walls facing the outside world, with high windows and closed doors, isn't much concerned with the quality of public space. A culture that builds porches and yards, open to the world for all to see, is one that values and embraces the commons. In talking about public space and equality, I'm describing the milieu in which I grew up. It was the water in which I swam, so I couldn't have described it until it was taken away. I took it away from myself: I didn't have to go to Cairo but I did. This fusillade of reality was what I'd pursued.

As with the guns, we talked about the harassment at first. We never said we were outraged, never talked about how it made us feel, never wondered out loud what it was doing to our heads. We wanted to be tougher than that, because if we weren't tough, we'd have to go home. We talked about the harassment as an annoyance. Making it an annoyance reduced and contained it. We talked strategy at first, talked rings and long pants and fake boyfriends, when we still thought strategy would work. We found private ways to contend. I braced myself every time I left the house, prepared my mind to keep the asteroids out. I learned to move briskly and always as though I knew where I was going, to never ever make eye contact with a male between the ages of five and eighty-five, and to filter the torrent, distinguishing salacious invitations from honest advisories. This filtration of bad from good, as though we could separate smoke from a heady hit of nicotine, was the trick: If you shut yourself away too much, you shut out the whole world, and there were delightful things here too. There was hospitality and humor, wizened skippers plying the Nile, the calm of the desert on the edge of town. It was a lesson in splitting off self from self, on how to hive a hard shell away from one's core and keep the two apart. If I didn't dissociate this way, putting away the harassment as a tiny part of my existence, it would have overwhelmed me. And to pack it away was a kind of triumph. I felt a bullheaded determination not to let it get the better of me. I thought I would be a coward if I ran home to a more comfortable place.

The panic subsided. We observed that mostly we were not physically harmed; this was the new bar by which we measured the world. We'd submitted. We stopped talking about the men, just as we'd stopped talking about the poverty and the guns. There was nothing new to observe, nothing to be done.

ON PROMISES
chapter six

*G*raham *was moving across* the world toward me, a glowing dot on the map in my head. I tried to push him out of my mind so that I wouldn't be overtaken by longing. The danger was that I would become so hopeful, so excited, that if he then failed to materialize, the blow would be too crushing. I hadn't seen him in more than a year, and one of my coping strategies was to focus on the time and place where I was. I couldn't live with my head somewhere else. I had to embrace my surroundings, because this time was only going to go by once, and I didn't want to spend it wishing for things to be different.

No one had email back then. Graham's progress reports appeared in the form of postcards and aerograms in my mailbox in the student lounge. They had him boarding the Trans-Siberian Railway in Beijing at the time of my arrival in Cairo. Then he was in Moscow, from where he sent a postcard of St. Basil's Cathedral. From there he took a train to Istanbul, where he planned to board a boat. I couldn't make long-distance calls from my apartment, but I could receive them, and Graham called late at night a few times, from jangly phones in train stations and ferry terminals, on lines that ticked and hissed and cut off when the paid-for time expired. From Istanbul, he told me, he would arrive, give or take, in two weeks. The date was uncertain because he wasn't sure of the ship's schedule, and once he disembarked at Alexandria he'd still have to make his way to Cairo.

A group of students I knew was planning a boat trip out of Hurghada, a small town on the Red Sea. Graham's arrival was imminent, but I didn't know exactly when it would happen. I couldn't bear it. I couldn't stand my own anticipation any longer. So I decided to go away and forget the waiting.

On the first weekend in October, eight of us—two Egyptian, two French, four American—took an overnight bus down to Hurghada, where our ringleader, Sharif, had chartered an inelegant but roomy motor yacht with a captain and first mate. For three days and nights, we sailed out and back into Hurghada, swimming and snorkeling, sleeping on the boat or deserted beaches, and eating grilled fish and drinking rum. I chased one of the French students, Xavier, who had no interest in me, which made me chase him harder. I talked to him every chance I could, urging him to swim with me, and trying to impress him by playing chess, which he won. His lack of any romantic interest in me whatsoever, his resistance to even befriending me or flirting back, gave me a focus and a challenge. While I fretted over Xavier's disinterest, I was, at least, not thinking of Graham. Rejection by Xavier took my mind off my biggest fear, that Graham would reject me by failing to appear.

One night our crew left us on an island with little to eat but lots to drink. We were cold but managed to build a fire. I finally wore down Xavier and we made out roughly on the sand, then had dry, drunk sex. Afterward he said he'd never felt so sick. I hoped that he just meant from the rum, but it cut me that I'd elicited nothing in him, that he would still not even put on a pretense of liking me. I'd never had sex with so little feeling, without even desire. I felt stupid. As we motored away from the island the next day, my sweatshirt blew off the deck and I dove after it into the turquoise water. I was hungry and hung over. I swam hard and down, chasing the white blur, but it sank too far too fast. I surfaced, resigned, but saw that the boat hadn't stopped to let me climb back on board. I looked to the shore, maybe a mile away, a yellow line on the surface of the water. I could swim it if I had to, I thought, but then what? It had no people, no fresh water. I looked back to the boat, which had grown smaller, then back to the island, then back to the boat. Finally it began to turn in a painfully slow arc.

In Hurghada on the final day, we had a long wait until our bus left, during which I called Michelle at our apartment. She answered quietly and paused. I could tell she was dragging the phone into her room, and my heart jumped at what this meant. She spoke to me in a whisper. "He's here."

My mood soared. I felt magnanimous even toward Xavier, and played another round of chess. My anticipation had tipped over the knife edge from pain to joy. I no longer needed to distract myself by every means possible. On the way to Cairo, our bus broke down, as Egypt's long distance buses generally did. I rapped my fingers on the window and stared out at the desert. We arrived at the central station at four in the morning, and I shared a taxi as far as Tahrir Square, then proceeded on foot. Qasr al Aini Street was deserted in the dark, and the *thwack* of my leather flip-flops echoed against the walls. Though I lived here, and was the hostess, I'd let homebody Michelle do the welcome. I'd arranged to be the one coming home with a backpack in the dark of night.

I turned into our street, and into my cement lobby, where the *bawab* slept in a corner. I climbed the single flight to our floor, and on the door to our apartment found a taped note from Michelle, advising me to act surprised—she hadn't told Graham that I knew he was here. But I didn't have sufficient rein on myself to act one way or the other. I let myself in, and could see across the dark living room that the light in my bedroom was on, and that there was a guitar on my lumpy green sofa. I went in. He stood in the half light near the bedroom door, hair around his shoulders, in loose blue cotton pants. I stopped several feet from him and we stood and stared. After a long while I set down my backpack and stepped toward him, and we held each other without words, reconciling all those phone calls and letters with flesh.

❀ ❀ ❀

We didn't sleep that first early morning, just talked until noon, and then he came to class with me. The guards didn't give him a second glance as we passed onto campus, nor did the teacher in my crowded, dim classroom. That night Graham lit a candle beside my bed, now our bed, a wide wooden thing with a headboard painted in pale yellow and faded gilt. We found that we could lie together, talking in the dim light and ardently kissing, for hours, but were shy about sex itself. It seemed almost beside the point. We slept from exhaustion, woke, and slept, as though we'd been through an arduous trip.

He began to tell me about his journey, and again I saw images as though they were my own recollections. He'd moved from Thailand back to the east coast of Australia, where he worked in a restaurant that played Nina Simone. He tried speed, stayed up for three days, punched a wall, and slept for three more, all of which upset his housemates. He was in Brisbane when I told him for certain that I'd be coming to Egypt. From there he plotted his route: the flight to Hong Kong, then the "slow boat to China," which he delighted in saying, though neither of us knew where the expression came from. He spent cold vodka-infused weeks on the train across Siberia, and saw Moscow in the first flush of capitalism. Because he was there and everyone was doing it, he stood in line outside of a new Estée Lauder store, and bought eye shadow that he gave to me. He took a train to Istanbul, sleeping through Bulgaria. Then another boat, which had stopped in Haifa, where passengers were banned from leaving the port's customs zone, and finally Alexandria. Ultimately me. I was heartened, flattered, and impressed by this odyssey made on my behalf. I absorbed it as proof of his love. At the same time I understood that the goal of the journey could have been something else. A voyage has to have a destination to give it shape and flavor. We quest for something desirable, but we also desire quests. I was wanted, but Graham also wanted to want.

❋ ❋ ❋

Traveling with a lover creates a sense of forward momentum where it might not otherwise exist. The relationship adopts the motion of the physical journey, eliminating the risk of boredom and making the travelers complicit. It shows each person in a new, maybe sexier, light. A journey can drive two people apart, as they realize the different ways they handle fender benders and lost luggage. But if it doesn't, it binds them in a filament of romance and camaraderie.

We didn't know we were creating a crucible, just that there were places we wanted to go. Unknown territory was practically a command, a dare that couldn't be ignored. We shared equally in wanderlust and so didn't need to explain it to one another. We just needed to get on the bus. As soon as my midterms were over, we did.

We went to the Sinai, to St. Catherine's Monastery, to Alexandria. Each time we returned, Cairo welcomed me with its overbearing hug. It was too much and it was home. Some of the American students who'd begun the school year with me would go back to the

United States in January, after just one semester. I couldn't imagine leaving. I felt like I was just sinking into Cairo, finally letting it take over. I had no homesickness whatsoever.

Between trips, Graham and I talked about the fact that he wouldn't stay in Egypt. Another kind of boy—one with a parental safety net, or a desire to study Arabic or start his first novel—might have amused himself for longer. If he'd been more like me, he might have lingered. But for Graham the only things in Egypt were travel and me. He wanted or needed to go back to Vancouver. He was making plans for his next adventure, and it wasn't mine. Our differences didn't concern me; I loved him without reservation.

✻ ✻ ✻

The El Madina hotel, in Siwa Oasis, remains the cheapest place I've ever stayed, at two and a half Egyptian pounds a night, or seventy-five U.S. cents. The foul bathroom was down the hall from our cell-like room. At night Graham lit a mosquito coil, and instead of setting it down to burn, he toured our room in his boxer shorts, climbing onto beds and chairs, chasing insects. Whenever he found one he held the burning poison up to the bug until it fell from the wall. I watched him from the bed, a book unread in my hands, patient, knowing that he'd come to me soon. He came when his conquest of the mosquitoes was complete. The bed was too narrow for two people, and there were two beds in the room, but we didn't want to be apart. The rough blanket became tangled among our legs while we fucked. We weren't shy anymore. We had to fuck everywhere we went, at least once per hotel, at least once every day, as though making each place our own. We slept embraced, as if a centimeter between us would be too much. Whenever I hear the words *romantic hotel*, I still think of the El Madina.

My mental image of an oasis was of one or two palm trees and a pond set amid a vast and endless desert. Only the second part of this image applied to Siwa. It was perched in the northeast corner of the Sahara, about as vast and endless a desert as there was, but it wasn't small. When Graham and I climbed an old tower on a hill, we could see that the date palms stretched out for acres, a sea of dusty green, and that there wasn't just one pond but several bodies of springwater, each one feeding networks of makeshift irrigation. The town was a tumble of low sandstone buildings, many crumbling in the dry air, which gave the whole settlement a soft, organic look, as though human life had bubbled up from the ground. It was a place that supported life, on the fringe of an unimaginably huge expanse that didn't. It was the inverse of an island in the sea.

I'd seen scrubby deserts and hard, flat deserts, but I wanted a "real" desert, the kind I'd seen in cartoons and read about in books. I wanted to see an *Arabian Sands* desert, a Tintin desert with dunes like meringue. So we rented bicycles and followed a road to the edge of town, then kept going. The road became a track, and the track got softer, until it was lost in sand drifts, and our bicycle tires sank and refused to roll. We laid the bikes aside and walked on a little, until we were amid dunes higher than our heads. I couldn't resist: I climbed to the top of a dune and then took a giant leap off its peak. I was airborne, arms spread, then crashed into the forgiving powder.

It was dusk when, pedaling back into town, sand falling from our spokes, we were stopped by a sight we couldn't make sense of. Rising on the eastern horizon was a giant orange sphere, too big to be the moon, too big even to be the sun. It seemed as wide as the whole oasis, as wide as Egypt, lighting up the sky with its glow.

It was the moon after all, but like I'd never seen it. The desert air was playing a trick of refraction, doing something that could be explained by physics. As the orb rose further, it appeared to shrink and become less orange, but it remained a full, glowing ball, and as we returned our bicycles and got dinner from an open-air café, right up until we retired to our room for the night, we kept pausing to stand and stare. It was as though a hieroglyph had come to life. We vowed that the next night we'd take pictures.

Back in our long and narrow room, I got under the blanket and Graham lit a mosquito coil to begin his campaign of insect terror. I watched him.

"What do you want?" I asked.

"What do you mean?"

"What do you want? In your life." I felt awkward saying it.

"I want to be wild; I want to be free," he said. He leaped from a chair to the floor, then added, "Do you love me?"

The paradox of love is that to have it is to want to preserve it, because it's perfect in the moment, but that preservation is impossible, because the perfection is only ever an instant passed through. Love, like travel, is a series of moments that we immediately leave behind. Still we try to hold on and embalm, against all evidence and common sense, proclaiming our promises and plans. The more I loved him, the more I felt hope. But hope acknowledges uncertainty, and so I also felt my first premonitions of loss.

The next afternoon we walked around with our cameras. Palm trees. Crumbling buildings. Donkeys. We came upon a group of five children, siblings, all dressed in the same garish fabric, a floral print on a bright yellow background. I imagined their mother: She'd somehow scored a bolt of cloth; maybe her husband had picked it up in Alexandria and presented it as a gift. A practical and frugal woman, she'd used every last inch, sewing dresses for her daughters, shirts for the little boys, maybe a head scarf for herself and cushions for the home. Graham and I wanted to take the children's pictures. The oldest child, a girl of around nine with a toddler on her hip, herded the rest of them in front of the camera, and began to negotiate precociously. Fatima didn't want money, or pens, or candy. She wanted copies of the pictures we took. We said we'd give them to her, but she held up a hand so commanding that we put our cameras down. No, really, we had to send her pictures. She'd been trying and trying to get some, but she was still waiting for a foreigner to come through. We explained about developing film, that we wouldn't be able to do it until after we left. Fine, Fatima said, she'd give us her address, and we had to mail her the photos.

"You must," she said.

"We promise," we told her, ballpoint address tucked into my notebook. It was rudimentary: her father's name, Siwa Oasis, Egypt. We raised our cameras.

Before the sun went down, Graham and I climbed back to the crumbling tower we'd visited two days earlier, and up to its roof. We were prepared for the night chill in scarves and sweaters, and we had cameras and tripods, the better to hold still while we captured the moon. We waited, but it didn't come. Maybe it was just rising later, we told each other, still hopeful for the vast orange ball. But the sky became dark. Eventually an ordinary little white, waning moon appeared on the horizon.

Photographers, like writers, want to pin things down. Not entirely happy with the flow of time, we try to capture and explain, to seize moments and then hold them up to the light for examination, savoring what's passed. The photographer Henri Cartier-Bresson, afflicted with a wanderlust that took him to West Africa at the age of twenty-three, said he wanted to "'trap' life—to preserve life in the act of living." Every photographer, every tourist taking a snapshot, wants to do something like that. Photography is one way we try to stop time.

We regretted not capturing the great orange moon, even though we knew photographs wouldn't be like the real thing, wouldn't convey the awe we felt when we first saw it come up over the horizon. What I regretted more was not being able to capture our own state, not being able to preserve us, right then, in amber. Even if I could have stopped time, I knew it wouldn't have the desired effect, because something essential would be missing, some sharpness of focus made possible by the fact that life was fleeting.

❀ ❀ ❀

A week after we left Siwa I accompanied Graham to the airport late at night for one of the bizarrely inconvenient departure times imposed on foreign airlines. We stood holding each other, crying, until finally he had to go beyond the security gate. I wiped my eyes with the back of my hand as I stepped out of the airport, into the scrum of taxi drivers and their black and white cars, shouting out fees of twenty pounds. I had exactly six in my pocket, less than even a fair price. But our good-bye had left me stony and unafraid, nothing could hurt me more, certainly not hitchhiking home. I was all too convincing in my willingness to try my luck on the highway. When I started out on foot, one of the taxi drivers relented on price, saying he was worried for my safety, and gave me a ride.

Neither of us did keep our promise to Fatima, nor eventually did we keep our promises to each other. I'm harder on myself for the first. The pattern was set. Travel equaled longing equaled love.

ON MAKING FRIENDS
chapter seven

I *befriended Mona early in the school year.* She had tight dark
brown curls that came from her Arab side. Her father had been
a Palestinian professor, killed in Beirut when she was eleven. Her
mother was an American heiress. After the family left Beirut she'd
attended an English boarding school and then Oberlin College.
Now she was a year-abroad student like me. The admission that
embarrassed her the most, the one she made me agree not to tell,
was that she'd been a debutante. It was a concession, she said, to her
grandmother on her mother's side.

Over the summer she'd studied Arabic at Middlebury College, which was renowned for its summer language course where it
banned students from speaking English. We now shared a class in
the colloquial Egyptian dialect, where the professor used a repeat-
after-me method, and never moved much beyond the niceties we
already knew. One day, on a hunch, I suggested that we instead have
lunch and go play backgammon. I didn't know her well, but sensed
there might be a chemistry of the kind I'd failed at with Michelle.

I took her to my favorite *kushary* place on Qasr el Aini. *Kush-*
ary was a wonder: seasoned lentils, chickpeas, fried onions, and
rice, served in a heaping portion in a metal dish. A bowl cost one
Egyptian pound, or around thirty-three cents; another pound got

you a small bowl of rice pudding for dessert. Mona could sometimes eat two bowls in a sitting.

I liked Mona's confidence, which was occasionally punctuated by flights of alarm and seriousness over things I didn't find alarming or serious—for example, she avowed that you could get AIDS from the toilet seats at the Semiramis, because prostitutes used them. Mona had been fearless about lacrosse at boarding school, and now was fearless about roving around Cairo. She was fearless about speaking Arabic too, even though she wasn't very good. She was dogged about learning it, but the reasons for her obsessive study emerged only slowly. Like most girls I'd met in college, I didn't believe that I had any important stories to share, though I hoped one day to acquire some. Mona believed that she did have important stories, ones that went beyond boys kissed and majors chosen, but she held on to them until she thought you could appreciate their significance.

Mona demanded regard. But she also gave it, believing that her friends didn't just happen to be special to her, but that they were people who really mattered. She liked my confidence too. We both aspired to be steely, and sensed that we could push and prod each other in that direction.

We moved on from the *kushary* restaurant to a backgammon establishment. A whiskered and weathered man, balancing a tray of steaming glasses, dramatically gestured us to an open table, calling "over here, over here." He whooshed a few other patrons out of the way, who, politely and nodding, removed themselves. The dominant sound of a Cairo teahouse is the slap of hard plastic pieces on playing boards, a *clackety-clack* that rises above the conversation and exclamations and televised soccer. We ordered tea and a water pipe with apple-flavored tobacco. I'd been a nicotine virgin before Cairo, and so the first few hits always went to my head. We played the version of backgammon we knew, the one Americans learn, which begins with all the checkers on the board. If an opponent's piece lands on yours, you have to take it off. You then roll the dice until you can get the piece back on, and when you do, you begin the journey again at the farthest point from home.

Several customers closely watched our game. A bony neighbor with a finely tooled brown face issued a general challenge; Mona immediately accepted. His friends gathered around to watch. He beat her once, then again, and again—but by the third time she was playing a respectable game, holding her own and eliciting impressed mutterings of *"aiwaaaa,"* an elongated "yes."

"Do you know how to play another style?" her opponent asked. And he proceeded to show us. You start with all of your pieces *off* the board rather than on it, and move them on with each roll of the dice to start their horseshoe journey. The other key difference is that instead of being sent back to the beginning when your opponent lands a checker on your own, you stay in place, paralyzed, until the enemy piece moves on. This version of the game opens up new questions of strategy. Being immobilized halfway around the board can be even worse than being sent back to the beginning, where the possibility of movement at least presents itself at every turn.

❋ ❋ ❋

Yemen, as Mona and I perceived it from Cairo, was far away, isolated, poor, traditional, religious, possibly violent, a boondocks even by the lights of its own neighborhood. It was farther, and that was where we wanted to go.

The books also showed a unique and surpassingly beautiful architecture of sand-colored minarets and towers frosted in white.

They showed stair-step terraced green fields of a kind that, like the architecture, didn't exist anywhere else. The Romans called the region "Arabia Felix," happy Arabia, for its agricultural riches. Yemen was a land beyond the mountains, the home of the Queen of Sheba.

Scooping from our metal bowls of *kushary* one afternoon, and talking about the upcoming winter break, one of us said, "Let's go to Yemen," and the other said yes. There was a dare in this discussion, an I-will-if-you-will aspect. But there wasn't a voice of caution between us. Once the possibility was admitted out loud, we had to go.

To our fellow American year-abroad students, our decision required no explanation. Their eyes shone with admiration; we were trumped in our adventurism only by a trio who planned to spend their winter break in northern Sudan. To the Egyptian and other Arab students, our act seemed senseless, like planning a trip to Appalachia when we could have gone to Paris. To our parents we emphasized that this was an extension of our geopolitical studies.

We went to the Yemenia airline office on Talaat Harb Street, where, dismayed at the price of the Cairo–Sanaa run, we haggled over cups of tea with the general manager, who gave us a generous discount. Mona's uncle sent her the only known extant English-language guidebook to Yemen, an out-of-date Lonely Planet. She didn't have time to read it, so she handed it over to me. I packed my bag and crammed on the plane.

ON BEING AN ALIEN

chapter eight

The taxi deposited us at dusk in front of the millennium-old Bab al-Yemen, the gate to the old city, as merchants were closing up their stalls. A swirl of people was hurrying away. Beyond the wall rose stone towers seven or eight stories high, each one decorated with patterns made of white plaster. White arches surrounded the windows, and as darkness fell, the white zigzags painted along the rooflines appeared to glow.

The people around us were mostly men. Young and old, every one of them wore a patterned sarong, a Western-style sport coat, a cloth head wrap, and a large curved dagger sheathed at his waist. A few women traveled in pairs, their human forms invisible, but their cloth tents riotously colored in a radiating pattern of red, blue, yellow, and green.

We stood and watched, and began to feel that everyone else was staring back at us. A little pocket of space formed around us as though we were a disturbance in the current. We shouldered our backpacks, walked toward the gate, and stepped in.

On a plaza just inside, we found a dark, smoke-filled teahouse. The door was low, which made me feel overgrown, but once inside I thought I might have shrunk. The water pipes created a hallucination: They were more than double the height of the *sheesha* pipes in

Egypt, topped with enormous clay bowls big enough to serve soup. The effect was as strange as if chairs had suddenly doubled in height. Because Yemenis are short, the pipes looked even more outsize, towering over their seated and reclining users. When the proprietor offered us tea, we pointed at one of the pipes.

"*Midaq?*" he asked. We nodded uncertainly. "*Midaq!*" he cried across the dim room, and someone else repeated the cry, and it went back toward some invisible tobacco-preparation area. The proprietor directed us to a cot against the wall, and our pipe was procured: a brass tank the size and shape of a pineapple, topped with a four-foot-tall wooden stem, painted black and decorated with tiny white dots. We leaned back on our cot. From here I felt I could finally recede and watch without being watched; at least a man stepping into the tea-house might not immediately notice the two foreign girls in the corner. Most of the patrons had one cheek swollen, as though it contained a tennis ball. Branches of glossy green leaves, like laurels, were piled everywhere. The leaves were the national intoxicant, *qat,* and several neighbors offered us some from their stash. Still grappling with the long coil of our pipe, though, and conscious that the task of finding a hotel bed lay ahead, we decided new drugs were a step too far.

It was soon clear that the delicate pipes and honey-soaked tobaccos of Cairo had not prepared me for Yemeni shag. The waiter piled dried brown hunks that resembled slabs of evergreen bark into our bowl, then seared them with coals. After a few inhalations my mind unfastened itself and floated toward the top of the room. I was first giddy, then nauseated. "I'm just not going to move until we leave," I said, and passed Mona the mouthpiece. Time slowed down. Other patrons asked us questions, green spittle flecking their lips. Where were we from? Yes, yes, Amreeka. George Bush bad. People good. The sort of split anyone could understand. Canada, I offered, but got no flicker of recognition. Where would we stay. Did we need a place. We stopped answering, and they stopped asking. It didn't feel rude. Later I would recognize this moment as the beginning of the glazed period. It occurs three-quarters of the way into any *qat* session. Quiet descends and everyone becomes philosophical.

When we left, the night air was refreshing, the drizzle welcome. We ambled down a narrow alley. Little squares of stained glass in blue, red, and green dotted the walls, until we emerged into the modern part of the city, where we found a businessmen's hotel on Ali Abd al-Mughni Street. Nothing we could afford ever had a private bathroom, but our room was clean and had a balcony. We slept the fulfilling sleep of the deeply tired. In the middle of the night I was awoken by a surreal wail. It was coming from outside. I sat up, confused. It sounded like a siren. "What the fuck is that?" Mona asked from her bed. I stumbled toward our balcony door. The city had turned off every light, so all I could see was pitch-black. I slid open our door, and the keening became louder. It was clear and pure on the night air, taking up the sky. I wondered why people weren't coming out of their homes in alarm. I was half-asleep. And then the familiar words began to resolve themselves. God is great, God is great. My disorientation subsided.

We knew about the call to prayer, had heard it for months. It crackled to life five times a day, part of the din of Cairo. It sounded different in a silent, dark city. Nothing competed for God's attention. It was 5:00 AM. I went back to bed.

❋ ❋ ❋

After that first night we wore head scarves when we went out in public, something we never did in Cairo unless we were visiting a mosque. This didn't make us look less foreign, because we still wore jeans and long coats. Our head coverings were ad hoc, pulled from existing wardrobes. Mona wore a Palestinian *kaffiyeh,* and I wore an old Spanish scarf, black with roses. The local women were fully tented, with their faces and bodily outlines obscured. Almost every woman wore a multicolored sheet in the same radiating pattern, with the extra fabric clutched in front by an invisible hand. I wondered if the garish print was a trend, or if it had been around forever. Over their faces each one wore a piece of black, red, and white tie-dyed silk, which clashed aggressively with the other fabric. Occasionally we saw women who, rather than the kaleidoscopic garb, wore black from head to toe, which was the style in Saudi Arabia. All-black was seen as a sign of upward mobility—of a family that had money or had been abroad.

We didn't blend in. Our scarves made us less obvious, a little more ambiguous in our perceived origin. They made us more comfortable; the few times our hair was exposed we felt naked and vulnerable. I've met European women in conservative Muslim countries who've told me not to cover my hair, on the principle that I should act at all times as an ambassador of liberal values. But I regarded it practically. I hoped it might ease my passage through public space more effectively than anything did in Cairo. It also meant I didn't have to think about my hair.

❀ ❀ ❀

We encountered our first masturbator in Sanaa. We were sitting on a low wall outside a mosque, looking at a map. He appeared in a doorway, maybe twenty yards away, exposing himself from between the folds of his skirt, staring at us and throttling his penis. I nudged Mona, and we jumped up and walked away. We looked back; he was following us. We sped up, and kept checking over our shoulders until we were sure we had lost him.

We came across the second one in Sada, a northern Yemeni town on the fringe of the Empty Quarter, where we were walking around the high city wall. We came to a tall parapet, and I turned to look inside it. I don't know who was more surprised, he or us.

A few days later we caught a group taxi going from Sanaa to Manakha. It left just as the sun started to go down. We'd secured the front seat, which we thought was the optimal position, with knee room, window control, and a safe barrier between us and the other passengers. I got the window—it was my turn—and Mona took the center.

It got dark, we drove into the hills, and Mona dozed on my shoulder. Sometime later I noticed that our driver was grunting. I turned on a penlight, pretending to read, and then turned it in the direction of the driver. My suspicions were confirmed.

"Enough!" I yelled. We ordered him to stop the car. We yelled at him, hurling insults. ("You're ugly! You're a dog!" were among the few in our linguistic range.) We got out and looked around. We'd stopped in remote mountains, so storming away was not an option. We ordered two young men into the front seat and joined the oldest-looking one on a rear bench. The car of eight riders accepted the proceedings with mysterious equanimity. No one spoke up in our defense, but no one argued with us, either. While the car reorganized itself to meet our demands, several passengers stood and stretched their legs, looking resigned, as though patiently waiting out a flat tire. I felt like a ghost, able to affect events in the world of the living, with a rattle here or a knock there, but never really believed to exist.

❀ ❀ ❀

In Manakha one of the other passengers, now cordial and helpful, showed us where to find the only open hotel. It was in an old family home. We bargained with the proprietor, Ahmad, and he led us up a steep, narrow, uneven stairwell, until we reached the very top of the house, the room called the *mafraj,* with windows to take in the tower view. I woke with the sun streaming onto me in different colors, shining through the blue and red stained glass. Outside our door I heard the rhythmic swishing of someone sweeping a straw broom across stone. The sweeping went on for so long that it seemed impossible that the small landing could be that dirty. Jumpy about lurkers, I decided to open our door and meet the suspicious party. I found a girl. She straightened and stared directly at me, as if to ask what had taken me so long. She called down the stairs for our breakfast, then approached the room and peeked in. Her eyes paused on every object: sleeping bag, backpack, hiking boot, camera. She said her name was Faiza.

Mona and I took breakfast on the roof, seeing the town by daylight for the first time. It was built into the mountainside in the cradle between two peaks. There were no power lines, no cars, and no roads other than the one we had come in on. The buildings were rough-hewn versions of those in Sanaa: sand-colored with white patterns painted on, zigzags and diamonds and crosses. Below and around the town, terraced rice fields had sculpted the hills into jumbo steps. Stairs for a fairy-tale giant, or a god. Once again, my visual perspective was thrown off. Things were not the right size.

After breakfast we set off. We climbed through the terraced fields, passing hamlet after hamlet, each one balanced more precariously than the last. It was as though, in the absence of roads and power tools, the local builders had developed a single skill: how to make a village as inaccessible and well-defended as possible.

When shadows started to slice across the hillsides, we looked down and saw a sea of white mist below us. The clouds climbed as we descended, so that soon we were enveloped in their cool vapor. During the rest of our descent, the veil parted and closed, each time revealing something different: a hamlet, a valley, a bend in the trail.

Faiza, sister of Ahmad, cooked and served our dinner. There were other family members present, a mother and another sister, but it was Faiza who toiled the most. She was fifteen years old and divorced. Ahmad granted, without further explanation, that this was unusual—not the marriage but the divorce. After we ate, Faiza returned to the *diwan*. "You came from Sanaa?" she asked us. Yes, I said, adding that we studied in Egypt. Everyone had some concept of Egypt—it was the source of Arab soap operas and movies. Faiza had never left the area around Manakha, Ahmad explained. As soon as he left she asked about our hair—Mona's was bumpy like hers but she found mine oddly straight, and wanted to touch it. She unwrapped her head gear to show us hers. We heard men coming up the stairs. In a blur of panicked movement, she retied her head scarf, an impressive task at high speed, involving an elaborate series of folds and knots. Later she showed us how to tie the black, slightly elastic rectangle that women used as the underscarf. When tied properly, the part of the underscarf that covered the face could be lowered without disentangling the rest, which simplified eating and speech. When women went out they added another layer on top of it, the face-covering *niqab*.

The next morning Faiza came to watch us again, this time dispensing with the charade of sweeping. I tried to think of something to say to her, but having already covered our marital status and hair, we were left with little common ground. I thought about the conversations I had with Mona, our classmates, and Graham, and realized that nearly every single one could be distilled down to a central theme: aspirations. What we wanted, what we planned, who we wanted to become, and how we were going to get there. Even in the gossip and the cheap thrills—the who-slept-with-whom, the pursuit of alcohol and drugs and weekend adventures—we were always talking about our own wishes. The fundamental assumption of my own agency underlay everything I thought and did. It was difficult to get into a different frame of mind and to imagine what I would talk about once there. I couldn't even ask Faiza if she hoped to marry, for at fifteen she had already failed at that one permitted ambition.

"Do you like Manakha?" I finally asked, groping for a connection as she fluttered her fingers over a pink cotton sweater lying on a windowsill. My words immediately struck me as lame. It was like asking her if she liked life.

"I have to work a lot," she said.

❀ ❀ ❀

One day in Sanaa, Mona and I were in the front seat of a shared taxi, waiting to depart. Suddenly a man rapped on our window. He was compact, brown-skinned, and mustachioed, like most Yemeni men, but wore a Western suit, and spoke careful and correct English. He had the offbeat enunciation of someone who had studied the language, but hadn't heard it spoken very often by natives.

"Please, would you ride with my family member?" he asked. Behind him was a small figure draped all in black, complete with face-covering *niqab*. This didn't strike us as a strange request. We'd angled to share the crammed benches of intercity taxis with other women, or had paid extra to have a whole bench to ourselves, apart from the men. So we moved to the back bench, where I took up my seat next to the black-clad woman, while the man who had knocked on our window, whose name was Abu Bakr, sat in front. Our taxi left Sanaa for Taiz.

All I could see of her were dark almond-shaped eyes with long lashes, set in unlined skin. Based on this I formed a picture of a great beauty. Abu Bakr's young wife, perhaps. My attempt at conversation went nowhere: I said hello, she said hello, then she looked out the window. I wondered if it was shyness or if she disdained me.

A half hour into our drive we could feel the sun beating on the windows. I felt sorry for our seatmate in the black layers. She took off her gloves and I looked at her hands. They were soft and pudgy, and I realized that she was a child. Mona and I pulled down the window screens, blocking out the sun and any prying eyes, and pushed our scarves back off our heads.

The child, Shafa, was Abu Bakr's niece. She was twelve, and Abu Bakr was taking her down to his home in Taiz to visit her cousins. Abu Bakr taught English and Arabic as a foreign language in Sanaa.

"Isn't that quite young to be wearing the veil?" I asked Abu Bakr.

"Yes, it is," he said. "She did not want to wear it, but I made her. I will not let any member of my family go uncovered, because I am con-serv-a-tive." He uttered the last word with effort, as though he wasn't quite sure how to pronounce it.

"Are you sisters?" he asked. Several Yemenis had asked us this, even though we didn't look alike. I wondered if the question was rooted in other people's hope, on our behalf, that however far from home we'd wandered, we must at least be kin.

❋ ❋ ❋

By the time we arrived in the highland city of Taiz, we'd accepted Abu Bakr's invitation to stay. His home was a newish structure built in the old style, a multistory maze of rooms and staircases. He shared it with his wife, his mother, two brothers, the wife of one of the brothers, and an assortment of children. When Shafa arrived indoors, she tore off her veil, and revealed herself to be not the ethereal and aristocratic beauty I'd first imagined, but a plump and round-faced preteen whose skin was just starting to break out. She embraced a cousin, who carried a set of plastic ponies with pink and blue hair. They ran away up some stairs.

Abu Bakr's wife, Ismat, was our age, twenty, and had been married six months. She was Djibouti-born, half-Egyptian and half-Yemeni, with gray eyes and high cheekbones and a cautious air. His sister-in-law, Hoda, was older, heavier, and more cheerful. They gave us our own large room with carpets on the floor and cushions lining the walls, and—a great luxury—our own bathroom with a shower and a flushing Turkish toilet. I had my first shower in five days. We laid out our sleeping bags in the middle of our room.

Accepting an offer of Arab hospitality is like committing to a first-class train ride. You'll be well-cosseted, but you can't get off in the middle, and so are stuck with your seatmates for the duration. Several women brought us breakfast in our room the next morning. Then Abu Bakr appeared and informed us that he was taking us sightseeing.

From 1948 until 1962, Yemen was ruled from Taiz by Imam Ahmad, the second to last in a line of hereditary kings, who lived in a hilltop palace. It still sits on the highest hill, with the town tumbling down around it. Imam Ahmad had been both a despot and a modern man. He'd updated the military, suppressed tribal revolts, and, up in his palace, collected modern curiosities like blenders, blow-dryers, and a phonograph. Despite a life of cutthroat court politics, he died peacefully in his bed, and the palace, now a museum, was preserved untouched. His curiosities were protected under glass in yellowed rooms, frozen in 1962.

The nation outside, with its strange architecture and costume, its missing technology, its profound apartheid of the sexes, also seemed to be trapped in time. That, though, was an illusion. Yemen was already globalizing, but in ways I couldn't recognize, because I thought the direction of change was always toward Westernization. I thought modernization meant that for better or worse you ended up with a Pizza Hut. There was one in Cairo. We foreign students disdained it, but it was popular with upper-class Cairenes. Many of Yemen's outside influences, though, came from sources I couldn't identify, since they weren't the signatures of my own culture. After President Ali Abdullah Saleh lent support to Iraq in the 1991 Gulf War, Yemen's wealthy neighbor Saudi Arabia retaliated by throwing out hundreds of thousands of Yemeni guest workers. They brought home new ideas about dress and worship. Veterans of the Afghan wars, who had gone to fight the Soviets with the *mujahedeen*, were also coming home, with new interpretations of jihad. By 1992 the Yemeni bell jar had long been broken. On the whole this was probably for the best. Most people don't benefit from remaining hidden and isolated, suspended in time, illiteracy and illness preserved along with their otherworldly beauty.

After visiting the palace we walked to a zoo on its grounds. Tiny cement enclosures with iron bars, some sunk into the ground, lined a small courtyard. The stench from the cages was acute, the animals thin. Mona drew her scarf across her face, feigning modesty, to block the smell and hide her expression. We dutifully toured the yard, trying not to look horrified. A mangy hyena prowled listlessly in a cage. Another contained a skunk. Two golden female lions had been granted the largest space. One paced back and forth while the other stood with her face pressed up against the bars, as though straining to push her head through. Why was it, I wondered, that I looked at these animals and saw them as suffering, while others—like members of a nearby family who were laughing and taking pictures—apparently did not? You could regard the creatures as pleasurable spectacle only if it didn't occur to you that they were sentient. In the final cage a brown and white monkey stood clinging to a metal bar with a bright red erection on display. He screamed and screamed, making the sound of human rage.

We left the zoo with relief and followed Abu Bakr to a nearby promenade with a view of the city below. It was Friday, the day of rest, and more families had come up to take the air. As we strolled along, Abu Bakr told us that he planned to marry a second wife, and was looking for a foreigner who spoke English or French, perhaps a European or a Canadian. I took this in with exasperation. His education and interest in foreign ways, along with his possession of a young, beautiful, and recently acquired wife, hadn't suggested an aspiring polygamist. Now his hospitality seemed to have been a means of prospecting for number two, someone who could maybe even get him a foreign visa. "It might be difficult to get a European to wear the veil," I said. She wouldn't have to, he replied, and I got the feeling he had mulled the question over. He saw himself as a reasonable man. "Do you think Ismat would mind if you married again?" I asked. He shrugged. "Maybe for a few months, but she would get used to it." Abu Bakr said he wanted to study in North America. I told him he might find it difficult to live there. "But I am progressive," he said.

He dropped us off at the busy marketplace and instructed us to be home by one thirty. "Okay, Dad," Mona said after he was out of earshot, and we giggled like teenagers allowed to roam the mall. We were regressing from independence. We moved past vegetable sellers sitting on the cobblestones, up a street lined with stalls each dedicated to one product: fabrics, Qurans, silver jewelry, daggers. I wanted one of the finely knit black scarves like the one Faiza had shown us, that tucked around the head and face. The first fabric stall we came to sold them, packaged in shiny plastic envelopes. Mona and I each bought one. At a jeweler's I bought a coin from the time of the Imamate, now useless, with a loop welded on so that I could wear it around my neck.

We arrived back fifteen minutes late and joined the menfolk in one of the *diwan*s; the women were still making lunch. As foreign women, we were a sort of third sex, allowed, like Ottoman eunuchs, to pass between two worlds. Ismat and Hoda emerged from the kitchen and served plates of rice and chicken on a long cloth laid out in the middle of the room, presenting Mona and I with forks, procured just for us. We thanked them but set the forks aside, wanting to prove our competence with our hands. After we had all had our first helpings, Ismat, Hoda, and Abu Bakr's mother, whom everyone called Ummi, sat down and joined us.

After lunch Abu Bakr said he was taking us on the family expedition to his home village, where his father lived with his other wife, along with several of his brothers and their families. Mona and I put on our head scarves and overcoats. Ismat and Hoda put on their long black cloaks and *niqab*s. Ismat wore an additional layer that hung over her eyes, sheer enough for her to see out but too opaque for anyone else to see through. Protected against the dangers of visibility, we piled into the car.

Abu Bakr's brother's *diwan* was more rustic than the clan's Taiz home, with carpets on bare stone and a dirt yard outside. He served us Vimto, a purple soft drink that tasted vaguely of berries; Mona loathed the beverage and made me drink hers, lest she offend by leaving her cup full. We clustered with Ismat in a corner with our Vimto and cookies. She asked us if we were married; we said no. "It's better not to be married," she said. "Do you want Abu Bakr to marry again?" I asked, wondering if bigamy might not be such a bad thing, if it might get her off the hook for wifely duties in some way. "No, of course not," she said. I now felt a sense of complicity with Ismat, but I saw no point in mentioning the plans Abu Bakr had shared. As fascinated and appalled as I was, as much as I felt compelled to ask questions on the margins, it seemed irresponsible to stoke conflict in a family machinery I didn't understand. We asked her if she liked wearing the veil. She said no, and pointed out that she hadn't worn the *niqab* before marrying; Abu Bakr made her do that. She had been to high school and studied English and French. Now it was her wish to study at the University of Sanaa and become a teacher. If Abu Bakr went to Canada to study there, she said, she wanted to do that too. I suddenly hoped fervently that this would happen. Life depended on the husband, I now saw, and she was lucky to have one who might take her abroad. In Canada she could escape if she wanted to; it was set up to facilitate that kind of thing. I imagined myself in her shoes, biding my time until one day, Abu Bakr at work . . .

He roused us from our corner. We walked from his brother's place to another house and another *diwan*. Then we moved on, bound for a third. Mona asked why we were going from house to house. "So they can see you," Ismat said, and I saw her smile for the first time. We were a sort of gift from Abu Bakr to Ismat, a learning experience and Friday diversion. A sense of responsibility came over me, and I resolved to power politely through my creeping exhaustion. Everyone else wore slip-on shoes, but Mona and I wore hiking boots, which had to come off at every door. We came to the threshold of the third home, in the courtyard of which at least twenty women and children had gathered; the women were unveiled. On the steps, flanked by Ismat, we met several women in receiving-line style, and imitated their gesture of pressing hand to heart. The oldest, small and gnarled, was the matriarch of them all. The women brought us a blanket to sit on in the courtyard, and more tea. The grandmother kept bringing us out more pillows and blankets, until one of the younger women told her to stop. We sipped and talked. Abu Bakr had disappeared, and I wondered when he would come to collect us.

When he reappeared, more tea was procured, and the grandmother and some of the younger women began chiding him, their chorus of voices rising in unison. The old woman went indoors, and he explained to us that she was mad at him for not warning her that foreigners were coming, so that she could have prepared gifts. Mona and I were nodding sympathetically when the old woman reappeared in her doorway and came waddling toward us, hands outstretched, proffering a dozen eggs tied in a red plastic bag.

Mona hit her limit and burst into hysterical laughter. I smacked her on the back and pretended she was having a coughing fit. We were so convincing that the old woman then brought Mona a glass of water, which caused her to laugh harder. I thanked the old woman for the eggs and we retreated. On our way back to Taiz I held them carefully in my lap.

❋ ❋ ❋

I sensed initially that Hoda, Abu Bakr's sister-in-law, disapproved of us; she hadn't deigned to speak to us at all on the first day. Maybe she thought we aimed to marry one of the men, or maybe she thought we were a corrupting influence on Ismat, the newest inductee into the household, with all our talk of university and confusion over veils. Hoda seemed to be a much happier person, much better adapted to family life, than sullen Ismat. By Friday afternoon, though, she'd warmed up to us, and told me I looked pretty with my new Yemeni head scarf on, the one I'd picked up in the Taiz market. She promised that after dinner she would beautify us by hennaing our hands.

There are many ways to color the skin with henna; the method here was to dye the palm of each hand rust-red. Hoda sat down in front of us in the *diwan* with a pot of mud, and ordered me to extend my left arm. She caked my fingertips and palm, then placed a ball of the red mud in my hand and had me close it in a fist. "You have to stay like this," she said, then speedily wrapped my hand up in a swatch of silk and tied it at the wrist. By the time dismay could register, I was already bound. Mona, who was watching, asked with trepidation, "How long?"

"Three hours," Hoda said, and reached for my right hand. Mona went to brush her teeth before her opposable thumbs were rendered useless. Once the ends of our arms had been reduced to stumps, we settled ourselves into the cushions and Hoda tuned the television to an Egyptian movie. The family turned its eyes to the screen. Chubby-faced Shafa was there, with one of her cousins, Fatima. Ummi and Hoda were there, and two of Abu Bakr's brothers were present, one with a child curled in his lap. Only Abu Bakr and Ismat were missing, and I found myself wondering how she was, and wondering, against my will, about the marital bed, whether it was happy or dreadful or somewhere in between. After a time I forgot that I had no use of my hands, and feeling sheltered and calm, let my eyes flutter shut.

❋ ❋ ❋

The next day, like free people, we left. We took a bus to Aden, didn't much like it, and so, high on liberty, decided in an instant to head back north. I saw that I might never understand certain things. However far I went, I wouldn't forget that I was a visitor. I couldn't forget that I could walk away. However deeply I sank—into situations of my own devising, or even real trouble—I would be conscious of an escape hatch, of the ability to call my embassy, my parents. Despite my great privilege, or maybe because of it, I couldn't resist wandering out to the edge. It was like when I'd tried to get myself lost in all those Spanish campgrounds, just to feel my pulse race. I was still pursuing the excitement of disorientation.

ON ADAPTATION
chapter nine

*M*ona and I spread our recent purchases across our beds and looked at them. We were back in Sanaa with a day left in our trip, staying in our hotel on Ali Abd al-Mughni Street.

We each had

- a rectangular knit black scarf, about three feet long;
- a shorter rectangle made of silk, black with a tie-dyed pattern of red and white circles;
- a pair of voluminous pants that gathered at the ankles;
- a cotton square, large enough to serve as a queen-sized bedspread, printed in red, yellow, blue, black, and green;
- flip-flops;
- safety pins.

"So," Mona said.

"So," I replied. We were daring each other again, psyching ourselves up. We were about to become deviants and fakes. We were going to go all the way.

❀ ❀ ❀

Strange things were happening to us. We were watching ourselves shift and adjust, watching suppressed feelings rise to the surface. We reacted to things first, then thought about them later.

At a hotel one night, Mona had stepped out of our room to use the sink in the next-door washroom. In the washroom was another door, leading onto a toilet, and while Mona was washing her face she realized that there was a person in the water closet. She called to me and asked me to bring her head scarf. As I went to do so, a man emerged from the toilet. Mona jumped, I jumped, and we ran into our room; she still had soap in her hand and water dripping from her face. "Please! No scare!" called the man. We slammed our door shut. Adrenaline coursed through me for having been seen with a bare head. We looked at each other and fell on the bed, the residue of panic giving our laughter a hysterical pitch.

On another day, in a group taxi, we had taken the front while several boys of nineteen or twenty had taken the bench behind us. They tried to talk to us from the moment they got in, but we crouched down into our coats and ignored them. In parry after parry, they trotted out all the phrases they had learned in foreign languages—German, French, English. I concentrated as best I could on my book, until one of them said, "Can I fuck you." This was, of course, nothing new, but my carefully cultivated immunity cracked. I twisted in my seat and lunged with my hands; I found purchase on his neck. All the anger of the last four months rose into my throat, and it felt good to finally let it take over. In a haze, seething with energy, I watched my hand until drops of blood appeared where my nails entered his flesh, and I felt Mona pulling me down in my seat.

They got out.

"Do you have the address?" Mona asked, as we looked at our new clothes. "Address" was a misnomer; they didn't really have them here. You either knew your way, relied on the kindness of strangers, or got lost. But I had directions to the Peace Corps compound on a piece of paper. We had met a volunteer, Aaron, and he had invited us to a group dinner.

"Let's do it," I said. I put on my pantaloons, which were dark green with gold embroidery around the bottom. They zipped up at the hip, and I felt like I was locking myself in. I grabbed my long black knit scarf and centered it on top of my head. With the first fold, I wrapped it around my forehead, pirate-style. Then I tucked it and brought it under my chin, as Faiza had shown me, twisted it and brought it across my face, just below my eyes, and then brought both ends around the back of my head for a final knot. Mona and I looked at each other, our heads now encased in black, expressions invisible. Just like that we'd erased the thing we most identified with ourselves, our faces. We'd become vacant canvases. I thought about how we treat people as blank slates anyway, projecting onto them what we want to believe. The less visual information available, the more we can project, just as I'd imagined chubby little Shafa to be a great beauty.

We picked up the tie-dyed rectangles. Positioning one end in a horizontal line just under my eyes, I tied the two top corners behind my head. Now I was painting my canvas with the local colors. In the West we talk critically about conformity, about the pressure to look a certain way, but it never goes as far as this. Extreme veiling, the kind practiced here on the Arabian peninsula, wasn't just for hiding features. It turned individuals into an undifferentiated mass.

The final addition was the bedspread expanse of cotton. I gathered mine up and draped it over my head, looking in the mirror to try to imitate local women. They held extra fabric over their arms, and clutched the whole thing together in the front. "My ankles are too dressy," I said. I wished I could wear my hiking boots, which made me feel tough and protected, but I slipped on the leather flip-flops instead. Our creations were complete.

"How do we get out of here?" I asked.

"Quickly," she said. I still didn't believe we were going to do this. I felt like a child playing dress-up. Did we have to take our game outside? But it was too late; we'd issued the mutual challenge.

We flew down the stairs, stifling a laugh as we passed the front desk. The hell with them, I thought, we weren't breaking any laws. As far as I knew.

We turned right out of our hotel door, along a busy shopping street in the new part of the city. I stopped laughing, but my heart beat faster.

"Just walk, just walk," Mona said, sounding alarmed, and breaching her own commandment that we should speak no English.

My breathing slowed, but I still felt befuddled—there seemed to be a din in my brain blocking out the street sounds. Then I remembered why I couldn't hear: There were three layers of fabric over my ears. I couldn't see very well, either, with my peripheral vision blocked by the bedspread. I concentrated on walking at a normal pace, and we settled in beside each other. I tried not to adjust, shift, fidget, itch. Everything seemed wrong. My fabric was dragging on the ground, I was too tall, my feet were too pale, my ankles too sparkly.

The sidewalk was thronged at the end of a business day, with men and women poring over watch displays, electronics, and bins of shoes. Most of the women were dressed exactly like us, the same garish patterns covering the same bits. I tried to ascertain funny looks, sideways glances.

I turned to Mona and shrugged. *"Mish mushkeela,"* I said. No problem. She didn't answer, but then she probably couldn't hear me. I thought maybe she looked worried, but then I couldn't see her face.

We turned right onto the dirt road that led into the old city, a mini-*souk* lined with vegetable stalls. This was interesting, I thought, although not as much fun as I had hoped. I couldn't shake my simmering anxiety. The problem, I realized, was that while I knew what local women looked like, I still had no real idea how they behaved. I didn't know their signals and postures, or what they did when. As an obvious foreigner, I knew who I was in the street and how I reacted to things. I knew that if my conduct was eccentric by local standards, it was the accepted eccentricity of a foreigner.

Mona started showing far too much interest in a display of tomatoes, and then, to my horror, asked how much they were. The vendor either couldn't hear or couldn't understand her. She reached up under her tie-dyed veil and pulled down the hatch of her under-scarf, and tried again, to no avail. Hubris had taken over a realistic assessment of her ability to communicate. I admired her nerve even as it dismayed me. She kept trying to talk to the tomato man until finally I tugged her on toward the old city.

A few minutes later I was pretty sure we were being followed. And, either because we were nearing the old city or because the shopping day was coming to a close, there were suddenly many fewer people around. In fact, there were no women, none except for us. And it was dusk. Since our first night in Yemen, which now seemed like a distant, innocent time, we had hardly ever gone out at dusk. The two young men were definitely following us. I bowed my head to Mona's and told her. We sped up. They sped up. We turned a corner, they followed. My skin bristled with fear.

The confounding thing was that we had no idea why we'd been

singled out. Being harassed for being Western was at least reassuringly predictable. Maybe these two had seen through our disguise, but maybe not—it was hard to say which would be worse. Maybe local women who stayed out after dusk got followed all the time. Maybe only hookers stayed out after dusk. Maybe they thought we were some girls they planned to meet. I was ignorant, and this was a stupid idea. As myself I knew what I did: I told them to scram, yelled shaming words, or raised my fist in their face. But I had no idea what a Sanaa woman did.

"Left," Mona commanded, and I followed; we were trying to lose them now, handicapped by the looming darkness and our muffled ears. We'd entered the old city, and were on a street lined with sandstone four-story homes. And suddenly, we realized, we were at a dead end. I hoped for a moment that they hadn't followed us into the alley. But then we heard them coming up behind us, one of them saying something I couldn't understand.

"Don't turn around yet, don't turn around yet," Mona whispered loudly, just as I was about to. I saw what she meant; the logic of instinct kicked in. I didn't turn around but instead made a fist with my right hand. I remembered something Graham had taught me years before—why had he taught me? I couldn't remember. It was so much more useful than telling me that dangers lurked. When you make a fist, he had said, don't hold your thumb under your fingers, or you'll hurt it when your knuckles connect with a jaw.

We let them come close.

"Now," Mona hollered, and we both turned around. I swung and hit a shoulder, and the impact ran up my arm. He exclaimed and fell back, undoubtedly more surprised than hurt. We ran between them. One of them shouted something after us. We ran back to the end of the alley, hearts pounding, then right, and right again. My thighs burned and I thought I'd never run so fast, though really I'd just never run like it mattered so much. I held my fabric up in my arms so that it didn't trip me up.

When we had made a third turn, we slowed down and looked over our shoulders. There was no one there, and no sound in the street except for the smack of our flip-flops on stone. As mysteriously as they'd begun to follow us, they'd disappeared. We didn't know why they'd started or stopped. We didn't know who they were—they could have been cops, rapists, bored teens. Conceivably all three.

Now night had fallen, the streets were deserted, and the moon lit up the paving stones. Our panicked turns had gotten us completely lost. I pulled out the hand-drawn map one of the Peace Corps volunteers had made. The compound was near a well-known mosque, but the map was drawn from the point at which we were supposed to have entered the old city. The streets didn't have names, nor the houses numbers. We wandered in silence, down alleys too narrow for moonlight, between walls punctuated with stained-glass squares lit up from within. My heart stopped racing, and I saw that the windows were beautiful. When we turned onto a broader street, we saw a white-trimmed minaret and two domes catching the moonbeams. I lifted our map again.

We ran down the street and reached the tall metal gate to the Peace Corps compound. Our host, Aaron, came down to the guardhouse, a forbidden beer in his hand; he was wearing a Grateful Dead T-shirt. "There you are," he said cheerfully, a walking piece of America, and instantly we'd crossed worlds.

We stepped into the courtyard, and before the door had clanged shut Mona and I were clawing at our clothing as though the fabric were burning skin. I pulled my black scarf violently back, almost choked myself, stopped to untie the knots, and threw it away from me. Mona dashed her bedsheet to the ground like she thought she could break it; I wrestled mine into a ball and stepped on it, and finally yanked my tie-dyed face cloth, which had fallen around my neck, off over my head. Aaron backed away and watched our frenzy from a distance until we settled down. He had female Peace Corps colleagues in Yemen; he'd seen them go quietly nuts. Then he led us to a room where we flopped into plastic chairs, and silently, solemnly, handed us cold beers.

❋ ❋ ❋

We landed in Cairo in the middle of a weekday with the feeling of returning to civilization. I felt welcomed into the dry, sunny heat, the honking and dust. In the taxi from the airport we decided we had to eat before parting ways. It took only a moment to decide: We asked the driver to take us to Pizza Hut.

ON REENTRY
chapter ten

*W*hen *I returned in midsummer* from Egypt to Vancouver, I took a job as a hostess in a downtown restaurant called Penny Lane. It was never quite busy enough. I stood for long hours at the podium by the entrance, and when that grew too dull I sat down and rolled silverware into napkins, which at least resulted in the satisfying accumulation of piles of bundled cutlery. The manager was not at all impressed that I'd spent the past year in Egypt, a fact that drew only a blank stare in the interview, after which I moved on to emphasize the one time I'd worked briefly—and unsuccessfully, moving slowly and forgetting orders—as a waitress. You could explore all kinds of different worlds, I now saw, but couldn't necessarily reconcile them to one another. This didn't bother me at the time. I could infiltrate the worlds of rich Egyptian kids, or strict Muslims, or Spanish nightclubs, or the young and aimless wait staff of my own hometown, who were themselves ramblers from elsewhere, Quebec and Ontario and Australia and Britain. I took pride in being a chameleon. Still, it felt strange to let Egypt slip so quickly behind me, as though I'd lost a limb and continued merrily on my way. There had been no debriefing. One day I was in Cairo, school having ended, most of my American friends already gone. The next I was in Alexandria, Virginia, where I was stopping to visit my half sister on my way home.

Just one instance of reverse culture shock lingered in my mind. Within hours of my arrival, my sister and I went out walking among a milling summer crowd on a boardwalk on the Potomac River. The weather was hot and humid. I bought an ice cream for four dollars, stunned at the price. And then I noticed the girls in sports bras, which stunned me even more. They were wearing their underwear in public; they were nearly naked. Disbelief passed over me, then disdain at their immodesty. Egypt had beaten a new sensibility into me. I'd been one of those girls a year earlier. I remembered cleaning my new Cairo apartment in a sports bra when two friends had come over, and how I hadn't even put on a T-shirt. Our modesty or immodesty was all arbitrary, I thought. Capable of growing in whatever direction was dictated by our surroundings. But once we were trained, once our culture was all in place, it was hard to dislodge.

Graham was living in his father's trailer home and working as a park ranger, and many nights I drove out to White Pine Lake to pick him up. He closed up the park and finished work at eleven. He had to meet me at the gate to the park to let me drive in. One night I pulled up to the gate, which was at the side of a winding wooded road, to find him standing next to his truck, buck naked except for his work boots. I burst into laughter and drove through. It took him a minute to close and lock the gate, and the whole time I watched him, wondering if a car was going to come cruising along the public road at any minute. I was enchanted by Graham's abandon. I thought maybe it was an impossible thing for a girl to feel, but I wanted it for myself anyway.

I went back to Seattle to begin my senior year, and Graham moved back to Whistler, the mountain town where he'd spent the previous winter. He'd saved up for a season lift pass and planned to spend as much time as possible on a snowboard. When he was in

Egypt he'd sometimes talked about going to college, but now he only mentioned the possibility occasionally and without much conviction. His enthusiasms were strong—powdery snow, photography, teaching himself the guitar. It was hard for me to see where these would go. I didn't judge him, because I hadn't solved the riddle of where I was going, either. I began to see that the future self he was creating might be radically different from my own.

Still, we were dutiful to our love. It was like a religion with two members, and whatever doubt we felt, we paid it our devotions. He took the Greyhound bus down to Seattle, or I drove my Ford Escort to Whistler, which I could do in about four hours with no stops. I was an alien in his home, a four-bedroom condo with eight housemates. He had his own room, the smallest one, with a single bed that we shared. I had a clunky laptop computer and piles of folders. While he was at work I set up shop at his kitchen table and pounded out my senior thesis, to be titled "Saudi Arabia and the Reunification of Yemen." His roommates passed in and out and talked to me about the snow conditions; I made a point of being *au courant*, my small way of fitting in.

It was he who seemed to first question what we were doing, to have the nerve to say, "I don't know how I feel anymore." I proclaimed that I was still very much in love, but this was in part because I didn't want to admit the possibility that it could just go away. Falling out of love for the first time is as surprising as falling in love. It's even similar: There's the bewilderment at the heart's revolutions, and a sense of finally understanding what people have been talking about. Only instead of feeling like you've been granted a superpower, you feel like it's been taken away.

I told Graham that I would finish college as quickly as possible, and that then we could be together. But when I discovered that the

U.S. State Department offered college internships, and that if I won one I could spend the next summer abroad, that happy pretravel conviction came over me again. This time it wasn't just one trip dangled in front of me but a whole possible career, one that would let me roam the world. I would travel, learn languages, and . . . well, I had only the vaguest idea what diplomats did. They went places, I knew that, and I longed to feel the slip-slide of unfamiliar territory once again. Graham was surprised when I told him I was applying to go abroad. I knew that choosing departure would be different this time.

I wrote a statement explaining to the State Department that I wanted to go to Kabul. I wanted to go because of romantic novels like M. M. Kaye's *The Far Pavilions,* because of Rudyard Kipling, because of history classes on the Great Game, because Afghanistan was different and difficult and far away. Graham was neither aggressive nor pointed as he questioned me about my desire; he merely observed that we would be apart again. "I might not even get it," I told him. "You will," he said, and I knew he was right. Despite his mildness, I felt angry and provoked as two things clashed inside me. There was, on the one hand, my dreamy vision of being with him. On the other hand was my feeling that this internship and all it represented—going abroad again, finding my own path—was an absolute right. Though still merely an idea, I felt that it was a part of me I had to defend.

I was at Whistler with Graham's roommates when my mother called with news: The United States had no diplomatic presence in Afghanistan at the time, but the State Department would be pleased to assign me instead to ten weeks at the consulate general in Karachi, in neighboring Pakistan. I jumped up and down on the sofa, yelling "I'm going to Karachi!" Everyone told me this was cool. They had no idea where it was, but they had a world map on their living room wall, courtesy of Graham, and I stood on the sofa and pointed it out. In any case, they understood that I would embark on a wished-for adventure, and wished-for adventure was a currency we had in common.

It was then, in the dead of winter, when I decided I would go away again, that we both began to understand that we would break up. I'd made a choice, and it was not to try for love, with all its risk of pain, but to travel.

For months after Graham and I broke up, we stayed in touch by telephone and letter, and then for years afterward I would think of him in a longing way. I would imagine that he was watching over me, and I would make choices based on whether or not they would impress Graham, who would never know about them anyway. I would feel like I was surpassing Graham: He'd inspired me to travel, but I would go beyond.

❋ ❋ ❋

In the spring I went to a small house party with college friends on Seattle's Queen Anne Hill. This was the kind of thing I'd only recently started doing—between my year abroad and all the time I spent visiting Graham, I didn't have many friends in Seattle. Most of the people at the party went to my university; I shared classes with a couple of them, Arabic with Terry and political science with Jeff. Then there was Terry's girlfriend, her best friend, and her best friend's boyfriend. I liked them all and they liked me back; they were even a little impressed with me in exactly the way that the Penny Lane manager was not. I had established my credentials as an adventurer. But I didn't know them as well as I wished I did, and I felt grateful to be included. I now saw that this was a hazard of being away all the time, this failure to entwine myself with people in one place. But maybe it didn't matter: I'd soon be away again for another three months. And then who knew what. I still didn't think much of Seattle.

We took ecstasy and stayed up all night, lolling on the floor like a litter of puppies, sharing our waves of euphoria. A tall man with long blond hair arrived; he caught my eye because he shared Graham's look. The new man's name was Stu, and he arrived with a woman whom I later learned was his girlfriend. Stu had dropped out of college, where he'd dabbled in architecture, engineering, and ethnomusicology, and was now rebuilding a house for his great-aunt.

He sat down next to me and didn't leave my side until the morning. We talked the entire time. I told him about Egypt and Yemen, and he told me about the time he'd spent in Thailand and Bali, mostly with his girlfriend, who seemed to be keeping her distance on the far side of the room. In Bali he had spent months studying wood sculpture, carving and whittling with a teacher next to a stream. He had wanderlust too. When I told him I would be spending the summer in Pakistan, he seemed genuinely impressed and excited; he talked about *qawwali* music and the *tabla* drum. I lay back and listened, at ease, letting him tell me about the place where I was going.

The next day Stu's girlfriend moved out of their houseboat. The night on Queen Anne had been some kind of final straw after four years, open wounds, an affair on her part with an Israeli she met in India, and a slide into friendship and recrimination. She and Stu broke up, and he asked a friend for my number and called me after two weeks. In the following month we grew close.

I was of two minds about the fact that we'd met on ecstasy. Did the chemical euphoria mean that what we had was fake? Or had it just opened us up faster than would have happened anyway? One of the greatest love stories of all time is about a potion. Tristan was sent on a trip to Ireland to fetch Iseult, his uncle's betrothed. On the sea journey back to Cornwall they swallowed the elixir, and after that were powerless to control their love.

The spring was still chilly, and we lay on a mattress on the floor of his houseboat, in front of a wood-burning fire. We did more drugs, mushrooms this time, with my new group. By bestowing his love on me, Stu had confirmed me in their circle. I wrote papers and took exams. Stu had grown up in Seattle, as had his parents, as had his grandparents, all four of whom lived nearby. I let him be my anchor. The night before I left, he stayed over at my loft and helped me wash a sink full of dishes that I didn't want to leave for my roommates. Then I was off.

ON ESTABLISHING AN INTERNATIONAL CAREER
chapter eleven

The heat took me in its fist. Jane, a freckled consular officer on her first tour, had come to see me through customs and take me to my assigned home. We rode in the back of an air-conditioned car across Karachi, where for miles the buildings bristled with rebar sticking up from the roof, as though the whole metropolis were waiting for another story to be added on. Dense traffic belched exhaust into the bright haze, and when we stopped, vendors selling newspapers and flower garlands rapped at the windows. Motorcycles buzzed by carrying families of five. From the low-lying sprawl we moved into broad avenues and colonial facades, and finally turned into a gated lane. Tucked in the middle of the city's thousand-plus square miles, it felt far away from the buzz.

The consulate general, in its wisdom, had given me a two-story, four-bedroom house, with formal and informal dining rooms, a roof deck, a walled garden with mango trees and a well-watered lawn, and servants' quarters occupied by a man named Taj, his wife and daughters, a few chickens, and a cat. A guardhouse flanked my gated driveway, occupied in shifts by leather-faced old gentlemen, called *chowkidars,* who had red-dyed beards. My house in turn sat on the narrow lane of consular homes.

After Jane left, Taj proposed a deal, to which I agreed. I was obviously less work than a normal diplomatic family. For a reduced rate—and the right to keep living in his quarters until more lucrative residents arrived—he would do my laundry, shop for groceries, and prepare meals. I felt like a cheat. All my traveler's ideas about self-sufficiency evaporated, and now I found myself with a servant who, to my astonishment, called me *"memsahib."* I associated the word with all those novels about the Raj.

I climbed up to the roof, but could see little of the city beyond the white-walled homes of the compound around me. In the flat bright sky, the black silhouettes of birds made lazy, loping circles. Cormorants flew in flocks, while birds of prey—eagles, kites, and vultures—hunted alone, periodically dive-bombing into the city below. I tried to count the birds but stopped at fifty-five.

I felt disoriented and alone, all the more so when Taj served me *chicken biryani* on formal china and silver at the head of the dining room table. This made me feel excruciatingly self-conscious, so I asked him to bring all my subsequent evening meals on a tray to my room. Laundry would take some negotiation too: Taj's rule of thumb seemed to be that, when in doubt, an item should be both ironed and starched. I started doing my underwear in my bathroom sink.

After dinner my first night I pulled an armchair up to my second-story bedroom window. I wanted to feel the heat again, so I opened the window up to the evening air, which was still sauna-like, and let it wash over me. My distance from anywhere familiar weighed on me like a physical force. For thousands and thousands of miles, there was no one who was thinking of me. The summer stretched ahead like a tunnel.

❋ ❋ ❋

The next day I put on a skirt and shirt that I hoped looked professional as well as modest enough to walk around outside, thinking, wrongly, that one popped out for errands or lunch. Jane drove me to work. The first thing I noticed about the consulate general was the line of visa applicants. There were hundreds of them—men, women, and children—all wearing *shalwar khamis*, the national uniform composed of a long, loose tunic over pantaloons. The line stretched along one whole face of the building, which occupied most of a block, and around the corner, where it snaked between metal barricades. It wasn't moving.

As we entered the compound by car, a high metal gate opened to reveal a metal drum as tall as our hood, which slowly retracted into the ground. Before we were allowed to drive in, guards inspected the undercarriage using poles with mirrors on one end.

I was given my own office in the political section. I reported to Kevin, a skinny political officer with glasses and a beard. He'd been a high school history teacher in Connecticut until he'd passed the Foreign Service entrance exam on his third try, and so had a teacher's patient way of explaining things. Kevin gave me some newspaper clippings and phone numbers, and told me to start finding things out. This, apparently, was what political officers did. They found things out and reported them to Washington, writing memos on orange and black computer screens. Every memo we wrote had to be classified on a scale of "unclassified" through "top secret," but nothing, no matter how innocuous, was ever actually labeled unclassified. Washington wanted reports on environmental issues, which no one on staff had the time to do, so this nonpriority portfolio was handed to me. Kevin was working on child labor: Washington was concerned that the Pakistani workforce included children under fourteen.

❀ ❀ ❀

I saw Karachi from cars: congen cars, the Marines' car, the cars of new friends and friends of friends. The Mitsubishi Pajero was king;

every well-to-do city resident seemed to have one. A boxy, high-riding four-wheel drive, it made its occupants feel safe. The only place I traveled on foot was to the consulate general most mornings. It took me fifteen minutes on foot in the searing heat, across the manicured expanse of Jinnah Park. I saw the bloodred stains that spatter Karachi sidewalks, the juice spat out by betel nut users after a chew. Usually a few men started following me when I entered the park, and usually they provided a running commentary on my appearance, my availability for marriage, my interest in fucking, my Americanness, and whatever else was on their mind. They stayed far enough away that I could think of myself as a wild animal, and of them as incompetent hunters, not likely to really get a shot. I'd been prepared for this by Egypt, I reminded myself. I knew how to brace for impact, to let just enough in and shut the rest out. I was callused but knew how to feel in control.

Sometimes, when either the heat or the audience seemed like too much to bear at 8:30 AM, I just took the consulate general's shuttle van.

One way it was different from Egypt, and from the other Arab places I'd been, was in the absence of women in the streets. Instead of women in varying degrees of head scarves and veils, here there was simply lacuna. In upscale neighborhoods like Clifton Beach, families strolled together along the boardwalk in the evenings. But in most neighborhoods, the crowds were 80, even 90 percent male. I saw only the richest and the poorest women. The wealthy, educated ones—these were the ones I met—lived busy social and professional lives behind the walls of their homes and businesses, behind the tinted windows of their cars and their bodyguards' guns. The second group appeared like shadows at car windows: a figure in a full burka the color of the road, holding out a withered hand to beg. A young woman with a too-old face, thrusting out a bundle of rags that may or may not have contained a baby.

Importuners at the window were a feature of car-bound life. There were hawkers selling cigarettes, newspapers, and strings of jasmine blossoms, and there were beggars. Paul, one of the Marine guards, had this trick he showed me one night on an outing to Snoopy's, a Clifton Beach ice cream parlor that the Marines had nicknamed Snoop Dog. Paul pretended not to see the beggar as the man approached and pressed his face and hands to the window—and then, *wham*, Paul turned and slammed his hand against the glass. The beggar jumped back in terror; I gasped, and the Pakistani driver didn't react. My first instinct was to laugh, because Paul's move broke the tension, turned the ever-present encroachment into a joke. Then I felt appalled at myself for laughing. I wasn't supposed to be like this; I didn't want to treat people like things. But I was now complicit in terrorizing a beggar.

On my first weekend Jane invited me to the Karachi Yacht Club with her friend Zeba, a Karachi native. En route we wanted gum, cigarettes, and bottled water. We pulled over in front of a cluster of stalls, and dusty urchins immediately swarmed the car; with calm authority Zeba rolled down her window, handed coins to one of them, and asked him to fetch what we needed and keep the change. That was how things worked.

❋ ❋ ❋

A creaking wooden motorboat carried us across the slick brown-gray water from a parking lot to the club, which occupied all of a small rocky island. Here the black birds of prey circled in even greater numbers, feeding on the detritus of the vast port.

In their island isolation, yacht club members could behave

more or less as they pleased. Some of the men and women lolled in shorts or bathing suits. Jane introduced me to Kamran, the twenty-one-year-old son of a Pakistani father and a German mother, who had a dark tan on sharp cheekbones, gold-flecked brown hair, and green eyes. A heart-shaped tattoo with the word *Becca* adorned his left bicep. "I was in Boston for three years," was the first thing he said to me. His last name was Qureishi, indicating the tribe of the Prophet; for all I knew he could have been a direct descendant. But everything about him, down to his fashionable surf shorts, suggested a desire to be something else. He had probably been "Cam" or "Cameron" in Boston, eliminating the foreign sound. He would quip to his friends in Urdu, but had committed to American-inflected English as his linguistic home base. His looks worked in his favor; he was handsome by any cultural standard and ethnically unrecognizable. But America, it seemed, had fallen apart from him. Becca had been a forbidden Puerto Rican girlfriend who had moved into the apartment his parents financed. (Her parents hadn't been any happier than his.) He'd played to excess and flunked out of Boston University. Between the girlfriend and the grades, his parents had yanked him home, and only now was he realizing the extent of his mistake. His friends would be going back to their overseas schools in the fall, while he would be staying in Karachi. He spoke vaguely of going to Germany at some point. He was doing a lot of sailing.

Kamran invited me to race with him that afternoon. As the regatta got under way, we cruised away from the KYC in a 420, a two-person sailboat. Kamran manned the tiller while I followed his directions. We tacked back and forth between anchored container ships, sometimes coming so close that I could almost touch the steel side. The ships were hundreds of meters long and towered over us like apartment blocks; when we came that close in our tiny vessel it was like approaching a man-made planet, nerve-racking and thrill-ing. Kamran explained that whenever one of them started pump-ing water out of a stern hatch, it was readying to heave itself into the shipping channel and make its sluggish way out to sea; in other words, we should get out of the way. Karachi had once been a fishing village called Kolachi-jo-Kun, which was hard to picture now that it was one of the biggest ports in Asia.

Afterward we sat drinking lemonade with his friends, young Pakistanis home from university in England or America. These kids who slipped naturally into the middle class when they were over-seas, walking to campus or staying in dorms, lived in fortified man-sions here at home, where they were waited on by servants. For me it was the reverse: In a poor country, it was so easy for a middle-class American or Canadian—or citizen of any Western nation—to fall in with the rich. From the canon to pop culture, we shared a language. We shared a sense of entitlement so ingrained that we couldn't have told you it was there. We shared ideas about individual autonomy and girls' being allowed to wear miniskirts. Here, as in Egypt, I found the high protective walls an affront at first, but whenever mental exhaustion took over, I was relieved to retreat behind them. Here, as in Egypt, being so welcomed by the rich kids gave me an inflated sense of myself, as though I were wealthy too. But then again, by global standards, I was.

✾ ✾ ✾

Jane dealt with American citizens imprisoned in Karachi. She couldn't get them out of jail—they had, as a rule, broken the law, often in relation to drugs—but she visited them, relayed messages to their families, and tried to make sure they had competent lawyers.

Jane's colleague David was fresh from Yale and freshly married to Nirit. He and his wife both had brown hair and pale skin, and when Nirit wore her glasses, they could have passed for sister and brother. He was a New Yorker, and Nirit was an Israeli-born American. When David was assigned to Pakistan for his first tour, and they applied for Nirit's diplomatic passport, it arrived showing Iceland, alphabetically just one country away, as her place of birth. Nirit, who was studying for a master's degree in conflict resolution, had just returned to Karachi for her summer break. David worked in the trenches—issuing visas, that is, or, far more often, declining to issue them. That snaking line that formed every morning outside the consulate general reached its conclusion at David's window.

Stephen worked in the political section with me, but his job was harder to ascertain. He was tall and twenty-seven, with wavy brown hair, and his office door—complete with nameplate and title—was directly across the section's foyer from mine. I watched his morning routine from my desk. He would pick up his newspaper from in front of his door, throw it into his office, close the door, and leave again. He spent his days beyond a different door, one with a coded lock, with the techies who handled secure communications. Stephen would reappear only at lunchtime in the cafeteria, where he was friendly and laid-back. One day I asked him, while sitting around a table with a group, "How come you're never in your office?" He didn't answer. I asked again, but then Jane turned to me and asked me how my cheeseburger was.

The next day Stephen came to my office and handed me a *Dilbert* cartoon he'd cut out of the newspaper. Catbert was working on a top-secret project, and said to Dilbert, in the last frame: "Just move along now. There's nothing to see here." Later Stephen told me that when he scored a coup at work, he went home and poured himself a scotch, alone.

✿ ✿ ✿

David and Nirit invited me out several times with their friend Ahmed, an entrepreneur and sports car aficionado who had lived in California. Ahmed told us about a business idea he had had: Car jackings were an ongoing problem in Karachi. Typically masked gunmen would force the driver out of his car and take off with the vehicle. With an ineffective police force and plenty of potential culprits, victims were never likely to see their car again.

On a trip to California, Ahmed discovered the LoJack: It was a device you attached to the underside of your car that sent out a radio signal, making it possible to pinpoint the car's location if it went missing. Perfect, thought Ahmed. Surely every car owner in Karachi would want one of these. He contacted the manufacturer in California and retailers in Pakistan, calculated his potential profit, and made plans to import a first shipment.

Somewhere along the way, though, as Ahmed was extolling the LoJack to his contacts in Karachi, a more experienced businessman took him aside. And Ahmed realized that he dare not import the LoJack if he wanted to continue to live in this town. The missing cars would be found, all right—in the driveways of government ministers. No one needed that kind of trouble. Ahmed abandoned his plans.

✿ ✿ ✿

A local Christian activist had been trying to get the political officers' attention, and so Kevin passed him down the ranks to me. I called Mr. Masih, who had a list of places he wanted to take me. After my first few weeks on the job, it began to dawn on me that I had a luxurious freedom: Within certain restrictions, like staying in or near Karachi, I was free to make an appointment and go off and ask people about what it was they did. I began to stretch my legs. This hardly seemed like work, but more like an extension of traveling. Usually I booked a congen car and driver, but sometimes I just took a taxi, or had the source pick me up himself. People, I realized, were eager to talk to me. However tiny and powerless I was in reality, I was seen as the ear of the U.S. government.

And so I visited a polyester factory, where the owner gave me a tour and let me watch the machines that melted plastic pellets into strings of thread. He wanted lower tariffs on his exports. I visited a judge in her chambers, who seemed exhausted and distracted, waving flies away as she discussed her family court caseload. I had my driver stop on a bridge in the middle of Karachi, so that I could get out and confirm to myself what I thought I had seen. Along the banks of a riverbed in the middle of the city, there had sprung up a *kachi abadi,* one of Karachi's slums. Ramshackle huts made of tin, wood, and flapping sheets of bright plastic lined the two banks, and the residents went about their lives, cooking over smoky tin stoves, playing on garbage heaps, and selling betel nut and Coca-Cola to one another. The water that ran between them had shrunk to a mere stream, within and around which rivulets had formed, and it was these that had caught my attention. Winding between sandy islets and trash were streams of fluorescent purple and glowing turquoise, making their lazy way to sea.

❋ ❋ ❋

Kamran's friend Obaid belonged to a new boating club on the Malir river, and had a car to get us there. He was proud of his car stereo and always sped. The first time I met him he told me to call him Obi, "like Obi-Wan Kenobi!" The two of them invited me to go water-skiing. I knew, from my research, that a tannery upriver dumped its effluent into the wide brown expanse, but I could now see that that was beside the point, just as it made perfect sense, now, that environmental issues had been handed over to the intern. Things that could kill you slowly receded in importance compared to things that could kill you quickly.

I was attracted to Kamran for his sheer beauty, and because he was—more or less—native to this place. He was a cultural bridge, familiar to me through his striving to be American, yet able to show me parts of Karachi I wouldn't have found on my own. They were all places that he thought were attractively shiny and modern—the boating clubs, the sushi restaurant at the top of Avari Towers, the elaborate liquor-fueled parties in private homes. It was David and Nirit's friend Ahmed who took me to eat unbearably hot chicken tikka from a street stall; another Pakistani friend who took me to the Sufi shrine of Abdullah Shah Ghazi, which was candy-striped and lit up like a carnival ride; and a Scot with whom I hitched a late-night ride in the cab of decorated cargo truck. Kamran didn't see these things as interesting. He had neither the native's pride of place nor the foreigner's appreciation for the exotic. Still I thought of him as a prize, a jewel to tuck among my things like a souvenir. He must have thought of me as a trophy too, with my undisguisably foreign appearance. Looks, I discovered when I kissed him, didn't translate into the kind of physical spark I wanted, the kind I had with Graham, the kind I felt the first night I met Stu. Maybe he discovered the same thing, but that didn't stop us from going around together.

❀ ❀ ❀

I began to feel duplicitous. My contacts thought they were getting the U.S. government; I had no way to convince them that while I worked inside that building with the guards and barricades and trudging, patient lines, I was utterly without influence.

I felt this particularly with Mr. Masih. He wanted to show me the plight of Christians in Sindh Province. Pakistan is mostly Sunni Muslim, with Shiites, Hindus, and Zoroastrians the biggest religious minorities. The Sunnis are in turn riven along tribal and political lines. Lost in this demographic patchwork are a tiny minority of Christians. Most of their forebears had been low-caste Hindus, and their conversions hadn't saved them from entrenched poverty.

On our first outing Mr. Masih took me to a slum of narrow concrete alleyways lined with dingy square homes, where the stifling heat settled into a stillness disturbed only by the flies. He introduced me to a mother and her four children; she sat listlessly and glassy-eyed on the floor as if stunned. Mr. Masih propelled me into her cubbyhole and urged me to talk to her, so I shook her hand and asked the first rote words that came to mind.

"How are you?" She twitched her head and flicked a fan in front of her face. When we emerged from the mazelike slum and were driving back to the consulate general, Mr. Masih explained that this community, lacking title to their land, was about to be bulldozed by a developer. Could I stop it?

"I—I'll look into it," I stammered, but then that seemed like a lie, so I said, "No, I don't think so."

"You see the problems my people have," he said.

"Yes."

"There are many churches in America, I think."

"Yes."

"Maybe you try to do something."

"Yes."

Hashish and marijuana flowed freely through Karachi nightlife, but the Pakistanis couldn't have cared less. They got much more excited about alcohol, which was illegal and had to be smuggled in. The American diplomats, on the other hand, talked nervously about the marijuana—not that they would partake, of course, but they had tried it once in college—while not giving a second thought to their own easy access to alcohol, which came through the commissary and foreigner-friendly hotels. David told me once that he couldn't possibly be seen at an Afridi party, as the Baluch family were known hash exporters; one of them, David said, had packed the sticky stuff into the shape of a chair and sent it off as furniture. While David erred on the side of caution, the teenage son of the deputy chief of mission, who lived next door to me, smoked pot in his bathroom and sent it to his friends in Washington via the APO U.S. Post Office in the consulate general.

One night we drove in a two-car caravan to Sandspit, the long, narrow peninsula that partially shelters Karachi from the Indian Ocean. As we drove west, we passed through a sprawling district of light industry and few lamps, turning from one dark street into another until I was sure that Ahmed must be lost. And then little lights flickered ahead on either side of the road. Maybe candles, I thought. As we got closer, each yellow pool illuminated crouching men, swaying like druids. None of them cast so much as a glance at our sturdy Pajero; it was as though we were invisible. The men stared at their flames, which leaped up from lighters and makeshift gas stoves. The flames heated small cones of aluminum made from old soda cans, and at the bottom of each cone, brown liquid bubbled on the heat. I watched a slack-jawed man tilt his head back against the wall in the spectral light, his arm extended, a needle hanging off the crook of his elbow.

After the industrial zone the buildings petered out into wooden huts, and everyone in the car started talking again. We arrived at the point where the spit met the mainland, and here it was possible to imagine the city as a onetime fishing village. Ahmed lowered his window and said, as he often did, that the world would be a better place if everyone would just turn off their air conditioners for a few hours a day. Fishermen came out of their huts and offered to sell us things: a cooked meal of crab or fish with rice, or a case of contraband beer. Ahmed stopped the car, and we loaded two cases of beer into the back of the Pajero. You had to buy when you had the opportunity.

The spit was a hundred yards wide, with a dirt road running most of its length. We drove out a mile or so and got out. Nirit and I took off our shoes, cracked open beers, and sat down on the sand. A full moon dappled the rolling surf. Ahmed scoured the beach for turtle tracks, finally settling on his stomach to keep an eye on the water's edge. And then we all saw what we had come to see: one of the great beasts herself, prehistoric and guileless, five feet wide under a hard, shiny shell. She lumbered up the beach to lay her eggs in the sand, programmed to reproduce against all odds. And now I felt unalloyed pleasure at the sand, the surf, the moonlight, and the turtle. Beauty is so uncomplicated to love.

❋ ❋ ❋

Mr. Masih had another trip in mind for me. It was far outside the city, in rural Sindh, someplace the congen drivers didn't go. So Mr. Masih picked me up in his little beater of a sedan that had no air-conditioning or working seat belts. We headed north on the main road out of Karachi, dodging riotously decorated cargo trucks. Whenever two truck prows bore down on us at once, which happened often, Mr. Masih careened onto the shoulder and back again without losing speed.

He took me to a brick factory. Men and women squatted in square fields of mud and water, working in family groups. The women and older children shaped the bricks out of the mud, kneading, slapping, and patting them into rectangles, and then laying them out in rows to dry. Smaller children fetched water in buckets to keep the mud muddy, and kept an eye on the toddlers. The men collected the dried bricks, some in wheelbarrows and some using a carrying device that would have worked on a pack animal: a board slung across the shoulders with sacks hanging off either side. They took the bricks to the kiln, five hundred yards away and dominated by dun-colored chimney, where fires baked the clay into uniform hardness.

Mr. Masih took me to a dusty courtyard and introduced me to the manager, who offered me tea, and they explained how things worked. The families were technically paid by the brick, but at minuscule rates, and they were all working off debts that made them indentured laborers. In a typical case, a father had borrowed enough from the factory owner to pay for a daughter's dowry. Now the family worked off the debt brick by brick. "They will not pay it in his lifetime," Mr. Masih. "Not even in his children's lifetime."

They were, in effect, slaves.

❋ ❋ ❋

The Shiite holiday of Ashura fell in August. There would be marches in the street to celebrate—or more accurately to mourn, since the day marked the death of Hussain, grandson of the prophet Mohammed and rightful inheritor of the Caliphate as far as Shiites were concerned. He was killed in battle at Karbala in 680. Someone had a house on one of the streets where demonstrations were expected, and I drove there with David and Nirit and a few others. We milled around in the street as the crowd built up, and then retreated to a second-story balcony, where we could look through the tree leaves to the street below.

Clutches of women in black stood around beds of hot coals, ululating and cheering each other on. They took turns walking barefoot across the coals, the female way of self-inflicting pain on this day. A sea of men in *shalwar khamis* of the purest, brightest white surged around them. The crowd eddied below our balcony and resolved itself into a circle around a group of men, who started to dance. Each one had an instrument in his hand: a hard leather-wrapped handle with glinting metal at one end. The dancing men curled in on themselves and then arched, curled and arched, over and over.

I didn't understand how the instruments worked until I saw the first bright streak of blood, a jagged crimson line across the white fabric of one man's back. Several lengths of chain were attached to each handle, and at the end of each chain was a metal blade, sharp and thin enough to slice skin with the slightest pressure. The instruments glinted in the sunlight. As graceful as a rhythmic gymnast, one man balanced on his left foot and bent his whole torso backward, right arm over his head, raining the blades down on his own back. The faster the men moved, the more others joined in from the sidelines, and the redder their lacerated garments became. Their faces looked agonized or ecstatic.

The next day Kamran's friend Obaid took us to go water-skiing on the Malir River, blasting "Blister in the Sun" from his car stereo. He skippered his family's speedboat for us, but declined to get in the water himself. Kamran gave him a hard time about that, then suddenly stopped. Later he explained to me: Obaid was wounded from the day before. I was surprised that a person who spoke my cultural language could also be a person who went to extremities of religion that I didn't understand.

✵ ✵ ✵

I spent a lot of time in my room, in the chair I'd pulled up to my window, which I would open in the evening to let in the heat and look at the circling birds. Here I thought about Graham sometimes, but Stu was sending me vivid and ardent letters, and my thoughts turned more and more to him. Stu was available to me in all my aloneness. I called him—by placing a request with the congen switchboard, then waiting—and told him about my work and the people I met.

In an early phone call I asked Stu if he wanted to join me in Pakistan during the month I had between finishing my internship and returning to school. He agreed right away to come. I thought this said something promising about him and about us. A person who would fly halfway around the world—Karachi was precisely a twelve-hour time difference away from Seattle—for romance and backpacking, on short notice, struck me as the sort of person with whom I belonged.

Nevertheless I felt awkward and confused when he first arrived. After thinking of him for a couple of months, reading his letters, and talking every week or so, it was jarring to have him materialize. It seemed to be almost a rebuke, a warning that I should be careful with my wishes. As we rode in a consulate car from the airport back to my luxurious catacomb, I gripped his much larger hand with my own and stared at him in surprise. I made myself fuck him right away—to put any awkwardness quickly behind us, to break the tension, to establish myself as in control and unfazed. I thought that it would orient me, or get us back to the relationship we had started before I left. It was not especially enjoyable, but pleasure, I figured, would come later.

Stu could not have been more easygoing as he waited out my

last few weeks of work, going wandering by himself into the city, to bazaars where I in my sheltered diplomatic life hadn't ventured. I envied his maleness and his six-foot-four frame, attributes I thought enabled him to go about the world at ease. He came back from his adventures with odd treasures from the building trades: brass hinges, a compass from a ship, centuries-old locks and keys. He would use them all, he said, to build a home. One day Stu told me how he'd wandered to some distant point in the city and then returned by *tuk-tuk,* one of the three-wheeled open taxis, a form of transportation forbidden by the consulate general's security chief. The chief had called me to his office one day to run through a list of no-nos, which included leaving the Karachi city limits and any travel to Yemen. On the other hand, he'd been letting his daughter date Marines since she was fourteen, according to the head of the Marine guards, who shook his head in disapproval as he told me.

The next time Stu and I went out, I insisted we take a *tuk-tuk.*

❋ ❋ ❋

Inspired by the fluorescent rivulets running through the slum, I filed a report on Karachi pollution. It was picked up in a global weekly roundup compiled in Washington, meaning that maybe it passed before the eyes of an assistant to an assistant to an undersecretary. But most likely not. It was dawning on me that I didn't want to be a diplomat after all. I didn't want to be David in a year's time, stamping visas at the head of an endless line. Nor did I want to be Kevin, the political officer who was my supervisor, who was feeling thwarted in his work on child labor. Congress had one idea, which was to ban all imports of carpets from Pakistan. Kevin thought things were more complicated. "There aren't any schools," he pointed out. I concluded that foreign service officers didn't have much influence.

Nor did I want to live as I'd been living. I understood the point of barricades but didn't want to live behind them. If I went as a diplomat to all the places I thought were so exotic and weird and difficult, I would end up in a string of enclaves.

This ebbing away of professional direction didn't yet worry me much. I had to complete my final quarter of college after I returned to Seattle, and I could think about it then. What I most wanted to do was travel more, without an end date or obligation in sight. I wanted to wander and feel free.

At the end of the summer, the Pakistani kids I'd met started returning to Florida and Boston, London and Leeds. Jane's prisoners still enjoyed the hospitality of the Pakistani government. Stephen still worked down the hall, behind the locked door, listening to who knew what. And on my last day of work, the line of visa supplicants making its way to David's window looked identical to the line when I first arrived.

ON DIFFICULTY
chapter twelve

"*I*t's *not possible*," *I said*, with a theatrical shrug of my shoulders. We refused to pay that much for a ride from Chitral to Gilgit.

It was dusk, and Stu and I were sitting under a tree, next to a green Jeep, haggling with the driver. To be more accurate, I was haggling, while Stu nodded his assent. By the time we'd left Peshawar, the Mos Eisli of the Northwest Frontier, we'd both adopted the *shalwar khamis,* and the more comfortable I'd grown among its folds, the bolder I'd become. The driver lowered his price for the third time, and but still I said no, and stood up to walk away. Stu hesitated. We really did want the ride, after all, on a road that wound through steep river gorges toward the Karakoram range. I might have been blowing our chance.

Finally the driver relented.

I still wasn't subtle at the game. I didn't understand that you had to spar, not just punch someone out. I often failed to start with a low enough offer, one that I could then magnanimously let rise. I was bullheaded, adamantly opposed to signaling submission. Once I'd won, showing that I was useful and tough, I could relax and let Stu make me feel safe again. I thought of all those explorers from centuries past, the Wilfred Thesigers and the Freya Starks, and how they always seemed to have entourages of native guides. My modern twist on safety-in-numbers was to bring a boyfriend. I felt guilty for failing to be independent. Independence was still my burning ideal. Most of the time I felt reliant, so whenever I could, I tried to prove myself by driving a hard bargain.

❋ ❋ ❋

In Gilgit we met up with David and Nirit and rented another Jeep with a driver. I let David, the diplomat, do the hiring. The Jeep took us as far north as a guesthouse in Sost, which, though it was still eighty kilometers from the Chinese border, served as Pakistan's customs and immigration post. Mountains rose behind the wooden guesthouse and all around us. The peaks were white, permanently frozen, and looked edible. Our chests felt tighter when we breathed; I associated the sensation with the cold, but it was because there was less oxygen to go around.

From Sost we shared a bus that had come up from below carrying several dozen Pakistani traders. The road took us along cliff sides above steep canyons, and once we had to drive over a sloping pile of dirt and rock that had tumbled down onto the road. As the bus tipped to a forty-five-degree angle, we discussed how we might escape if it went over, and decided that climbing out the windows would work best. David said he would push Nirit out first, and she said, hell yes, she would go first. Even the Pakistani tradesmen who took this route all the time looked nervous, shifting in their seats with wide eyes. But the driver and the conductor, who had gotten out to direct him over the hump, took us safely back onto the road.

The actual border was at the Karakoram Pass, at an elevation of 18,176 feet. We dismounted briefly on an expanse of glacial moraine, where the snow-covered bowls and peaks rose headily around us. The bus took us on to a Chinese border post, where we sat around for several hours in the bright dry sun, waiting our turn to pass through customs. Then we switched to a Chinese bus, which took us on to the town of Tashkurgan. It was a dry, cold little outpost where each of the few street corners had a pole mounted with a speaker, which at regular intervals blared martial music and crackly announcements. We and all the other bus passengers checked into the same government-run hotel, our way station en route to the city of Kashgar. It was a drafty, many-storied building with high-ceilinged unlit halls. The four of us shared a room; the bathroom was down the hall. It had no door and was not gender-specific, and every toilet held an unflushed pile of shit. Our dinner was composed of gelatinous dough balls, birds I thought were too small to eat, and Tang. I thought we'd reached a new low, but after dinner Stu collapsed. He'd been getting headachey during the day from altitude sickness, and now became so pained and delirious that I wondered if we should turn back.

But part of me also felt like Stu needed me now, and I liked the sensation. I wanted to take care of him. I'd been dependent on him, and now he was dependent on me. As I watched him in the night, drying his forehead with my towel, I concluded that turning back wouldn't get us to a lower elevation any more quickly than going forward. It wouldn't get us to anywhere easy or comfortable or familiar; we'd come way too far for that. We would continue on to Kashgar.

❁ ❁ ❁

The forces that fuzz the edges between cultures had left Kashgar relatively untouched. The highest mountains in the world lay to the south, to the west was the international border with Tajikistan and Kyrgyzstan, and to the north and east there were vast plains. The clocks captured the strangeness of the place: There was no local consensus on time. Officially the whole country operated on Beijing time, but by the rotation of the earth we were several time zones away from the capital. So if you were observing national time in Kashgar, it would seem, for instance, like the sun came up much too late in the morning. Some establishments solved this problem by running two clocks side by side, labeled "Beijing" and "Kashgar."

We checked into a hotel that seemed to be independent of the government, a sloppy warren of rooms in an apartment block. Stu had started to feel better almost as soon as we left Tashkurgan, and after a nap, at nightfall we went out to the nearest square, which had filled up with food vendors, and ate our way from stall to stall: sizzling kebabs, spicy noodles, and bread rolls the size, shape, and consistency of bagels. The faces looked Eurasian; the people were Uighur. The men wore embroidered skull caps. The women were present, pushing bicycles along and exposing their ankles and faces. They had fused fashion in the most jarring possible way. A typical outfit included trousers in a traditional multicolored *ikat* cloth, a black lace dress, a drab blue blazer, and a red chiffon scarf. Calf-length sequined skirts were popular, as were brown polyester head scarves.

Here we met the China travelers: Swedes and Britons and Australians who had backpacked the length of the country, on trains and buses, and had the stories and scars to prove it: flights of rapture over the Terra Cotta Warriors, food one-upmanship that always ended with fried insects, public humiliations involving diarrhea and the language barrier, and always, when they learned that Stu and I were headed back south to Pakistan, the earnest insistence that we had to see the rest of the Middle Kingdom. How sweet it would be, I thought, to change plans like that on a whim, but we had plane tickets, and diminishing funds, and I had a nagging last few credits at school. I didn't think of what my degree was *for* anymore. I'd eschewed diplomacy, but didn't know what to do next.

The young foreigners at the western end of China were the toughest of travelers, and they were proud but easygoing; the whiners had been weeded out a thousand miles back. They were thin after many months on rice, stubbled if male, and they knew which of the Chinese fire waters were drinkable and which to avoid. They had plans—travelers always had plans—to go on to Central Asia or up to Urumqi or eventually Mongolia. None were headed for Pakistan.

We rented bicycles and rode out to the edge of the town under a late summer sun, leaving behind a muddy riverbank and continuing on a poplar-lined road. We came to a mosque tiled entirely in shades of blue. With its glinting domes it looked like its cousins in Isfahan and Istanbul and Damascus, and I reflected that we'd come to the far northeast edge of Islam, beyond which different gods prevailed. A muezzin in a white turban came to call the faithful to prayer, and Stu and I got out of his way but watched him from a distance. He positioned himself in an archway leading into the mosque and, without benefit of a microphone, raised one hand to his mouth and began. He chanted not in Chinese or Uighur but in Arabic, the language in which the angel Gabriel was supposed to have transmitted the Quran to Mohammed. I felt the soothing presence of the familiar, a touch of comforting continuity in this land of sequined dresses and Chinese bagels and government *diktats* about time. He chanted: "God is great. God is great. There is no God but God, and Mohammed is the prophet of God." His voice rose on the breeze and mingled with the rustle of the trees. No one came to pray.

We spent a few days wandering around the Kashgar market, where you could have riding boots cobbled in front of you, or buy a snow leopard pelt. And then, the day before we were to leave, we gathered in the late morning at an outdoor restaurant table with David and Nirit and some of our new friends from the hotel. There was a Swedish couple, Lars and Annie, both tall and bespectacled; a Torontonian who spoke very good Mandarin; and a gaunt but chipper Englishman with a shaved head named Nick. He had a Balinese silver bracelet like Stu's, and wore a Maori bone carving, like the one Graham had given me, at his neck. We thought we were iconoclasts at the far edge of the world, but here we were in uniform, like members of any clique. Breakfast rolled into lunch, which rolled into beers, which rolled into wondering what the dish that claimed on the menu to be spaghetti might be like. It was my twenty-second birthday.

When I told everyone, we decided it was a fine excuse to start trying the liquors. Stu poured us both thimblefuls and we toasted. It felt like a burning fuse had hit my throat, but I made myself swallow and smile. We told stories about our trip, making my haggling in Chitral now sound funny. Somewhere along the way we'd become a couple who finished each other's sentences.

Everyone was talking about other countries they'd been to, name-dropping like social climbers. I mentioned that I'd backpacked around the Middle East. Lars and Annie had traveled through Central America and climbed the pyramids at Tikal. The Canadian began talking about spiders in the Outback. We were pleased with ourselves. We'd gone the farthest. There was nowhere farther or weirder than Kashgar.

"Australia," Nick said, rolling his eyes. "It's all about sex and lager." We laughed, impressed with our own sophistication. We weren't like that.

I didn't say it, but I suddenly wanted to go to Australia immediately. I was tired. Tired of catcalls and menace, beggars and bureaucrats, men with guns. Tired of proving I was tough enough. I wanted police officers, if there were any, to be concerned for my safety. I wanted to be in a place of freedom and ease, where chasing boys and beer, or not chasing them, was a matter of personal choice. Nick's words lodged themselves in my mind. I wanted sex and lager.

LUCK

And you may ask yourself,
What is that beautiful house?
And you make ask yourself,
Where does that highway go?
And you may ask yourself,
Am I right . . . Am I wrong?
And you may tell yourself,
My god! . . . What have I done?

—Talking Heads,
"Once in a Lifetime"

PART TWO

ON SETTLING DOWN
chapter thirteen

The little house was at a T in the road, where Palatine met Northwest Forty-first. Palatine came down the hill from Forty-second, and we joked that an out-of-control car might barrel into the living room one day. The neighborhood was up-and-coming. From the back deck we had a view across the channel to Queen Anne Hill, and with a pair of binoculars we identified the house where we had met a year before. "A single metaphor can give birth to love," Kundera wrote in *The Unbearable Lightness of Being,* and under Stu's tutelage, I began to see metaphors everywhere. Seeing that house across the channel confirmed that the universe meant for us to be together.

If you stood on the edge of our bathtub and looked out a small window, and the day was clear, you could see the white peak of Mount Rainier in the distance. The house itself was cramped and ugly. On a whim, with no sense of consequence, I painted the tiny bathroom teal and fuchsia. It was a poor choice, but we figured we wouldn't be looking at it for long. We had plans to make the place beautiful.

We often made love early in the morning, as the gray wet light came up and before I took the bus to work, and my memory of that hot happy secret carried me through to the afternoon. Surely a half hour of pleasure before the day began was partly the point of life.

This was important, because most of the rest of my life bewildered me—the tedium of my new job, the fact that I lived in Seattle. I'd answered an ad in the newspaper looking for a "customer service representative" for an export shipping company, a person that in an earlier era would have been called a clerk. It sounded international and so possibly exciting; maybe, I thought, it would involve travel. But instead I answered phones and photocopied bills of lading at a frantic pace, until seven o'clock at night, just in time to FedEx them to Hong Kong or Le Havre or wherever, so that they would be there when someone on the other side went to pick up the cargo. We were a sort of travel agency for stuff. Eventually they hired a new girl to do my job and promoted me, making me the chief booker for South America and Australia–New Zealand. I took pride in having my own two regions, and was also embarrassed by my pride, so distant did my job seem from whatever it was I was supposed to have been doing. I couldn't remember what my ambitions had been. It felt like I'd misplaced the manual for postcollegiate success, and, after sixteen straight years of education, had lost all sense of what I wanted to do. The business of creating an adult life was difficult to think about, so I preferred things that distracted me or, ideally, overwhelmed me. Anything to push thought aside. Stu overwhelmed me with his constant presence and his seeming confidence—confidence about me, his next building project, his ability to transform our house, and our plan to sail around the world. I wasn't really sure about the sailing plan and whether I had signed on to it or not, but I didn't need to think things through thoroughly, because he was sure enough of everything for two.

Stu had unnatural certainty. At twenty-five he was still learning how to use this trait to his advantage, but it gave him the ability to convince almost anyone to do almost anything. His size confirmed him as a dominant force: He was six foot four with broad shoulders, like other college rowers. But unlike them, he'd dropped out of the university, unable to pay. His parents, who were just twenty years older than he was, had declared their responsibilities over when Stu and his sister finished high school, and when I met him they'd just moved to Delaware, from where they planned to start their own trip around the world. But Stu still had a tightly knit family nearby: On his mother's side his grandparents, uncles, aunt, and cousins all lived in the Seattle suburb of Kent, while his paternal grandparents lived in the southwest corner of the state. Stu was firmly rooted in place. Among my extended family only my parents lived in my hometown, which my brother and I had now both left. My mother's kin were still in Oregon, and my father's two siblings and their children had scattered. Both of my parents had settled far from home, in another country, with no family around.

When Stu and I talked about buying a house and remodeling it, the idea seemed exciting. My parents helped with a down payment, and at the age of twenty-two I cruised heedlessly into home ownership. Around the same time, one night on the couch after we'd been out to dinner with friends, Stu asked me to marry him and I said yes. This seemed exciting too. I explained my new situation to myself and others in rational terms: He was a builder, and while we were a little young, we would soon be married, an assertion that suggested solidity. If I was honest with myself, though, which was not all that often, the appeal of buying a house with Stu was not that it was sensible, but just the opposite: There was something manic about the headlong rush, and that was what made it so compelling. Through the traveler's mind-set of being open to experience, I grabbed more and more and more of it.

Like a distant rumble, it crossed my mind that I was closing doors. But it was hard to take seriously the idea that anything was irreversible. I'd been raised so that I would have every opportunity, and now, even if I didn't know what to do with my choices, I believed that they were all still available.

Upon moving in, we ripped up decades-old carpet to reveal a hardwood floor. We accepted donations and gifts from relatives—a couch, dishes, even a crystal cake platter as a Christmas present from my aunt. It would never be used, but it amused us. The cake platter underscored my sense that I was performing a charade. I was quite sure I would never be the kind of person who needed a cake platter, and yet I gave a convincing impression of someone who would. We displayed our treasures from Pakistan, like a brass water pipe and a *tabla* drum, on our black particle board shelves from Ikea. The carpets we'd bought in Peshawar covered our floor, next to the sturdy brown couch from my parents. The souvenirs were the first items we pointed out to any friend who came over, which only happened occasionally, so comfortable were we as just two.

Sometimes I tried to write, usually little stories set in Egypt, but on weekends we always had projects to do. We had to clean out the basement and take loads of building debris to the dump. We would spend an hour or two in Home Depot. On our return trips we drove all over the city in Stu's pickup truck, stopping to look at houses we liked, homes that could inspire our own. I hadn't spent a lot of time thinking about houses before, and now Stu's taste became mine. He liked clean lines, fine woodwork, and unusual surfaces like dyed concrete and weathered metal. Once we got home there was no time left to write. This bothered me a little. But in the bigger picture I didn't worry that much about time, which seemed to be in great supply. We were rich with it and could afford to throw it recklessly around.

Stu and I always went grocery shopping together, a ritual I found soothing, even soporific. We bought cilantro and green onions and limes, and made fresh salsa from our own recipe. We disdained the store-bought kind. He taught me to make the dishes he knew, like killer-hot Thai shrimp curry; I taught him to make the dishes I knew, like tabouleh; and sometimes we learned a new one together. On weekends and evenings we were never apart. We lay on the couch, embracing and watching television. Every now and then I felt a twinge of suffocation, but I didn't like separation, either. We'd spent so much time alone together, so quickly, beginning in Pakistan and continuing right after we returned, that I still didn't know very many people in Seattle. The friends and college acquaintances I'd managed to cultivate, between time abroad and trips to Whistler, all seemed to have gone away. Kim was back in Germany; Jeff had gone to Washington, DC, to look for meaningful work; a few had joined the Peace Corps; and at least one had gone off to law school. I sometimes thought I should have done any of the above, but then Stu was right there in front of me, blotting out thought. And now I had a house—I couldn't just walk away. Every now and then a fisherman friend of Stu's would have a barbeque, and we would lie in the grass, eating king salmon flown fresh from Alaska, grilled with lemon and thyme.

His circle was scattered with young men starting careers as fishermen or builders. They seemed to know what they were supposed to do, but their girlfriends and wives were less sure. Several worked as waitresses or baristas, and if they'd finished college, they had office jobs like mine. Some of them were already talking about having babies; I felt more likely to build a spaceship and fly to Mars. When anyone asked us about children, Stu and I told her that we were on the "ten-year plan." A year or so after moving into the house, I overheard Stu telling someone "the nine-year plan." "What?" I asked. "When did it become nine years?" And he pointed out how long it had been since we started saying ten. I thought his literalism was funny, since I didn't quite believe we were using up time.

I felt out of place, maybe even more than I had in Egypt or Pakistan. It was harder to know who I was in Seattle. Anywhere exotic, as a permanent stranger, I could define myself against everything around me. In *The Global Soul,* Pico Iyer explores why he feels so at home in Japan, an alien and unyielding "uniculture" that will never regard him as one of its own. Iyer comes from India, England, California, the globe. He comes from cultural fluidity. And so Japan's rigidity makes him feel at home because it tells him where he stands: "It's not always easy for me to explain that it's precisely that ability to draw strict lines around itself—to sustain an unbending sense of within and without—that draws me to Japan. In the postmodern world, to invert Robert Frost, home is the place where, when you have to go there, they don't have to take you in." Egypt would never take me in. The boundaries that encircled me there had also made me feel at home.

Sometimes I felt like a tourist in my own life. I had tried living elsewhere, and now I was trying this Seattle, settled-down thing. It was just another place to visit. Part of me didn't believe it was *my* life, but rather thought that I was observing it from the outside. The difference between here and stranger places, though, was that Seattle would take me in all too easily. It disturbed me that my life looked so much like those of the fishermen's wives. I said I was going to travel, go to graduate school, go write, but now that was all just lip service. The masquerade was too real. What if I *was* like them? I couldn't bear the idea that this life might be my only one. I couldn't bear the thought of being ordinary.

Not that it wasn't a seductive life. On weekends we went to Stu's grandparents' second home on a small island in the San Juans, sometimes with friends, where we sailed and soaked in a wood-fired hot tub. Stu showed me how to split wood and patch a hole in a fiberglass boat. He had a knack for gathering food from the sea, and showed me how to set crab pots and shuck oysters. Stu, it seemed, had a knack for every practical skill. You knew you'd be safe if you were lost in the woods with him. I lacked similar abilities, and I hadn't met many women who had them, either. Nor had I known many hyperurban men, the kind who know the right cut of a pair of trousers but can't cut wood. (The coinage of *metrosexual* was far in the future.) So I associated Stu's savoir faire with manliness. I wanted to learn it all myself so that I could be self-reliant in the same way, so that you wouldn't mind being stuck in the woods with me. But to get there I needed to attach myself to a man so that he could teach me. It was a certain kind of trade: Without a romantic relationship, I didn't see why anyone would invest in tutoring me like this, long-term and for free, like a parent. Young people in every field—usually women—have extracted life lessons from older romantic partners—usually men. Stu wasn't much older, but he knew a whole world of things that I didn't. I liked that with Stu I got to learn things that would make me more independent of Stu.

At the island in the San Juans, glossy green water stretched away from the beach. Underneath there were powerful currents, hundred-pound lingcod, and even giant squid, but the surface was placid. In the foreground, seals basked in the sun on Posey, and across the channel the hump of Spieden, covered in long grass, took up the horizon. Stu taught me to pilot the Boston Whaler; he showed me how to watch for rocks when the tide was low, and how to slow, turn, and throw the engine into reverse, the most graceful technique for sliding up to a dock. When I wanted to be alone I took a neighbor's kayak across a slender channel and tooled around the water's edge. We slept in the cabin on the property reserved for the grandkids, and after Stu got up in the morning—always before me, always to do something useful—I lay in bed and looked out the windowpanes across the blue-gray rocks and strewn kelp, to the shimmering surface beyond. In the evening we would build a fire and Stu's family would gather and we'd eat fresh crab dipped in butter.

Everything I was supposed to want had suddenly accrued: the boyfriend, the job, the house, the weekend house, and the wedding plans. It had been that quick and easy. We lived that way for a year and a half.

ON COGNITIVE DISSONANCE
chapter fourteen

*A*s it turned out, I would be the car that barreled into the living room.

Stu was a proponent of marrying at his grandparents' island, with a pig on a spit with an apple in its mouth, but he said he would go to City Hall if that was what I wanted. I advocated City Hall because, as I told people, I didn't want to think about planning a wedding. The process seemed onerous and unreal. One of the few weddings I'd seen had been my cousin Kellie's extravaganza, which occurred right after I returned from Spain. She and her husband married straight out of college. The day before the wedding she threw all twelve bridesmaids an elaborate brunch, and on the day itself we wore emerald green satin with leg-of-mutton sleeves. A hundred guests toasted the couple in the penthouse ballroom of a Portland sky rise, and I wondered just where it was that girls learned how to do these things.

A few years later Stu's friends began to get married, and while the weddings weren't as elaborate as Kellie's, they were significant events, with gazebos in gardens and tuxedos on the boys. I was intimidated. A big wedding would have been like the cake platter writ large: I could probably give a convincing impression of someone who would have one, but it wouldn't feel real. I felt like everything that had occurred in my relationship with Stu so far had happened *to* me, by accident and without intent. I'd fallen in love, and things had taken their headlong course. But if I got married I wouldn't be able to pretend that it was happenstance. Marriage required a conscious choice, after which I would be called on all my declarations of intent. Marriage, as I understood it, was when you had to stop bluffing and go all in. You had to choose one man, and through him—as I understood it—one life. Our settled, committed, home-owning existence would stop being a grand experiment. I still wanted to believe that there were other possibilities.

As these thoughts began to well up, it was also easy to keep going along with the television on the couch and the weekend trips to Home Depot. I developed an internal life that contradicted the placid surface. I went back and forth, sometimes telling myself that I just needed to get comfortable. I loved Stu, after all, and he wanted to travel too—after the house was done. I thought maybe if I squirmed around enough, this life would feel like the right fit.

But instead of trying for peace and cooperation, I began to pry up our differences like they were loose floorboards. I picked fights over his pot smoking, which bothered me intensely for reasons I couldn't at first put my finger on. Addiction was a weakness, and I hated weakness. Later I would also see that my desire to control him came from a desire to control my own life, over which I seemed to have lost all command. Sometimes I found a small stash or a pipe hidden in the bookshelf, which made us both miserable. He hated to be caught, because I would get angry, and I hated myself in the schoolmarm role. We played a game of cat and mouse, in which I both sought to find evidence and dreaded the possibility that I would.

My own weakness was for him. I wanted to hold him tightly to me. I blamed the pot for his falling asleep on the sofa, which made me unhappy because then he wasn't with me in bed, and I couldn't fall asleep until he was. I blamed Stu for making me into a person I didn't like, who was insecure when he wasn't around. We were so enmeshed that I couldn't fathom losing him. It dawned on me that if I escaped the relationship, I might escape these feelings too. If I lost my love, I could lose my anxiety and anger, or so I suspected.

In my confusion, I began to understand how a person could go off in two directions at once. For someone who liked to please, it would be easy to end up with a concealed life. You just did what your boyfriend wanted, and got on with your own thing inside. You might end up with a case of cognitive dissonance, when two versions of your life came crashing together. Or the twain might never meet. Years later, when I would cry over some perceived contradiction in a lover's behavior, and ask him how he could have said X but done Y, I would try to forgive by remembering my own turmoil, without much success.

I found more things to pick on. I insulted him for his inability to do the dishes or hang up his clothes. I got mad when he came home late from work and didn't call. I asked when he would finish all the half projects he'd begun around our home, which, alarmingly, showed no signs of nearing completion. But none of these things were exactly the point. Underlying it all was my wish to go away again. The idea of roaming intoxicated me to the extent that I couldn't look at the glossy cover of a travel magazine, or browse the travel section of a bookstore, without getting a lump in my throat.

And so I developed my own secret. It just took a quick stop, every few weeks, on the way home to Stu. When I wasn't committing the act, I barely acknowledged it to myself. If I had, it would have exposed the fundamental contradiction of my life, my promise to do one thing while planning something else. I would have had to admit I was a sneak, even though I believed I was a basically honest person. I would have had to admit I was plotting escape, even as I embraced my Seattle life. My two worldviews would collide.

Our unspoken understanding was that our resources should go into the house. Stu's did: His time, energy, and the money he made from building jobs mostly went to our joint project. My secret, though, was that I'd opened a bank account apart from the one I shared with Stu. I was saving money on my own. Half of every paycheck went into my personal bank account. Aside from an occasional piece of sports equipment, I bought no luxuries—no clothes, no stereo or television, no upgrades to my Ford Escort. I was saving to travel like it was a silent fever. To pursue the thing she needed to do, Virginia Woolf wrote, "a woman must have money and a room of her own. . . . ." I needed money and a backpack.

My wanderlust had only been in abeyance, like a briefly dormant volcano. There was so much of the world I hadn't seen yet. There were lives—so many—that I hadn't experimented with. What if I was meant to be an aid worker, a dive instructor, a spy? What if I was meant to be a writer in New York? And forget even what I was meant to be. What would it feel like to just wander the world, free of all responsibility, knowing I could stand on my own two feet? I resented Stu for keeping me from all those other possible lives.

There was no noble purpose in my wish to go away, no practical aim. There was no longer the fig leaf of an internship, college course, or job. It was just eyes-glazed-over desire. I bought a copy of *Outside* magazine with a picture on the cover of a tiny teardrop island photographed from above. It was a white sand shoal fringed with underwater coral and set in a turquoise sea, part of the Whitsunday Islands, which sat just off the coast of Queensland. I looked up the islands in an atlas and ran my fingertips over the smooth, shiny page.

I saved the magazine, my own secret stash, so that I could revisit it again and again. He had his escape and I had mine too. The photograph was a physical provocation.

Around Christmas of my twenty-third year, I began to tell Stu that I wanted to take a trip. I told him—and myself—that I just needed this one adventure. I would travel with my high school best friend, Kristin, a scheme I tried to play off as wholesome, even though he knew her too well for that. I would go away for two months, or four at the most, and visit a place I'd always wanted to see. I likewise told my parents that it was just a short trip. Then I would come back to the house, get another job, pay my share of the mortgage, and get married. I had somehow—I still thought of things as happening *to* me—embroiled myself in all this responsibility, but they couldn't begrudge me this one thing. And I was nine-tenths convinced that a trip was all I needed. I would get this travel thing out of my system. The words "sex and lager" were still at the back of my mind, but I didn't mention that to Stu.

Once I had decided, you couldn't argue with me any more than you can argue against love. Stu, who not only loved me but believed in love, who believed in star-crossedness and soul mate-ism, made a valiant effort to understand. He raised more objections to a trip I took to visit my parents in February than he did to my Australia plans. But no one collapsed into cognitive dissonance just yet. We both maintained the worldview that said I would return. Stu was the one who drove me to the airport, and he began to cry as soon as he walked away. I thought to myself that I should be crying, but I couldn't summon the tears.

ON CULTURE SHOCK
chapter fifteen

*M*uch *as I wanted to get to* the sex and lager, I couldn't go there just yet. I had to dare myself again before I went to the beach. So instead of flying straight to Australia, I planned to first spend two weeks alone in Malaysia.

I avoided arrangements as deliberately as some people make them. I wanted the experience of landing in a new place with no plans, and considered hotel reservations a luxury for the weak. Conveniently, my attitude and my budget meshed. On top of the price of my plane ticket to Australia with a stop in Singapore, I had saved up a few thousand dollars. It felt like a fortune, but I knew I had to conserve.

For the first hours I slept, but by the time we were over the South China Sea, I was wide awake. I chatted to my seatmate, who was traveling with her young daughter and had a hotel reservation. Now I asked myself: Would it have killed me just to know where I was staying my first night? In midair I began poring over my guidebook, reading about youth hostels and studying a map, trying to commit it to memory.

When I arrived it was the middle of the night in that deep and alien way that is only possible when you've just landed in a foreign city on the far side of the world. The airport was bright and cool and efficient, and I followed signs to a bus stop. The heat walloped me as soon as I stepped outside, a heat that would have seemed unlikely even in the middle of the day. It was like carrying an extra bag, made of velvet and full of lead. The bus was cool, and I sat alert, looking out the window, mentally reviewing the street names and maps I'd tried to retain.

A Belgian approached. He was young and bald and wore a floral short-sleeved shirt; he worked as a tout for a youth hostel. The airport bus into the city, where he was sure to find a backpacker or two, was his regular run. Things would not be so hard after all. I was almost disappointed, and a dying ember of rebellion urged me to resist him, but I was in no position to turn down an extended hand. I followed him off the bus in a low, flat neighborhood of boxy identical buildings, and up a narrow flight of stairs to the check-in desk of a hostel. They had two kinds of dormitories, with air-conditioning and without, and I permitted myself to have the former, which cost one Singaporean dollar a night more. Every decision was like this: I was not allowed to take the easier, usually pricier, route. I needed to save money, sure, but cheapness was also a barometer of something else. It measured my ability to get by, satisfying that need to prove myself to myself, as well as to the judges and skeptics—other travelers, Graham, Stu, my parents; anyone who thought I wasn't tough enough—whom I imagined watching over my shoulder.

The Belgian disappeared and the clerk, a small young Singaporean Chinese, showed me to the dorm room. It was pitch-black at first, and I wasn't allowed to turn on the lights. As my eyes adjusted I saw that the room was enormous and windowless, lined with metal-frame bunk beds on every wall and more aisles of bunk beds across the middle. There were maybe forty beds in all. Most were full, populated with boys and girls from across the Commonwealth and Europe. The temperature was frigid, and the hostel's sheets were plain white, so that I seemed to have stepped into an institution of some kind, filled with incubating human life forms. I chose a lower bunk against a wall, tucked my pack under the bed and my money belt under my pillow, and fell into a deep, dreamless sleep.

I awoke to an English accent. A girl one bunk over was talking about a job interview. When I opened my eyes, I could see that she had on a white shirt and was pulling a suit from her backpack. She had a real purse and a plastic folder that contained a sheaf of papers. I wondered if her interviewer would have any idea that her staging area today had been this people warehouse, which looked every bit as neutral by day as it had in the middle of the night. I hoped not to have a job interview for a long time, but I liked the idea of a cool safety zone from where to launch oneself into the world. The room was emptying out, kids of nineteen or twenty-three heading off to their next destination. We were half-cooked, struggling to be born.

In the face of the English girl's clear direction, I remembered that I had none, and that I had none because I wanted none. This no longer worried me like it had on the plane. I didn't want to stay in Singapore, which was modern and expensive, and so out of sheer need to have some kind of a goal, I decided I would go north up the east coast of Malaysia. There was an island up that way, Tioman, that was supposed to have pretty scuba diving; maybe I would go there. I checked out and left my backpack at the front desk, and went out into the heat.

I bought a bus ticket to somewhere called Mersing. With hours to kill, I stepped into a shopping mall with a specific purchase in mind: I'd come away with no watch, and it had occurred to me that this was an oversight. On the road I would have planes, trains, and buses to catch, as well as time zones to negotiate. In the mall, which was multilevel and hexagonal, I found a watch that had an analog face, a bezel for counting minutes, and a lemon yellow plastic strap. The package said it was waterproof to thirty meters. It wasn't a splurge, I told myself, but a necessary and sensible purchase. The store clerk set it to 11:15.

❋ ❋ ❋

While standing in the customs line at the border, I noticed a German couple behind me who kept laughing, and before I could wonder what they were saying they switched to English and invited me into their exuberant little world. Where was I going? Where was I coming from? The boy, Stefan, had been working in a tiny fishing village on the east coast, and had just been down to Singapore to pick up Nela, his girlfriend, who, like him, was tall and sandy-haired.

Stefan described their destination. He was working for a Swedish boat captain, he said, doing archaeological work. It was very hush-hush. His best friend in the village was a Buddhist mechanic. Why didn't I come with them, and then I could go on to Tioman Island? Yes, yes, Nela said, maybe pleased to have another girl on board. I looked for the village in my guidebook; it didn't seem to exist. No buses went there, so we would have to share a taxi for the two-hour drive. I glanced at my bus, which had now crossed the border, and the line of passengers getting back on. I wondered if my disappearance would cause the bus attendant any consternation. Singapore was famous for banning chewing gum and caning juvenile delinquents, so it seemed possible that a staffer would chase down a missing girl. I felt surreptitious as I shouldered my pack and followed the Germans to the taxi stand. This was what I wanted: new people, whimsy, a strange place to go.

On the taxi ride Stefan and Nela told jokes in German, which they tried to translate for the Malaysian driver and me. None of them made sense—there was one about a farmer with many daughters and a chicken—but their laughter was infectious. Stefan had been fuzzy on where I would sleep that night, so I wondered if there would be a hotel or a host or a spare room. That kind of uncertainty might normally have made me anxious, but now it just seemed like part of an adventure. I got an internal flutter from thinking about it, the kind you feel when you've just rounded the top of a roller coaster ride.

I drifted in and out of the moment. As the landscape became more rural, I looked out at the fields and took pleasure in the curling palm fronds and multiple shades of green. Then a gear would shift and I'd feel surrealistic for a minute, like I was watching a movie in which, oddly, I was the star. Then the Germans' laughter would bring me back and I'd feel present in the car.

I'd almost forgotten where we were going when the taxi rolled to a stop. The village had one main dirt road. On one side wooden warehouses separated the road from the waterfront, and on the other side there was a barbershop, a restaurant, and a scattering of houses set back carelessly from the road, some screened by low palms. I stood there with my pack, and Stefan invited me to come meet Ah Chung. I would stay with him. A small red shrine was nailed to the front of Ah Chung's home like a birdhouse; two incense sticks burned in front of a gold Buddha. Stefan and Nela disappeared and told me they would meet me at dinner. I wondered if I was part of a trade or agreement of some kind, if Stefan had promised to bring a girl back from Singapore. Maybe he'd joked about it one night, teasing Ah Chung about his bachelorhood. Then, when he met me, Stefan thought what a laugh it would be if he actually pulled it off.

Ah Chung spoke little English but was courteous, even courtly.

He repaired diesel boat engines for a living and had the hands to show for it, but I couldn't tell how old he was. The house was one story, and painted inside in a color that had once been robin's egg blue. Ceiling fans stirred the air. It was a little cooler than Singapore; we were closer to the breath of the sea and the trees. He showed me to a tidy room and handed me a folded towel, and I closed the door behind me. I hadn't been alone since Vancouver. What with the flight and the time difference and my jet-lag-addled mind, I wasn't sure how long ago that had been.

When I went to bed later that night, I wondered if I should think of some way—a chair?—to barricade the door. I was a girl and he was a man, so the usual question hung above us. *The hell with it,* I thought, rejecting the ambient disquiet that afflicts girls who leave the nest. As if to reward my optimism, Ah Chung would be respectful to a fault.

❋ ❋ ❋

We had breakfast on the dock. It was a restaurant, insofar as someone was serving us food for which we would pay, but mainly it was a dock. We ate bone soup, and chucked the remnants between the floor slats, into the green water below. My sense of the surreal came and went again. One minute I was comfortably in place, and one minute I was watching myself. I imagined myself pulling on a new skin, stretching into it, wiggling my fingers toward the ends.

Seasickness, which affects even the hardiest mariners, comes from the contradiction between what the body feels and what the eyes and ears take in. A balance system in the inner ear keeps us steady on the ground, but when it tries to do the same thing on the deck of a boat, while we're looking at a pitching sea, the brain becomes disoriented and nausea is the result.

I think of culture shock as working in a similar way. The slow travel of yore gave wanderers time to adjust. In fast travel, we may jump across the world in eighteen hours, but the brain takes time to catch up. Jet lag is over in a few days, but culture shock lasts much longer and comes in waves. There's the initial shock of, say, suddenly finding yourself on a dock in a Malaysian backwater. Then there's the long, slow shock of staying in a new place, spending months or years discovering a new difference every day. In a new culture you stand on something more like water than land, and it goes on shifting under your feet. The cultures most similar to our own can provoke the greatest unease, because the differences are unexpected. When I would live in London years later, the initially familiar English would become stranger and stranger to me every day, until I would feel like they were communicating with one another via antennae, in a language I couldn't understand.

Stefan and Nela were going out on the boat with the Swede and invited me to come. Captain Lars, they said, would be grateful for the extra hands. I didn't know what we would be doing, but Stefan told me there would be diving and that was enough. I was away now, up for anything. Theoretically you can take on any old adventure at home, bungee jumping or spelunking or whatever. But you don't. The mind is primed by going away. Desire and appetite build and you feel like you can't miss a thing, because who knows when you're going to have just this chance again? Everything has to be tasted.

Rob, a crew cut English salvage diver, explained the deal. There was a wreck out there in deep water, a Chinese vessel that had sunk hundreds of years before. But there was a problem with the Malaysian archaeological authority. Rather than risk losing his booty, Captain Lars and his crew had plundered the wreck without permission, sweating and waiting on the estuary for the paperwork to arrive from Kuala

Lumpur. They'd retrieved hundreds of pieces of pottery, bundled them in heavy tarps and rope, and sunk them again in shallower water.

It's not easy to find things on the floor of the sea, even if you know where you put them. The loads were scattered, the better to avoid detection. Once we'd found the first one, Rob said, they would leave me there while he and Stefan moved on to the next, then Rob would surface and return with a cable. Rob explained all this while the three of us bobbed on the surface, holding on to the anchor line. I set the bezel on my new watch, Rob pointed his thumb down, and we dropped away from the sun.

The water was brown and murky; we were where the estuary met the sea. I could barely see the sand below me approach before I bumped it with my knees. Rob attached the end of a line to a rock near the anchor, and spooled it out while we followed him through the dark haze. I thought of Hansel and Gretel and their disappearing bread crumbs, trying to find their way back home. We came to a roped bundle, a foot tall and two feet wide, and Rob signaled me to stay put. He and Stefan kicked a few times and disappeared.

The current was strong as the sea sucked out the tide. I pointed myself into the onrush and held on. I breathed in and floated up, breathed out and floated down. I had no sense of passing time, couldn't tell after a while if it had been a couple of minutes or fifteen. I held my watch to my face and saw that it had stopped. *I'm on the bottom of the sea,* I told myself, prodding the soft areas of my mind to see if I felt fear. But fear requires imagination, and I wasn't imagining anything now. Mostly I felt calm.

❋ ❋ ❋

I hadn't even noticed the clouds gathering, but as we docked a rainstorm burst down. The dry clothes I'd just put back on, a sleeveless cotton shirt and a long flowered skirt, were immediately plastered to my body. I ran along the wharf, careful not to step into any of the gaps. My cheeks hurt, either from gripping the air regulator with my teeth or from smiling so hard. Everything was going the way it was meant to go.

Later that night I examined my watch and confirmed it was permanently stilled. I threw it away. It was the last watch I would own for ten years.

❋ ❋ ❋

Ah Chung was a diffident host, quietly generous in that way that makes you ask yourself why we aren't like that in the West, or if we are, why we outgrow it so soon. I'd never invited strangers to stay in my home or driven them around town.

I asked vaguely about the *orang asli,* the indigenous people who live in the jungle, and Ah Chung took me into the woods, to a witch doctor with a face like a walnut. The old man squatted in the doorway to his hut, which sat on stilts with a little ladder leading up. He asked me if I would like him to cast a spell, and, with Ah Chung translating, I said sure. Since I was a young woman, the witch doctor figured I would want a love spell. "He needs a food item on which to cast," Ah Chung said. Perhaps a teaspoon of sugar, the witch doctor suggested, which I would then have to feed to the object of the spell. I scrounged in my bag and found half a package of cough drops, purchased for the dry air on the plane. On whom would I like to cast the spell? I shrugged and thought of Stu. "I want him to love me forever," I blithely told Ah Chung. The witch doctor did his hocus-pocus, and I tossed the cough drops back into my bag. More magic and potions, like Tristan and Iseult.

I couldn't stay in place. Movement had brought me here, so movement, it stood to reason, would bring me more good things.

❋ ❋ ❋

Tioman Island was the kind of place billed as a tropical paradise. When I disembarked I walked down a sandy road, and checked into a beach hut alone. I was at a loss as to what to do. As I walked along the beach I felt watched and self-conscious, all the more so because there were few people around, and so I couldn't hide in a crowd. I sat and looked at the water—turquoise, sparkling—and a solitary four-foot-long monitor lizard lumbered into view, lazily swinging her reptilian tail before coming to a complete halt. She seemed to calmly consider the landscape, at ease in her habitat. I wondered how people got that comfortable with themselves.

Everybody talked about finding themselves, but maybe you had to get lost first. Any teenager of any intelligence, who is exposed to more than one culture, sooner or later asks the anthropological question: How much of who I am is defined by the world around me, and how much is something more innate? Is it ten to one? Fifty-fifty? The obvious way to find out is to move from one context to another. Putting myself in new situations, I thought, would act as a purifying fire, charring away all the dross and leaving some essential self. Philosophers and travel writers down the ages have explored the question. In his collection *Fresh Air Fiend*, Paul Theroux writes, "On my own, I had a clearer sense of who I was. . . ."

I wanted that clarity. Without my own culture, would there still be something left? Or would I burn away to nothing? Now that I was alone on the beach, nothingness seemed possible. With people around, there was always some obvious way to manifest yourself. You got dressed, got on the boat, tried a word or two of Malay. Alone I didn't know what I did. I watched myself watch the monitor lizard, who I bet didn't have this kind of problem. She was at peace, living her lizardy life. Far away down the beach, a few people ambled in and out of view. I feared that one of them might come close, not because I thought someone would harm me, but because I felt like there was no one at home in my body. I had no self to present; there was no one to show the world. She—I—had gone off to reformulate and was hopefully coming back. Sometimes you're at a loss for words; I was at a loss for self.

I thought of a book I'd once toted around in my backpack, one that Mona, during our travels in the Middle East, had given to me as a gift. In Jack Kerouac's *On the Road,* Sal Paradise reflects on the moment he woke up, around sunset, in a hotel in Des Moines. He thinks:

> . . .*that was the one distinct time in my life, the strangest moment of all, when I didn't know who I was—I was far away from home, haunted and tired with travel, in a cheap hotel room I'd never seen, hearing the hiss and steam of outside, and the creak of the old wood of the hotel, and the footsteps upstairs, and all the sad sounds, and I looked at the cracked high ceiling and really didn't know who I was for about fifteen strange seconds. I wasn't scared; I was just somebody else, some stranger.* . . .

❋ ❋ ❋

When I got to Kota Bahru, a city on the northeast coast, I was relieved to be alone in a crowd instead of alone-alone. I checked into my own room in a cheap hotel with walls that didn't go quite to the ceiling, and went out at dusk. A night market of food stalls was just opening up, and near it, I sorted out coins and dialing codes to make my first call to Stu since I'd left. There was a delay on the line, but we worked with the rhythm. He told me he was fixing up the terraces in the backyard, and I tried to describe the scene around me: The women wore the most colorful head scarves, in pink, yellow, and poppy red. The stalls served spicy noodles with fried eggs on top. When I got off the phone I felt like a lifeline to comfort and company had been cut off. I jangled around in my pockets, counted out more change, and placed a call to my parents.

"Grandma died," my mother said, and I could hear the quaver in her voice. Grandma Celia had been eighty-three years old and ill for many months, since well before I left. I felt sad mostly for my mother, but I didn't know how to express it. Being far away is a boon for people who are bad at expressing things. I heard myself say, "Oh no, oh no," but the din of the night market rose up around me. They were planning the funeral; I wondered if my mother wished I would return for it, but neither of us raised the possibility.

Recently I'd seen my grandmother only a few times a year. Because I missed seeing my family go through the loss, and missed the ceremony, her death would never seem real to me; it would just feel like a longer and longer stretch since I'd seen her last. From my distance the loss was theoretical, and though I couldn't have said so, I preferred it that way. I felt relieved to be so far away, because I was excused from grieving. I felt nothing but tenderness for her, but there was an emotional emancipation to being here and not there. Even though I didn't believe in God or heaven, I could childishly go on believing that she was still around.

When it happened, the specific timing of my grandmother's death seemed like a footnote: She died just after I went away. But a lesson would persist as I formed and unformed long-distance relationships over the years. Going away could free you from feeling too much.

ON CUTTING TIES

chapter sixteen

I found Kristin, as agreed, in front of Singapore's luxurious Raffles Hotel, which didn't allow our scruffy kind into its lobby. She'd been to Indonesia with her boyfriend, Jeremy, and was now marveling at the scope and variety of her bug bites. She held up her welted limbs for me to see.

Kristin was home, comfort, familiarity. We'd been best friends from the age of fifteen, and we'd stayed close even after I left for college and she started university in Vancouver. Our birthdays were a month apart. She knew about every romance and sexual adventure, knew all the things that my boyfriends and parents did not. We'd snuck out to downtown nightclubs in her father's Gran Torino, and snuck off to the birth control clinic on the bus.

We never fought but we misunderstood each other often, so different were our tastes and goals. We almost never liked the same boys, and for a career she wanted to do something with money. She hadn't moved away from Vancouver but she took big trips; she had visited me in Egypt and would visit other places I lived. We both regarded our buddy trip to Australia as a sort of last hurrah, a bachelorette party before we got old, which, with the wisdom of our twenty-three years, looked like it was going to happen very soon.

There was copious employment to go around for young people on "working holiday" visas. You could waitress or temp; there were even signs advertising for workers in the lobby of our twelve-dollar-a-night hostel in Sydney. It was like it had all been set up just for us. When the Australian social critic Donald Horne wrote *The Lucky Country* in 1964, he meant the title as an ironic indictment of his homeland. Its citizens just happened to get lucky, he was trying to say, insofar as they could get rich on natural resources without having to innovate much. Australia was "run by second-rate people," he wrote, though fortunately for them, the place was difficult to screw up. But Australians merrily adopted his term in the positive sense, and it came to mean that the country was charmed, sunny, well-endowed—and far from the problems of the world. To travel in Australia was a little like that.

Once I took a look around Sydney, I knew I couldn't stay. I'd just been living in a rainy city on the Pacific, going to an office every day. So I urged Kristin north, but not before she'd worked a few shifts in a nightclub in the red light district. There she met a customer, Jason, who unlike the rest of the patrons was young and attractive, small but perfectly formed, with sandy, floppy hair and a tight black T-shirt. He was high on who-knew-what, something euphoric and chatty. He gave Kristin his number and told her to come up to Noosa, the Queensland town where he lived. We caught a bus up the coast to Byron Bay, slumping against each other, saving our money by traveling overnight.

Everything was so easy. The availability of work. The twelve-dollar-a-night places in every town, with shared girls' rooms and breakfast included. The English guy who appeared at the bus station in Byron Bay and ushered us to a hostel. A dozen other travelers got off the bus and we followed him like baby ducks. We weren't on a guided tour, but we might as well have been. It was like a conveyor belt through an amusement park ride.

Outside the hostel there was a sandwich board with a menu of bookable activities and trips in ascending order of danger. Bicycle rental, surf lessons, white-water rafting, bungee jumping, sky diving. This was the kind of danger that was pursued here, planned out and guided by experts. During the day we walked to the beach, and at night we all went to the same bar. In the morning we crowded next to each other at outdoor picnic tables with our fried eggs and pancakes, like we were at summer camp. A brunette next to me with a Yorkshire accent wondered what to do about her boyfriend: He was insisting on coming out to see her, but, she said, he didn't understand: about the bungee jumping or about the options rolling out before her every day. I knew what she meant. We were the same people we were at home, but somehow here, in a different climate, we had permission not to be.

Ah yes. My boyfriend. Fiancé. In Malaysia I'd been too overwhelmed by my surroundings to think about missing him. When we talked on the phone when I was in Melbourne, we both cried. I told him the story about the witch doctor and the spell he cast on the cough drops. I thought at first that he would think it was romantic. As it came out I realized that telling the story was a mistake. Stu put too much store in spells and symbols.

I missed Stu without wishing that he was with me. As I moved toward the warmer weather I felt the thread between us spooling out and growing slack, like the line that connected me to the anchor at the bottom of the Malaysian sea. Kristin seemed to be going through something similar, trying to stay connected to Jeremy amid flickers of ambivalence. Sometimes, for convenience, we called them at the same time, ducking into side-by-side phone booths with our calling cards. I didn't know if we were doing it because we really wanted to talk to Stu and Jeremy, or to preserve the sense of being fastened. I mailed Stu letters and a couple of postcards; he asked for an address where he could send me a letter, but I didn't have one to give. Other travelers used *poste restante,* which let you receive letters held in the care of a city post office. That was how I'd sometimes sent letters to Graham, at a time that now seemed long ago. But I told Stu I didn't know where I would be from day to day.

We took a bus to Noosa. We stayed one night in the Koala Blue, and called our boyfriends back home. Stu had words to send me and insisted that I give him the hostel's fax number. I stood by the machine as the pages poured forth. One, two, three, curling into the tray. A fourth, a fifth, and a sixth. I felt a rising alarm. I felt responsible for this outpouring, and I didn't want to feel responsible. I felt exasperated that he would try to reach me this way, forcing me to pay attention to his words. He was assaulting my snatched freedom, my one breath of air before settling down, rather than letting me be. I took the pages and Kristin and I went to a café, where I bought an iced cappuccino with whipped cream, a special treat because it cost around an eighth of my daily budget. The pages were repetitive, manic, generously loving. They made me uncomfortable. Stu felt me drifting. He was on to me even from thousands of miles away, even before I was on to myself.

Kristin called Jason, the high guy from the nightclub in Sydney, and he invited us to stay in his house. Just like that we'd jumped the conveyor belt. Jason had an airy two-story place with tall windows and sliding doors, with a broad back deck shaded by eucalyptus trees, five minutes up the hill from a sandy swimming cove.

He lived with two housemates, Moo and Ben, both training to be chefs. Jason was a sometime waiter, with plans to open a nightclub, or start a T-shirt company, or move to London. There was a little spare room with a single bed, and Kristin and I took turns night by night, alternating between the bed and the floor. The first night we overheard Moo saying to Jason in the kitchen: "Backpackers? Are you serious?"

Kristin announced that she was almost out of money, and got a job waitressing at a restaurant called Mariposa. It was on Noosa's refined Hastings Street, where fruit and eucalyptus trees shaded low buildings in sherbet shades of stucco. Well-heeled tourists from Brisbane and Sydney dined on Hastings, in open-air cafés, before hitting the beach. Nearby enclaves were called Noosa Heads, Noosaville, Sunshine, and Sunrise, as though the city fathers had been addled by the gentle landscape and sunny days.

I decided to do nothing. Nothing because I'd always done something.

I swam in the cove and ran on the trail through subtropical forest, in a national park that began near Jason's house, and continued for miles out to a cliff over the ocean. I took day trips inland to nouveau hippy towns, with Moo on the back of his motorcycle. I went from the house to the beach to Hastings Street, and back to the house, where Jason rolled joints for his friends, girls and boys, on the back deck. There was Leoni, a bartender Jason had worked with down on Hastings Street. There was Summer, who had a breathy voice and yellow-blond hair. There was Johnny, the heir to a shoe fortune. He was younger than he looked, a forty-year-old who looked like he was sixty, but he still seemed too old to be hanging out with us, a haggard party boy who'd never stopped. His woman friend, Sandra, always showed up with him, guiding him like a nurse. One day Sandra said that she'd found him face-down in the sand the night before and taken him to the hospital. Everyone worried about Johnny.

I spent days as though I had a million of them, wasting them—it occurred to me—like I'd always wanted to. I wasn't training for anything anymore—I wasn't even working. I ate time like a gourmand king, not even trying to keep my appetite in check. Time has a different meaning before your first intimations of mortality, and mine were a long way off. I wasn't even in denial, which would suggest that somewhere deep down I knew what I was dodging. I didn't believe in death at all. If I did, I might have seen Johnny as a ghost from the future, a cautionary what-not-to-do. But I didn't believe I could ever definitively fail, because when time is inexhaustible you can always try again. There would always be a later. I could spend a spare seven hundred days in Seattle, because there would always be more days. I could spend dozens here in Noosa and it wouldn't mean a thing.

Jason's friends' talk bored me. It was almost, but not quite, fas-cinating in its dullness. They gossiped about the people they worked with, most of whom I'd never met. They talked about where to get pot and ecstasy. Jason talked about going to London and caressed the latest issue of *The Face*. Sometimes he would retrieve a back issue from the stack in his bedroom to make a point, like a father trying to convey a passion to his kids, but he was as successful as I would have been if I'd started talking about the Middle East. Jason was going to be a DJ, he said. Late at night I went back to my room and tried to sleep while dance music from the living room vibrated the floor. I had no idea how he paid the rent.

I developed a recreational crush on Jason, mostly because he was there, and because all the other women in his circle seemed to have one too. And somewhere deep down I knew I needed a catalyst, someone to jostle me free. I had to break the sexual bond of the last two years.

Jason didn't seem to mind either way, he could have gone with Kristin or me or neither of us, but I was the one who was around more. Nobody expected anything of anyone in this house, sexual or otherwise. It was the opposite of living in a repressed society: There, young men were aggressively, overwhelmingly, angrily horny all the time. Places like Australia were all-you-could-eat buffets of liberty, and so the young men were chilled out. And there was something gratifying about wanting a man who didn't care. It made you feel like you were exercising free choice. Stu had always been so certain of our joint destiny that I'd never had time to reflect. Maybe this whole trip was about wanting a chance to think straight.

I started trying to stay up as late as Jason did, watching him fiddle with his turntables. It was a paying of dues, required before the attention turned to me. How many girls, I wondered, had waited for boys to finish with their stereos, their videos, their guitars. But if I hadn't had to wait, my desire might not have accrued. And maybe his wouldn't have, either, if he hadn't first been admired. "Do you want a massage?" Jason finally asked. It was just unobvious enough, leaving room for either of us to retreat; people were always giving each other massages around here. He came around behind my chair and kneaded his fingers into my back. I moaned and lolled my head, and rolled it to the side so that my cheek touched his hand. Then he put his fingers in my mouth. He might as well have pressed a trigger. Now I'd want him inordinately for that one little act. I'd want him until my desire either dissipated or was denied.

One night Jason and I went down to Brisbane to go to a rave. The next morning Kristin told me that Stu had called the house and asked her why I was away. I was glad to have missed the call. Something in me had been finally dislodged. I tried to call Stu back at his grandmother's island home, but she said he had already left. She asked me how I was.

"Fine, fine," I said.

"Stu's been talking about your wedding," she said. "He's got this idea for a pig roast." *She's on to me*, I thought.

But I couldn't muster the feeling that anything mattered. I was carrying around my bruised copy of Kundera's *The Unbearable Lightness of Being*. He writes: " . . . the absolute absence of a burden causes man to be lighter than air, to soar into the heights, take leave of the earth and his earthly being, and become only half real, his movements as free as they are insignificant." I thought I'd detached from the earth and was floating through the air.

When Kristin had a day off, we went shopping on Hastings Street and bought identical miniskirts. They were checkered black and white and grazed the tops of our tanned thighs, and we nicknamed them the dish towels. She was several inches shorter than me, petite and athletic. We were both blond with green eyes, but hers were a pale, minty shade I've never seen on anyone else. We went out together like twins. We had both always had a mania for attention-getting and inappropriate clothes, but here nothing was really inappropriate. You could walk around in a bikini or go barefoot for days, and no one would mind.

About two weeks after we arrived in Noosa, we lay in our little room—it was my turn on the floor—and talked. I'd met her boyfriend, Jeremy, only a few times and had taken an instant dislike. He'd told me that he was spending time with her because he was a doing his psychiatric rotation in med school, and she'd seemed like an interesting subject. I never found out if he was joking.

I was getting tired of our long and tearful conversations with our boyfriends, and since the multipage fax, I'd let the days when I was supposed to call go by unnoticed. I wanted a partner in my abdication from life back home, and Kristin talked a good line about the guys she wanted to screw over here. Though Norwegian on her father's side, she was obsessed with Swedes, who were plentiful on the traveler trail. She wanted tall blond boys. So, I asked her, why didn't she just break up with Jeremy? "You're planning a wedding," she countered. "You might not be quite ready for that."

But I had no idea how to break it all off. I felt guilty about causing pain. I had a debt, one now being covered by Stu and a renter in the basement, but how long could I let that go on? I pushed it out of my mind. I didn't want any weight to intrude.

I swam every morning, or whenever I got up, in the little cove. I floated on my back, drifting and weightless, then lay on the white sand below the tangle of spiky pandanus and piccabeen palms. What if I just stayed, I wondered. I could get a job, something mindless, and never leave. What if I just chose pleasure, chose the beach and the sun. That's why people saved for retirement, wasn't it? And here it was rolled out before me, all too easy. "What then shall we choose?" Kundera asks. "Weight or lightness?"

It was Kristin, several weeks richer, who spurred us on this time. She might have been concerned for my state of mind, or might have felt some obligation to protect my engagement as long as it was still in play, or maybe she just wanted to get on with things. She was an aggressive sightseer, and a whole itinerary lay ahead. She didn't see the romance in doing nothing. We declared ourselves done with buses and tacked a note to the bulletin board at the Koala Blue. A Canadian named Bruce called; he was traveling north with his girlfriend, Liz, and he had a big sturdy Range Rover with a roof rack, the kind of vehicle Australians call a ute. For a share of the gas, he would take us farther north.

❋ ❋ ❋

The best kind of travel—the kind I wanted to experience—involves a particular state of mind, in which one is not merely open to the occurrence of the unexpected, but to deep involvement in the unexpected, indeed, open to the possibility of having one's life changed forever by a chance encounter. After several months of phone calls, letters, and that one long fax, I determined that my tie to Stu, which is to say my tie to home, was not letting me be completely open to the world. It wasn't letting me be entirely weightless. While I'd already come far away, I wanted additionally to be able to feel that any life was possible. I wanted to be different people, and just as much, to see what sort of core remained as I shifted from skin to skin.

Bruce, Liz, Kristin, and I stayed overnight in Yeppoon, a sleepy beach town near the Tropic of Capricorn. A flat, sandy island called Great Keppel was the designated backpacker destination here, and so Liz, Kristin, and I took a ferry over to spend the day. Bruce, who didn't think it was worth the price of the ticket, stayed onshore and tinkered with his engine. We planned to leave in the evening.

Before we left, while Kristin and Liz were in the supermarket getting bread and cheese, I stepped into a phone booth and called Stu.

I had to cut my ties, I explained, adding that I didn't want to get married and was not coming home. It was agonizing to hurt him, and frightening to think that this was it between us. We talked and talked. I knew that the other three were waiting in the car for me, but I couldn't bring the conversation to a close. When, after an hour,

I stepped out of the phone box, night had fallen and a full moon was on the rise. For a long time thereafter, the sight of a full moon would remind me how many months it had been since that phone call.

We drove through the night. Once you're north of Brisbane, to continue northward is to move farther and farther from the urban rhythms of civilization. Human settlement spreads out. Miles of cultivated fields or long wild stretches of nature take up the distance between towns.

I awoke when we stopped for gas, in a town where the houses had corrugated tin roofs that sloped down over the decks. It was called Marlborough, Bruce said, and then we moved on into cattle land and I fell back asleep, my head on Kristin's shoulder. I awoke again when we slowed through fields of sugar cane, which looked like high, thick, densely packed grass. We'd come more than six hundred miles north of Noosa and more than eleven hundred since I'd looked at Sydney and decided we couldn't stay. We turned northeast toward a village called Airlie Beach, where we parked on a hillside at two in the morning. The three of us girls stretched out in the back and slept there. When the sun began to beat on the windows, I awoke and climbed onto the roof. The dawn was pink, and a white field of sailboat masts undulated below. I knew instantly that I wanted to stay. This was consummation. I was now fully open to the chance encounter, the thing that could change me. I had finally unloosed my ties, and by force of will been born again. I was open to whatever the world put in my path.

ON BOYS
chapter seventeen

I said good-bye to Kristin and she climbed into a yellow station wagon with a pair of Swedes bound for Cairns. We promised to meet up later. I would catch up with her in the Northern Territories, or she would come back down here. The car pulled away and I looked down Airlie Beach's one main street, Shute Harbour Road. The buildings were painted and decorated to look different from each other—dark wood for the Hog's Breath Café, turquoise for the dive shops, pastels for the two-story apartment blocks—but underneath they were all made of cinderblock and corrugated metal. The architecture had a purpose: When a roof was ripped off in a typhoon, it was easy to replace.

Kristin had been a kind of tie to home, and now I was on my own. To stay I needed two things, a job and a place to live. They would buy me time on boats. The day she left I met a dark-haired guy in long surf shorts at the bar in the Hog's Breath Café, outpost of a chain that crammed its interiors with old signs and hubcabs, carefully strewn around to look haphazard. Stewie, who was twenty-three and a pleasant drunk, said he could hook me up. His name seemed symbolic. I let him take me by the elbow and lead me outside, where he pointed up the hill to a white house standing sentinel over Shute Harbour Road.

"You see the house with the red curtains?" he slurred. "We tie-dyed those ourselves." I told him they showed beautiful workmanship. "Come wake me up in the morning. Go into the house and it's the room with the sock on the doorknob."

At ten in the morning, I climbed the stairs to the front door, pretty sure Stewie would have forgotten me, but I had nothing better to do. Next to the door, nailed to the stucco, there was a black cursive sign that had once read "Airlie View," but someone had replaced the *A* with a *G* so that now it said "Girlie View." I pushed open the door and found a linoleum foyer, a living room with colorless wall-to-wall carpeting, and a giant television in front of the picture window that would have otherwise framed the bay. Grayish mattresses were stacked against one wall, for a makeshift sofa, and the tie-dyed curtains cast a rosy light on the dust motes and a potted marijuana plant.

"Hello?" I called and stepped inside. The house was silent, and I wondered if it was unoccupied, but I glanced in the kitchen just beyond the foyer and saw piles of dishes in the sink, and empty cartons and cans on the floor. A door led off the living room, and I was wondering if I should knock on it when a boy came out. He had long, curling, sun-streaked hair and a goatee and wore only a sarong. He was gold all over, and I looked away, as though from a bright light.

"The door was open," I said.

He rubbed his forehead.

"I'm looking for Stew?" I couldn't always bring myself to use the diminutives.

"The door with the sock on it," said the naked-chested man. I followed him and found the second door, which was cheap and hollow and also ajar. I peered into the crack and saw two men, one of them my acquaintance from last night, asleep on a mattress on the floor. I stepped back and knocked, listened to the silence of the house, and knocked again.

"What time is it?" Stew groaned.

"Hi," I said brightly and stepped into the room.

He stared at me.

"Beth? From last night? We talked about a place to live?"

"Oh yeah," he said. He scratched some part of his body under the sheet and looked over at the figure next to him. "That's Brendan."

My shrug came out exaggeratedly, as I tried to signal that whatever went on here, it was cool. Brendan was silent and still, hair splayed across the pillowless mattress, sleeping the sleep of the passed out.

Stew looked up at me.

"Bethy, give me five minutes, will ya?"

"Sure," I said, and retreated to the living room. Boys started to appear. They came out of bedroom doors, in from the backyard, in through the front. They were cheerful and disheveled and unsurprised. Stewie emerged and made introductions. They *were* surprised when Stewie said I wanted a place to live. They had had lots of people stay, but no girls. Seven or eight people resided in the house, give or take drifter friends, all in their early twenties. Most of the principal residents worked in the kitchen at the Hog's Breath Café.

The boy I'd met when I first walked into the house was Laurie. He was the tallest and finest of them all, and probably as a consequence, the most easygoing. He played music and kept a guitar and a didgeridoo in his room. My new friend Stewie was from Perth and had been on the dole, but now was getting some kind of government student subsidy so that he could train as a dive instructor. Nathan was the only serious sailor in the house, as well as the only one with his hair trimmed short. He'd done well in high school physics, he said, which made him so good on a boat. He had his own room in the basement and a girlfriend down south in nursing school. Brendan was a shorter, rougher version of Laurie, and was between bedrooms, catching as catch can every night. Muzz was nineteen and had just showed up; he slept on a bunk bed in the basement and collected the dole. The others treated him as a sort of pet and called him Muzzy, Muzzo, or Muzzer. Dutchie came into town from his job at a mine.

Later I'd meet a couple of orbiting girls. There was Tracy, a zaftig blonde with a crush on Stewie. She had an air of competence and a restaurant job. And there was a brunette they called "Crazy Dog Woman," which I thought was cruel until I found out that she had two big dogs. She came to try to have sex with Laurie. So did other women; it was generally known that if Laurie was sleeping naked with his door open, he was fair game.

The house was set to be torn down, Stewie explained, and the landlord had rented it to them for its last year of life. It was the cheapest five-room house in Airlie Beach. Behind the house there was a large, empty metal boat shed with a concrete floor, and two boys were moving out of it today, headed down to Surfer's Paradise. I could have the shed and a mattress for thirty dollars a week. I went and got my backpack from my hostel and moved in.

The house had a stove but no telephone or refrigerator. When someone bought beer it was necessary to drink it all at once. The boys threw their orange peels and fish bones out the window, and sometimes left messages for one another on the walls, which was ineffective because no one remembered to look for new scrawls. When I wanted to shower I tromped across the backyard to the open back door of the house, toilet kit in hand, as though in a campground. I carried my own toilet paper. I wore flip-flops in the shower for protection against the grime and mold, and stashed tea and noodles in the kitchen cupboards. I thought of Graham Greene's *Journey Without Maps*, where he writes, "There seemed to be a seediness about the place you couldn't get to the same extent elsewhere, and seediness has a very deep appeal. . . . It seems to satisfy, temporarily, the sense of nostalgia for something lost."

I quickly counted Stewie as a friend. He ate ketchup on rice when he was out of money, but after he picked up his government check, he was able to buy toilet paper, toothpaste, and tomato sauce, items he usually wrote on a list ahead of payday. "Clean bum, clean teeth, full tum," he'd say, settling onto the mattress pile and tucking into his meal.

I bought candles for my bedside, and secured them on the concrete floor with hot wax. The landlord's random belongings, stored and forgotten, were stacked along the perimeter of the shed: lawn chairs, a dishwasher, outboard motors. Though I had the most utilitarian space of all, it had a feature that none of the rooms in the house shared: I could shut it from the inside with a heavy metal bolt. No open doors for me, no random mattress guests. I craved total freedom, and I envied boys because I thought they could have it. But there was a way in which, as a girl, I could act free but never quite get there in my head. However many expectations I escaped and constraints I threw off, there would always be that nagging caution at the back of my mind that said I'd better lock the door.

❀ ❀ ❀

Finding a job wasn't as easy as I'd hoped. The town was tiny and remote, with fewer well-off tourists than Noosa. Budget travelers flowed through at a constant pace, but the restaurants and bars were wary about hiring them, because they tended not to stick around.

People who had proven they could stay six or eight months had the good jobs, the ones in hotels and on boats. After I'd asked for the manager in more than a dozen restaurants, the chef who ran the kitchen at the local yacht club agreed to hire me for two weeks, while someone else was on vacation. If my point in Noosa had been pointlessness, here I harbored an ambition: I wanted to get on the water. The yacht club was not a yacht, but it brought me closer to my goal.

I called the order numbers over a loudspeaker, and when the well-roasted patrons came up to the counter for their fish and chips or daily lasagna special, they asked me where my cute inflections came from. Having the icebreaker of a foreign accent was like finding a forgotten twenty-dollar bill.

❀ ❀ ❀

One day I ended up in the morning debrief, having followed Stewie into Laurie's room and been forgotten. I pulled back into a corner. Laurie was still in bed, and the house residents surrounded him, courtiers waking the prince. He'd moved the marijuana plant, which was communal property but too often raided, from the living room to his bedside. His didgeridoo lay right there beside him.

"I had all my dirty magazines out," Nathan said. "I was planning to masturbate, but my hand fell asleep."

"I came in here at just the right moment," Brendan said in his hoarse morning voice, talking to Laurie but playing to the group. "You were naked and she still had her clothes on, and she was all turned on. I really made her squirm. I made her think I wanted a triangle."

"You mean a threesome," someone said.

"You had your hands between my legs, mate," Laurie said. "At first I thought it was Dog Woman. Getting a bit twisted."

"Did you have a fat?" Nathan asked.

"No, Nathan, I didn't, not anymore," Laurie said, and added, "Brendan punched a hole in my door."

"Brendan, why'd you punch a hole in Laurie's door?" Stewie asked.

"Because I was pissed stupid."

"And what if it'd been my face there, eh?" Laurie asked.

"He woulda punched a hole in your face," Stewie said.

"And I woulda driven these scissors through his face," Laurie said, fingering the scissors he used for snipping buds.

"You know Laurie's had a woman the night before when he's got his guitar in bed with him," Nathan said, and everyone laughed.

"And if he's got the baseball bat, you know Crazy Dog Woman's been around," Brendan said, and they laughed more.

I didn't ask about what the didgeridoo meant. I felt included. I'd become Jane Goodall among the chimps, with the boys now saying anything in front of me or to me. Nathan told me he missed his girl-friend so much he was getting a callus on his palm. Brendan asked me which girls he'd have the best chance with. Dutchie, the mean one, told me someone-or-other better not find herself alone with him. "You know what I mean?" he growled, and I backed away.

❀ ❀ ❀

I went to a crowded backpacker bar with Tracy and Stewie and some others, the kind blasting U2 and serving a four-dollar beer-and-pizza special. I was restless. I lived in a house full of boys who talked about sex all day long, but I wasn't having any myself. I couldn't sleep with one of them, or I'd lose the status I'd carved out as snow-white-mascot-sister.

I decided early in the evening that I'd take someone home with me. I'd never reversed the order like this, deciding to have sex before I knew whom I wanted to do it with. I thought it would be a grand experiment. I watched the door until a group of Italian boys came in, one of them with long brown hair and baggy pants. He looked like a skater, and I thought he was adorable. For the sake of benchmarking my challenge, I told Tracy and Stewie that he was the one I was going for.

By the time we were leaving the bar, I was a little bored with the whole idea. The problem with trying to be hunter rather than prey is that boys are by and large easy lays. There's no thrill in pursuit. Before taking the Italian out back to my shed, I traipsed him through the house, showing off my catch. It was a typical late Tuesday night: Brendan making instant noodles, a couple of stoned girls watching a movie, some boys already gone to bed. While the Italian talked to Brendan in the kitchen, I went into Laurie's room and told him what I was doing. He foraged in his bedside drawer and gave me a fistful of condoms. I would use two. It would be just okay. The next day Brendan told me he couldn't have been more proud of me if I'd been his own daughter.

✾ ✾ ✾

One day as I meandered away after my yacht club shift, along a path that curved through palm trees and manicured grass, in no rush to get anywhere, a man skipped into view with a yellow flower in his hand. He was older, sinewy, and thin as a whippet; he had followed me from the yacht club. He presented the flower to me with a little bow, which instantly made me laugh. Then he asked me out on a date and told me to meet him at the marina.

I showed up at high noon on a day as blue-skied as all the rest. With springy, quick movements, Mark ushered me to a forty-foot fiberglass sailboat with sparkling clean white decks, a bareboat he'd borrowed from a friend at the charter company. Before we set sail, he went to his car and got a platter of sliced cheese, cured meats, and fresh fruit, cadged from a caterer friend. He threw off the lines, motored us beyond the breakwater, and raised the mainsail in a light breeze. He sailed like it was walking, chatting to me all the time. He glanced up at the weathervane and suggested we visit a shoal he knew, since the tide was low enough. The water was calm and clear: The Whitsunday Islands are protected by the Great Barrier Reef, forty-odd miles offshore, which acts as a sixteen-hundred-mile-long breakwater.

He asked me questions, and I explained my accommodations. "Really, a boat shed?" he asked. It did sound a little flimsy, now that I said it out loud. I was suddenly aware that not everyone in Airlie Beach was exploring that place where youth, poverty, and freedom reach their logical, feral conclusion. Adults lived here too. "So what do you want to do when you grow up?" he asked. He had an amused lilt in his voice, like he was teasing a child. He had sussed me out too quickly, like he knew that I knew that I wasn't really one of the boys, or a sailor, or likely to stick around very long. He knew that I was one of the many, many tourists, that this was all a flirtation and I would go and have a real life somewhere else. I was one of Airlie Beach's customers, friendly and cheerful and never to be heard from again.

But I was caught off guard enough by his question to say the first thing that came to mind: "Be a writer." I hated to admit to ambitions I might not achieve.

"What kind?"

"Um, writing about, you know, traveling. And stuff."

He laughed. Why did he keep finding me so funny? "Isn't that what everybody wants to do?"

I squirmed. "What about you—what do you want to do when you grow up?" If he could mock my age, I could mock his too.

Mark had all this game, the kind the boys in my house did not, because Mark, it turned out, was impossibly old. He was thirty-two. And he was embedded in a town that looked transient at first glance. He'd lived here for an unbelievably long time, six years, working mostly as a skipper, taking visitors around the islands for money. There'd been a girl and an engagement that had gone awry, and now she'd gone back south to civilization. Mark's mother mailed him books from Sydney, his link to a culture beyond boats. He told me that the newsagent in town carried a small selection of paperbacks in the rear.

Mark said he was thinking of finally leaving town. He was deeply tanned and had a permanent red sunspot in one eye. His skin, eyes, and ambition would eventually dissipate if he stayed here. You couldn't just live in a beach town like this forever, or at least you had to decide if you were the kind of person who did. Mark said he'd reached his conclusion. But he was still here.

I exulted in being on the water. My fingers skimmed the Coral Sea, and I looked at all the shades of blue, widening my eyes behind my sunglasses as though that would let me take in more. My happiness was doubled by the knowledge that the physical world *could* bring on this kind of pleasure. It made me content to know that I could be moved by nature, independent of human relations. It was a one-way relationship, but beautifully simple.

The water was so clear I could see the bottom even as it got deep, like I was looking through a tinted window. Mark pointed out islands to our west and south and told me little things about them. Whitsunday had the most sugary beach I would ever see. Hook was uninhabited, and Hayman was a luxury resort. The homely distant lump once called West Molle had been rechristened Daydream, and South Molle was being renamed Adventure Island, for the tourists. "But I still like to call it South Molle," Mark said. Captain Cook named the Whitsundays when he sailed up this way in 1770, before his ship foundered on the Great Barrier Reef. Later, on his final voyage, Cook landed in Hawaii, where his crew traded nails for sex, and he was killed by an angry mob.

Most good travel stories are about discovering the unexpected. The traveler goes abroad with an illusion, the illusion is shattered, but then she learns something new, and after assorted challenges and humiliations, she achieves a satisfying epiphany. When we dropped anchor on the leeward side of a white sandbar, though, I skipped straight from illusion to satisfaction.

It was the teardrop from the cover of the magazine. The very one. My mouth fell open and Mark smirked again, thinking I was just dazzled by the prettiness. But I was also thinking of the perversity of the fact that my airbrushed fantasy had come to life. Things are never just what you hoped for. We jumped into water so clear and warm that it was like jumping from air to air. The sand rose up under us, and we floated to where it met the sea and walked out of the water like creatures in an act of evolution.

We walked from the wide end to the tapered end of the disembodied beach, and Mark bent down to pick up a hard, brittle white object, which he put in my hand. I weighed it, wanting to please, wanting to solve his little puzzle. It seemed too light to be a bone. I felt again like a child as I looked up for explanation. He said it was the remains of a cuttlefish, a special find, and showed me how you could draw on it by scraping the calcified surface. We sat down and watched the sandbar shrink around us as the tide rose up, until the land was gone.

A few days later in his apartment, a tidy grown-up place with a balcony and a crisp duvet, Mark was retiring and shy, as though he didn't know what to do with me now that he'd gotten me home.

So I signaled the first move, moving my face next to his, letting him know that he could.

There's light sex and there's heavy sex. The first is weightless and meaningless, like a feather brushing your body, pleasurable but gone the next day. Heavy sex is more exciting, because it entails the risk of consequence. The risk might be of an immediate mishap (getting caught, falling off a chair); or of something more prolonged (ruining a marriage, falling in love). Risk is one of the things that gives meaning, and when we court meaning it heightens the sense of risk.

Jason was light. The Italian was light. Mark was light. They helped me escape all the heaviness back home. But all the lightness posed the same problem I imagine immortality would: If you could live forever, nothing would have meaning anymore.

❁ ❁ ❁

One day Nathan came home from sailing with a long, heavy, silvery fish. But no one felt like cooking, and there was nowhere to keep it cold, so someone laid it across the threshold of the open front door. That night we gathered in the living room to watch a movie, and my housemates and their friends passed around a cloudy glass bong. Whenever someone new arrived, he or she asked why there was a fish in the doorway, then suggested we put the thing in the fridge, whereupon someone on the floor said that we had no fridge, whereupon everyone on the floor laughed harder than they had the time before, until we were in hysterics.

Several days later I moved in with Tracy, to a fold-out bed in her living room, where the breeze wafted in through the sliding screen door, and potpourri scented the air.

ON BETRAYAL

chapter eighteen

I called my brother from one of the booths between the beach and Shute Harbour Road. He mentioned in passing that he'd seen Kristin—in Vancouver.

"What?" I asked.

I was dumbfounded. In my mind Kristin was still in Australia, working in Cairns or Darwin or who-knew-where. We were supposed to meet up. We were in this together, our last hurrah, our bachelorette. Now she'd gone and left the party. I thought that even if we'd temporarily gone separate ways, it was out of respect for each other's independence—for my sailing and her sightseeing Swedes—with the understanding that we'd reunite. I'd thought of her as a companion still, even though she wasn't here. She hadn't even told me she was going home. Granted, we had no way to reach each other, but she could have sent a letter to Poste Restante Airlie Beach. We should have talked about it first.

Sometimes in relationships, what we imagine about the other person is almost as compelling as the reality of who they are. Now I felt like I'd made up an imaginary Kristin. I'd allowed myself to believe that she shared my desire to be on the road. That she didn't want to go back to her boyfriend. I'd envisioned a pact to keep traveling, together at least in spirit, with no end in sight. I was hurt. I didn't see that there was something selfish in my hurt. I wanted her to be just like me, to do the thing I wanted her to do, regardless of what she wanted for herself.

I didn't even understand why she would want to go back so soon. Money was no excuse; there was plenty of work here among strangers. I was just getting started, just beginning to transform. I thought going home was weak. People who did were self-jailers, too scared to live without their bonds. They were geographical monogamists, in need of one place. They needed their habits and their things. They needed their people. I thought I didn't need any of that.

Kristin had gone home to her suburban condo, her two roommates. She'd gone home to her familiar place, the city with the mountains on the North Shore, which were unlike anything in this flat land. She'd gone back to the struggle to establish a postcollegiate life, with a career and all the rest. She'd gone home to friends, to parents, to Jeremy.

❋ ❋ ❋

From time to time, out of a sense of responsibility, I called Stu. One day he told me that he'd packed up all of our things and was leaving Seattle. He'd found a renter for the house, someone who didn't mind its tatters. In the same way that I'd lost respect for Kristin when she went home, Stu's decision gave me new respect for him. In my mind he'd become part of our hateful house. But when he said he was going to separate himself, I liked him better. I remembered that he had wanderlust too. In our very first conversation he'd told me about Thailand and Bali, and then at the merest suggestion he came to me in Pakistan. He was turning back into the person I first knew.

At the same time, he shifted the burden. He was abandoning what I'd abandoned, and now there was no one looking out for the problematic hearth and home. By staying there he'd enabled my freedom, giving me a gift that I'd overlooked. Now I'd have to think more seriously about the outcomes of what I'd done.

He flew to Fiji and hopped a sailboat to New Zealand. And with no warning, sometime when he was crossing the ocean, he did the most generous thing he could have done: He told me he understood. Two months after I made that full-moon call from the phone booth in Yeppoon, he mailed me a letter from Auckland, penned on a becalmed sea. Written on five small sheets of yellow notepaper, the letter read in part: "By leaving our safety net, we have thrown our souls upon the wind, exposing ourselves to all of the fears and dangers that we sought to protect each other from, and in doing so, we have made ourselves available to experience things that . . . border on the magical." It was like he was saying he understood everything I had done. It recast my betrayal as a kind of love, and I wondered if his version of events might be the right one. And so by setting me free, he began to reel me in again.

ON SPONTANEITY
chapter nineteen

I *got a job as a deck hand/cook* on a refitted former racing yacht that took tourists on five-day trips. I saw Mark for the last time on my first day of work, just after we had left the marina and were getting ready to raise the sails. I was sitting on the bow, attaching the hanks to the forestay, when I saw a small lime green sail coming our way. It came closer and I saw that it was Mark, windsurfing at high speed. He came within five meters of the boat and waved to me and called, "Bon voyage!" then made a graceful jibe. I yelled good-bye, he looped toward the boat one more time, and headed away. He'd finally made plans to move back to Sydney, and I knew he'd be gone by the time I got back to shore, and that I'd probably never see him again. Light as air as he'd been, he'd given me my all-time best first date, to the teardrop shoal, and now the perfect unburdened good-bye.

❁ ❁ ❁

The problem was, I wasn't much of a deckhand and could barely cook, and definitely couldn't manage tacos for eight at a forty-five-degree angle without getting seasick. I was too stressed to enjoy the blissful settings: Whitehaven Beach, so empty that it made our visitors feel like they'd discovered their own paradise; isolated snorkeling inlets; drinks by tiki torch on Adventure Island, nee South Molle. After finally getting the galley clean at 10:00 PM, instead of collapsing into my bunk, I had to socialize with the skipper and the guests. At 6:00 AM, before cooking breakfast, I tried to take a few minutes on deck by myself.

I was terrible at the job, which made me hate it. Permanent residence in paradise was looking unviable. It's typically believed that people in the service sector don't move into anything more cerebral because they can't, but the reverse is true too. I could be forced back to offices and keyboards by sheer incompetence at everything else. When the manager of the sailboat took me off after several weeks, I was at loose ends. I was no less of a tourist than any of the backpackers who passed through; I was just a different kind. I started to think about leaving town.

The day after I was kicked off the boat I went to a party at the Hog's Breath Café, the same place I'd met Stewie on the day that Kristin left, and he'd pointed up at the house. I began talking to an acquaintance—by now every face was familiar—at the bar. Shaun was one of a pair of American yachtie brothers who'd washed up in town years before. Everyone called them the Sepo Twins: Sepo was short for septic tank, which rhymed with yank. Shaun told me that his brother was getting married to a local girl, and that he himself had finally decided to leave. The next day. He was going south, all the way to Sydney. I asked if he needed another hand, to drive and cover the gas. He said yes, absolutely, he could make better time that way. I said I would come with him as far as Noosa, and we raised our cans.

I'd acquired a few things in Airlie Beach, and now I couldn't get my backpack closed. It's amazing how quickly the dust settles when you don't move. I decided to leave behind a mask and snorkel, some clothes, and a couple of books. I asked Tracy to mail them to me, and she said she would, and we both knew I'd probably never see them again. I inscribed a few numbers in the tiny black book I kept for the purpose, but the hastiness of my departure meant that I couldn't spend a lot of time saying good-bye, which was how I liked it. I'd be there one moment, and then, *poof*, I'd be gone. I romanticized the quick disappearance, but really I just hated the awkwardness of leaving. I hated the heartfelt statements that were required, and the declarations of intent that I already knew wouldn't come to fruition.

Why south instead of north? Now that Stu had released me along with himself, I didn't need to run from him anymore, and if I went south I'd be closer to New Zealand than if I went the other way. Then there was the fact that going north would have taken me into the wrong kind of new territory. I could have continued on the tourist itinerary, to Cairns, the Daintree, the Northern Territories, where the books all promised real live crocs. That's what Kristin had done before flying home. Then I could have gone down to Alice Springs and Uluru, nee Ayers Rock, nee Uluru. But taking that route would have suggested a kind of finality. Once everything was ticked off, the next obvious thing would have been to go home, and I didn't want to do that.

ON TAMING NATURE
chapter twenty

I *first heard about the Kokoda Trail* from other backpackers. It had a fearsome reputation: sixty miles of track, most of it no wider than a single person, passing through jungle and malarial swamp, and rising to a height of 7,185 feet as it traversed Papua New Guinea's Owen Stanley Range. From July to November of 1942, Japanese and Australian troops had done battle along the trail. More than seven thousand soldiers died, mostly from tropical diseases.

Though I'd heard the country spoken of up and down the Queensland coast as a dream or goal, I hadn't met anyone who'd actually been there. It loomed above Queensland on the map, across the Coral Sea, as much an idea as a place, all rumors of impassable jungle, tribal warfare, cargo cults, and cannibalism. In the remotest valleys of the island, which was shared between the nation of Papua New Guinea and the Indonesian province of Irian Jaya, there were supposedly even tribes that had never made contact with the outside world. The Sunshine Coast, on the other hand, the stretch of small towns north of Brisbane where I washed up after Airlie Beach, was in thrall to the march of suburbia. I even became a part of it.

I met Justin in a bar in the village of Sunrise Beach, where he stood out in a fringed suede jacket. He claimed he'd seen me before, at the cash machine in Airlie Beach, but I didn't remember.

A few weeks later I quit my waitressing job in Noosa and went to work for him. He had a landscaping company made up of himself, a small trailer, and a clutch of shovels and rakes. His mother was a real estate developer, and her company gave him all its business. After it razed an area, say a eucalyptus forest, to pour dark new asphalt and sprawling one-story homes, it hired Justin to prettily refoliate the area around the houses.

We drove around the developments planting nursery-reared bushes and palms, and unfurling strips of lawn that came in neat packages of one-foot-wide rolls. It was hot, wearying, physical work, but I preferred it to waitressing, because I didn't feel incompetent, and I could spend all day talking to Justin.

It was in the third conversation after we met, when Justin took me to dinner at a game restaurant and ordered the kangaroo, that he first mentioned Papua New Guinea. Before he had finished asking "Have you heard of the Kokoda Trail?" I told him that I wanted to go.

"Let's go," he said. "I have a friend there I've been saying I'd visit. She can help us sort it."

"Okay," I said, and that was that. Like when I'd made up my mind to go to Spain, or Yemen, the choice was instant. We started planning. Even our decision to have me work for him was in part, ostensibly, so that I could save money for the trip, which I couldn't finance on my diminished bank account. I had what John Steinbeck, in *The Log from the Sea of Cortez*, called "the curious boredom within ourselves which makes adventurers or bridge-players." Easy had become too easy, and I wanted to be somewhere hard again.

"Your adventurer feels no gratification in crossing Market Street in San Francisco against the traffic . . . Instead he will

*go to a good deal of trouble and expense to get himself killed in
the South Seas. In reputedly rough water, he will go in a canoe;
he will invade deserts without adequate food and he will
expose his tolerant and uninoculated blood to strange viruses.
This is adventure. It is possible that his ancestor, wearying of
the humdrum attacks of the saber-tooth, longed for the good old
days of pterodactyl and triceratops."*

Eschewing suburban Australia, we would leave for the South
Seas and expose our blood to strange viruses.

✻ ✻ ✻

Justin had been to Sydney for university, where he studied waste
management, and made a few trips around Queensland and one to
Hawaii. Like me, he was twenty-four, the age at which every other
Australian I met was saving for a lengthy trip abroad or just returning from one, but he was a homebody. He thought about entre-
preneurial plans or maybe getting another degree. But his dreams
were all based around where he lived. He even occupied the ground
floor of the large family home shared by his mother and teenage
half siblings, Aaron and Samantha. Just six months before we met,
his stepfather had been killed in a motorcycle accident, after which
Justin had moved back home to be an anchor for his family, and
they for him. His life made me think of the mug a bank manager
had given me when I left a part-time job in Seattle. It commanded,
"Bloom where you're planted," which I had thought contemptible,
and taken as a rebuke.

Justin was tall and broad-shouldered, with curly brown hair that
grazed his shoulders. He had a strangeness that suggested he was
either oblivious to what others thought of him, or that, at least, he

was living in a world of different social cues and fashions than every-one else. In daylight hours he wore a black patch over one eye; it had been damaged by a dog bite and now was hypersensitive to light. The patch aroused my annoyance. He had a legitimate and practical rea-son for wearing it, and yet I was convinced that he also liked the way it looked; he liked that it made him look like a swaggering pirate. Why else would he also wear long, blousy white shirts with crisscross drawstrings? I was even more annoyed that I, too, liked that it made him look like a swaggering pirate, a fact I would have never admitted for fear of mortal embarrassment. I suspected there must exist some discreet modern way of protecting a damaged pupil from sunlight. I wrote in my journal that he was "too much, too intense."

Justin was intelligent, but if you didn't believe in things like past lives or telepathy—and I was determined not to—you might have considered him crazy. I was torn; I thought his supernatural convictions were stupid but also seductive. He told me that the quick, intense bond we formed suggested we'd met in a past life.

He was a misfit: His closest friends were at least a decade older than him. He took to me because I listened attentively when he talked about his latest esoteric interests—a book about chaos theory, another about ancient Egyptian architecture. I took to him because he was a rich vein of knowledge amid the intellectual wasteland of chefs, waiters, and drug dealers I'd so far met on the Sunshine Coast. We fell easily into a sense of complicity.

Justin liked to listen to me too. "Tell me a story," became his favorite refrain, often spoken as we were driving in his Jeep or hiking up a trail. Whenever he asked, I tried to satisfy the request. I *should* have had stories to tell. But I was often at a loss. All of my experi-ences to date were piled up like shiny baubles in my backpack, but I had no ability to string them together.

Our planned trip expanded to encompass a grand tour of Papua New Guinea. We got inoculated by a doctor friend of his, Ken, who also gave us malaria drugs. We bought lightweight sleeping bags, hiking boots, and boxes of Band Aids. We trained, driving from Justin's house in Coolum down to the Glasshouse Mountains, gray monoliths that shot up from the flat coastland like fingers, where we ran up and down the trails. Instead of going back to my rented room in Noosa I began sleeping on Justin's sofa, a tweedy sectional in a tile-floored room with a patio.

Three things happened in the week before we were to leave.

The first was that Stu and I decided to meet in Auckland. I'd fly there as soon as I got back from PNG. Stu would help me out with the ticket.

The second was the change in my relationship with Justin. Our conversations were still geeky but his look had become longing, a fact I willfully ignored. To me our relationship was still fraternal, and I recoiled the night on Ken's balcony when he first leaned in for a kiss. I pushed him away and said "no." He tried to ask me something, but then Ken appeared with fresh Bundaberg and Cokes.

The next morning I braced for awkwardness, or another annoying romantic push. But everything continued as normal: We drove to a work site in his Jeep, had lunch at McDonald's, went for an evening run up a hill near his house. I basked in his attention—I could feel him watching me strew wildflower seeds across a patch of bulldozed dirt, or hike up a hill ahead of him, and I liked it. The fact that he'd so gracefully accepted my rejection made me more intrigued by him. A little later, while we were hanging around with his sixteen-year-old sister, Samantha, I counseled him on what to wear on a date that coming evening. He was taking a woman he had just met to the game restaurant. "That's where you took me!" I said. "Are you going to order the kangaroo?"

"Of course," he answered. "I like to establish baseline conditions." He smiled.

Samantha looked at us warily and said, "You guys are weird."

A week later I was planning to crash at his place again, and we each lay on one leg of his couch, head to head, watching the movie *Legends of the Fall*. In it Brad Pitt plays Tristan, the wild son of an early twentieth-century Montana family, who has a talent for taming wild horses. At one point, which would stick with me far more vividly than the rest of the plot, Tristan leaves his father's ranch and says good-bye to Susannah, who has an unrequited passion for him, to go find himself in the world, which takes years. The viewer is treated to a glorious montage of Tristan abroad: smoking opium with lolling Chinese women, carving on the wooden deck of a boat in the South Seas. The wise old narrator uses a metaphor about Tristan that I've always remembered. Water courses over rock, flexible and flowing, but when it freezes, it's so strong that it breaks the rock.

At the end of the movie we thought we'd been spoken to personally. We were like that! Willful and wild and so strong that others would break themselves against us rather than the other way around. Swept away on this mutual delusion of self-regard, Justin rolled over and kissed me, and this time I found it seductive. I was surprised, because I'd become blasé and bored in recent months. I'd told Justin that I'd gone "off men," and meant it. I hadn't realized the capacity for pleasure could reassert itself so easily.

The third thing that happened that week was that Patricia called. She needed his friend's name—mine—to help clear us through customs. He began to spell it, slowly.

"E . . . L . . . "

I watched him from across his bedroom.

"I . . . S . . . A—"

On realizing that my name was not "Elton" or "Ellis," she hung up on him. It was only then, after I questioned him, that Justin confessed to their past affair. Obviously, it was still a burning concern for her, but there wasn't much any of us could do at this point; we'd be arriving in New Guinea in a few days. I almost told him to tell her we weren't a couple, which almost felt true. But I refrained; the truth was I was excited and giddy about the new turn of events, wanting to grab Justin and bite him at any given moment. I wasn't about to pretend it hadn't happened. It was Patricia who forced me to acknowledge our status as lovers. Knowing that Justin might be desired elsewhere required me to take a position.

❋ ❋ ❋

They say that three kinds of white men go to Papua New Guinea: missionaries, miners, and misfits. Save for a few adventurers and anthropologists, the white women who turn up are usually following their husbands. Patricia was different; she'd moved to Papua New Guinea from Australia as a child, and the family had settled in Lae, on the north coast, where her father launched a software company. Patricia went to university in Australia but returned, and at twenty-seven was living in Lae, vice president of the family business.

Patricia and her friend James met us at the Port Moresby airport. Patricia was pretty in a milky way—in another climate she would have been called an English rose. She had a slim build and thick, dark-blond hair, but it was cut short in a way I thought was unflattering. She was dressed for modesty and comfort in the heat, not fashion, in loose trousers, a long T-shirt, and a vest.

"Welcome to sunny Port Moresby," she said, in what seemed to be a sarcastic drawl. The place was notorious for shantytowns and an obscenely high rate of crime. Patricia spoke in the slow cadences I associated with the tropics. She gave no indication that she'd recently hung up on Justin in a fit of jealousy, or that I was the object.

James had brown hair and the kind of deep, ruddy permanent tan some white people acquire when they're perpetually in the sun. He was from England, and had for five years worked as a mining company geologist based in Lae, where he and Patricia had become friends. Patricia had invited several people on the trek, and they'd been enthusiastic at first, but James was the only one up for it in the end. He'd hiked other trails in New Guinea and even spoke a few words of pidgin, and had done a lot of organizing for our trip.

Port Moresby, ramshackle around the edges and hilly, might have been unique among capital cities in that it wasn't connected by road to any other place in the country. The roads that led out of town all petered out somewhere in the jungle. Armchair anthropologists attributed all the thievery and rape and murder to the effects of rapid urbanization. Young people, mostly men, came down to the cities having only ever known their tight-knit tribe and its wars against other clans. In the city nobody was a *"wantok,"* a kinsman, so everyone was fair game.

We spent the rest of the day driving around Port Moresby picking up supplies: rope, more mosquito repellent, rice, dried food. At one point we traversed a wide and chaotic intersection that swarmed with people. Pedestrians surrounded the car, moving like atoms to their destinations in an inscrutable flow. It was a sensation I'd had before, in Pakistan especially: I was in a fragile glass pod of Western culture— of air-conditioning and pop music—submarining through an ocean of foreign bodies. I looked at Justin, who was literally wide-eyed. I squeezed his hand and felt something I couldn't identify, something I decided must be what mothers felt. There were things I couldn't experience for the first time, but I could enjoy someone else's discovery.

That night we stayed with friends of Patricia's who had a swimming pool. Taking a dip after dinner, Justin and I couldn't see any surrounding landscape because of the high cement walls, which were topped with shards of glass, but we could look straight up at the stars. I propped my elbows on the edge and leaned back. It all felt so good: the coolness of the water, the stars, a scent of jasmine on the air, and Justin. I tried to keep my mind focused on the pleasant present, but now my fear was coming on full bore. The jungle? For six days? What had I been thinking? I wanted to be the sort of person who would hike the Kokoda Trail, but that was different from wanting to do it, which I now wasn't sure about at all. I'd dared myself and now I was stuck. I was trying to prove something, but I wasn't sure what it was, or whom it was for.

ON LOVE
chapter twenty-one

*W*e entered a high-vaulted tunnel of green. We were a party
of seven, the four of us plus the three porter-guides Paul
had hired, Godwin, Samuel, and Yepuku. They wore T-shirts, long
shorts, and flimsy-looking sneakers, and each one carried a machete.
We wore T-shirts, long shorts, and heavy-duty hiking boots, and
each of us carried a day pack—except for Justin, who had insisted
on carrying *all* of his own equipment, tent, sleeping bag, and everything. *Of course he would,* I thought.

The trail began to climb right away. In these parts there were
supposed to be blue-necked cassowaries, horn-billed kokomos, and
bright little frogs that lived in the trees. That first day, though, the
jungle passed in a blur. Trekking on muddy, root-gnarled ground, I
spent the next few hours looking at my feet. My thick white socks
poked out of green and brown hiking boots, and gradually took on
the tone of the mud underfoot. Within just a few square miles, New
Guinean mud came in a rainbow of nuanced shades. Back on the road
it had been russet red. Here in the jungle it was more yellowish, with
stripes of beige and deep orange. Below my shorts my legs gradually
became streaky with sweat, dirt, and Bullfrog, an ingenious Australian concoction that contained both sunscreen and sufficient DEET
to kill mosquitoes but not, I hoped, humans, which had a sticky,

viscous consistency, and which I smeared on my exposed skin every time we paused. Light dimly penetrated the canopy overhead.

We ate ham sandwiches we'd made the night before on a cluster of smooth gray rocks by a stream, and after lunch set off uphill again. Then down. Then up. Calves stretched, thighs burned, shoulders ached. Ferns and twisted roots closed around us, and the whole jungle seemed to be a series of ridges. The trail was entirely unmarked by signage, and often our narrow path would come to what might or might not have been a fork. We would peer down these alternate routes, just as narrow and tangled and unmarked as the one we were on, and consult our map, but they never added up. After a couple of hours we had no idea if we had passed a major turn indicated on the map, or if it was yet to come. We consulted Godwin, Samuel, and Yepuku whenever we came to one of these choice points, and it was Yepuku who usually gave us the most confident-sounding answer.

By dusk, though, it was apparent that our "guides" had no better idea of the route than we did. We began to acknowledge that we were completely lost. *What are the chances*, I thought. But that's the beauty and terror of a natural place. On sidewalks and highways, even strange ones, you can make any number of mistakes and still be at your hotel in time for cocktails. Here, mistakes had real repercussions. The pressure of the wild made things matter.

A hard, pounding, tropical downpour began, powering right through the canopy. The trail became slippery underfoot, and so when we came to a stream we decided to stop. There was no clearing in which to set up camp, and while the tall trees were widely spaced, the undergrowth of ferns and vines was dense.

Suddenly Justin had a machete in his hand and was hacking at the undergrowth with big swinging arcs. I watched him for a second, then took Godwin's machete and started hacking too. The rain beat on our faces, soaking our clothes and washing off the sweat and dirt and Bullfrog, and I was amazed at the sharpness of the knife in my hands. One swipe and a solid mass of vines was gone, another swipe and another square foot opened up.

When we'd beaten down a square patch so that it was just a flat tangle of vines, Justin and I laid down our plastic tarp and set up our tent, still in the pouring rain, then threw our belongings inside and crawled in, leaving just our hiking boots outside under the fly. We laid out foam pads and sleeping bags, and took off one wet item after another. It wasn't dry inside, what with our pile of wet clothes and what seemed like 110 percent humidity, but it was less wet than it was outside. I lay down and reached for Justin tentatively, just to kiss his forehead. But I felt his erection against my thigh, and the incongruity of the situation—sex on the one hand, and on the other being lost in the encroaching, devouring environment—turned me on. Making love felt urgent, and while we did, images of our machete attack on the vines flitted through my mind, spurring me on.

❋ ❋ ❋

When Patricia told her father she planned to do this hike, he'd tried to dissuade her. When that proved impossible (was she any more certain about why she was doing this than I was? Was it to be with Justin? To prove something to him?), he gave her a handheld GPS. She pulled it out the next morning to try to figure out where we were. We learned that, as a device that functions by picking up a signal from a satellite, it was useless under a thick layer of foliage, and therefore would be useless along much of the Kokoda Trail. She put it away.

We packed up and retraced our steps up the skinny, slippery thread we'd followed down to our campsite the night before, to a point where the path was wider and better trodden. Using our maps, from there we regained what we thought was the trail. In the heat of midafternoon we came to a wide river and ate lunch on the shore— tinned tuna, onions, sliced tomatoes on bread. Afterward we laid out wet clothes from the night before on the rocks, and James lay down on a rock and closed his eyes. Justin busied himself building something with sticks, rocks, and a tarp that looked like a very large funnel. I asked him what it was. "It's for rainwater collection," he said, crouching down to adjust a stick. I reflected that this was exactly the sort of thing Stu would do, and that they would probably get along well—not that I would mention this to either of them. It was the sort of self-serving thing a bigamist wants to believe.

Patricia and I stripped down to our underwear and waded into the clear water to cool off.

"What's Justin doing?" she asked.

"Making something to collect rainwater," I said.

I shrugged and she rolled her eyes, which made me laugh.

"Boys will be boys," she said, and I felt like the ice was broken. Up until then we'd had only brief exchanges about rope, rice, and her GPS. Now we were in this together.

"When did you move back to New Guinea?" I asked.

"Three years ago," she said in that sleepy drawl. Any stress the trek might be causing didn't come across in her demeanor.

"And you want to stay here?" I asked. I couldn't figure this out. The place that to me was the most exotic in the world was, to her, home and safety and comfort. But it was so isolated, her community so small. Why didn't she want to leave, I wondered—move to Sydney or Melbourne? Didn't she want to meet men who weren't misfits, missionaries, or miners?

"I wasn't planning to at first, but business is good." She sold software systems. Her degree was in computer science, which suggested that maybe she'd always planned to come home and work for the family enterprise. She mentioned that she had a boyfriend, Rupert, in Lae, which answered the unspoken question I had about her relationship with her tent mate, James: definitely just a friend. I wondered if it was awkward sleeping side by side with him. But I was beginning to think that social awkwardness was a luxury of civilization, of which we were in short supply.

After Patricia got out of the water, Justin came in and joined me, and without discussion we swam upstream, beyond an outcropping of rock, so that we were out of view of the camp. I wrapped my legs around him like we'd been separated for years, and we kissed cool wet faces and shoulders, limb slipping on limb. We stayed away from the group only for a few minutes, but I swam back feeling reassured—that out here we still felt this affection and desire, and that even semilost and sore and tired, there was this basic pleasure in having each other.

After our swim, Patricia, James, and I studied the maps. The "guides" leaned over our shoulders, clueless. They were citified young men, bereft of that special radar that jungle residents were supposed to have. Like cannibalism and the loincloth, the ability to find one's way through untamed nature was a fading tradition in PNG.

We figured out that this was the place we'd meant to camp the first night—and that the village we'd hoped to gain by tonight was therefore still a day's march away. We decided to stay put for the night.

❀ ❀ ❀

In our tent at night, I pressed Justin for details of his relationship with Patricia. I gobbled them like a soap opera, like they had nothing to do with me. They'd met on a flight from Sydney to Brisbane. She was spending a week there for work, and they met up a few times. They slept together. They parted, he said, on the understanding that they would just be friends.

Lying on my back in the dark, I smirked at all the careful little agreements we articulated in relationships, about how "things" were going to "be." To Justin I just said, "Right."

To her, at least, it must have felt like a whirlwind romance: the speed, the disinhibition of impending separation. Maybe it had felt that way to him too, but if so, he'd forgotten or was hiding it from me; he sounded disinterested as he described their history. After their first meeting, they exchanged a few letters and phone calls. He really did want to visit Papua New Guinea one day—maybe this was the real basis of his interest in her. I could see myself doing the same thing, latching on to someone because he promised adventure. Six months after they'd met, she called and said she was in town. She summoned him to the Hyatt, the most luxurious hotel Justin knew, the place where his parents had entertained clients. He met her in the restaurant, and they had a sumptuous lunch, her treat. It dawned on him that her only reason for being there was to see him. The lunch—the whole visit—was her attempt to make him see that she was the one for him. He was too unnerved, he said, to savor the compliment. He'd been chased before by women, but he was alarmed in this case by the whiff of desperation he caught, the degree to which Patricia had inconvenienced herself to make her case.

He declined to come up to her room, and she flew back the next morning to her home in PNG.

"I think she wanted me to be a reason to move to Australia," he said.

"But what was it?" I asked.

"What was what?"

"What was it that"—I wasn't sure how to put this, but I

thought it might somehow answer questions I had about myself—
"what was it that drew her to you?"

"You and I, Beth—we affect people. We just do."

This flattered me a great deal, and so, now thinking pleasantly of
my own outsize impact on the world, I dropped the subject of Patricia.

Rituals fell into place. The next morning I filled my canteen from the
river, dropped in a purification tablet, and gave it a good shake. Then
I poured in powdered orange juice, which covered the tinny taste left
by the purification tablet, and shook again. I washed and dried my
feet in the stream, put fresh bandages on my blisters, pulled up my
socks, and tied my boots. And we started walking uphill again.

On the evening of our third day, at sunset, we arrived where we
were supposed to be on the night of day two, a village called Nauro.
We came out of the jungle and down a gentle slope to a wide grassy
flat dotted with huts made of sticks and fronds. Wiry children in
shorts and flimsy dresses ran up the path to meet us, and then gal-
loped alongside us as we descended, their ringmaster calling "this
way, this way." After being lost and not seeing anyone but our group
for three days, it felt like a glimpse of civilization. I was pleased to
see a pile of bananas and papayas. We negotiated to buy some fruit,
and for the luxury of an overnight hut. It was raised a few feet off the
ground on stilts and consisted of a pointed roof over a wide floor covered with woven matting, which creaked a little as we padded across
it in our socks. All four of us would share the same floor space, and
Patricia, I was pretty sure, shot me a warning glare before we turned
in, as if to say, "You wouldn't dare."

Godwin said he knew the way. He hadn't known the route we'd taken to get to Nauro, he explained, but this part after Nauro he had hiked many times.

The ground didn't get steep, which was briefly a welcome change, but it got swampy and swampier. I stopped to change from hiking boots into Tevas. Pretty soon we were more wading than walking. Someone had laid down logs as a path through the swamp, but the logs kept sinking underfoot. Some were so skinny and slippery that I fell off again and again, and finally just gave up and trudged through the opaque water. Maybe this was how you got through the jungle, by just giving in.

After half an hour of slogging through knee-deep water, I realized that I had no idea when it was going to end. If we kept marching forward, how long would it take to reach dry land? What if we went back? We weren't World War II soldiers under orders; we'd done this to ourselves. We plodded on, and the reed grass became so tall that I couldn't see far ahead. When I could see over it, the jungle looked to be in the far distance. "Watch out; the grass is sharp," James called from ahead, at exactly the moment I—dammit!—felt a blade graze my forearm. A scratch in these conditions was more than an annoyance; it was an opportunity to worry about tropical diseases festering in my sores.

Justin was the first one to realize that he had leeches on him. *Gross,* I thought, and quickly looked down at myself. There were three black dots on my calves.

Appalled, the four of us wanted to stop and remove leeches, but Yepuku urged us on. "Faster, faster!" he said. "They won't stick on you."

When we regained dry ground, we all sat down on a log and peered at our leech-covered legs.

"You can burn them," Patricia said, and we scrounged in our packs for lighters. I plucked one off with my finger. It left a small red welt where it had been sucking my blood.

"You can pick them off!" I said.

"Only if they're small," Patricia called back, experimenting with one of her own, finally not sounding sleepy at all.

James tried to set one of his on fire and we smelled burning hair.

Justin had two leeches bigger than quarters and was trying to decide between burning and picking.

"Let me try," I said. I held the flame to his leg and his skin and hair started to burn. It had to hurt, but he stared at me stoically, fondly, and didn't say a thing. The leech fell to the ground.

Ten minutes later we were leech-free and comradely, back in fresh Band Aids, dry socks, and boots. I'd slathered on another layer of Bullfrog. Its chemical, lemony smell had become a fixed mnemonic. I even knew its bitter taste from when I forgot that Justin was also slathered in toxic goo, and gave him a kiss.

A little later, back in the jungle, pleased with ourselves for having conquered a swamp, we decided it was time for a map check. And we soon realized that, relative to where we'd wanted to reach that evening, we were four hours off course.

No more listening to the guides, we swore. And we'd really better start using that GPS. Patricia and I were talking about whether one of us should climb a tree—we were the most agile— when a family of six appeared. They were all barefoot and walking at twice our speed. The mother and father had weathered faces that made them look elderly, even though they were probably no more than forty; life expectancy here was fifty-something. Every member of the family, down to a girl of about four, carried his or her own bush knife.

The father explained to Godwin, Yepuku, and Samuel how very far off the Kokoda Trail we were, and our nonguides looked genuinely surprised.

The *paterfamilias* and his eldest son then led us to a fork in the trail and pointed down one of the tines. He spoke in a local language to Godwin, who translated in a mix of pidgin and English. We had an hour-and-a-half walk ahead of us. We were to go up a mountain, back down the other side (this was sounding drearily familiar), and when we found water at the bottom, we should camp there for the night.

That was at about four in the afternoon. After a couple of hours we were still walking uphill. We stopped to eat cucumbers we'd bought in Nauro, then kept going. After numerous false crests—after each of which another, higher one suddenly appeared in the distance—we finally reached the peak of the highest ridge and began to descend the other side. That was about when the last of the light disappeared.

We got out our flashlights and began, gingerly now, to make our way downhill, and the locus of the pain in my legs shifted from my thighs to my calves. After waving our flashlights around at first, we learned to point them strictly at the ground, so as not to ruin our night vision. The path was narrow, steep, and covered in places with hard, tangled roots. Sometimes a muddy patch shifted underfoot. There was no possibility of going back the way we came, and no possibility of camping on the spot, so there really wasn't much to say. At one point Patricia remarked, as calmly as a scientist observing a lab specimen, "We have redefined stupidity."

James's flashlight sputtered out. He moved in closer behind Justin to take advantage of his light. The night became timeless. After a while I no longer had any idea how long we'd been trudging downhill in the dark. I might have been doing it my whole life;

this might have been my entire existence, and everything else just a dream. The pain, the repetitive movements, the bobbing lights. I no longer even felt tired. In fact, I felt okay. Maybe even good. I could keep going. I could hike forever.

We hiked downhill some more. Instinct was in charge now. The more evolved parts of my mind, sensing that they weren't needed, wandered off. I thought about Stu, sailing across the Pacific. How he must have loved that. I thought about a novel I'd discovered by a young Australian writer, *Praise,* and about what flakes all the characters were, and yet how they were deeply meaningful flakes because their flakiness was just a protest against life's meaninglessness. I thought about Kristin and knew that she could have handled this trek. We'd camped together as teenagers, and she was the more athletic one. I wondered again how she could have gone home.

✻ ✻ ✻

Godwin was saying something up ahead. He was agitated. "We're here, we're here!" I didn't believe it at first, but as I descended toward his voice I saw that we really were somewhere, if not at a spot that I would have considered a "somewhere" before this trip. It was a wide flat area next to a stream. With my newly trained eye and my mind on life's basic necessities, it promised food and rest.

I took this as a new challenge, one that filled me with energy. We would set up camp! Yepuku and Godwin built a fire. When the white-gold light sprang up, I saw that James was sitting on a rock looking vacant. Samuel was missing. "He very slow," Yepuku said without alarm.

Justin and I set up our tent and he crawled inside and lay down, booted feet still sticking out the flap. With James listless, Patricia and I set up her and James's tent, and James wordlessly climbed inside.

"Let's see, shall we have rice with soup powder, or soup powder with rice?" Patricia asked, unnaturally buoyant.

"Rice with soup powder," I said. "And as an appetizer, a cucumber!"

Godwin and Yepuku eyed us like we were crazy, which was becoming true.

When the rice soup was ready, Patricia took a mug to James, and I took a mug to Justin.

"C'mon, you should eat," I said quietly, and he struggled into a sitting position and accepted the soup, slurping from the top of the mug. I returned to the campfire and sat there with Patricia and Godwin, drinking my own soup and taking cucumber bites.

"I don't think I've ever had a better meal," I said.

Justin called weakly from the tent: "Are women stronger than men?"

Typical Justin: saying something that flattered me, but that I wanted to resist, because I felt myself so easily falling for the flattery. There's something suspicious about someone who's always stroking your ego—maybe this was why I struggled to hold my feelings for him in check.

"Evidently," Patricia said. Just then there was a rustle and Samuel emerged from the bush, and sat down silently with us at the fire. Then James called from his tent. "Do large-breasted women have bigger brains?"

What we needed to get through this was no longer physical strength. That had stopped mattering hours, maybe days, ago, when we all exceeded what we'd thought were our physical limits. We'd all pushed ourselves through pain and exhaustion. I remembered how, when we first stepped into the jungle outside Port Moresby, it had felt like going into a portal to a different world. Now any one of us, Godwin, Samuel, and Yepuku included, would have taken an escape hatch.

Now it was psychological strength that mattered, the ability to stay calm and keep pushing ourselves. I would never set any records on lung capacity or muscle power, the things that made me resent boys because they had so much more. But maybe I had an advantage in tenacity. Maybe I wasn't faking it anymore. I hadn't been sure, but now I knew for a fact that I wasn't just saying I could do something like this, I wasn't just trying to be cool or make a point. All that was irrelevant now. I was really sitting here, lost in the jungle, probably hundreds of miles from the nearest road, at risk of illness, injury, and unfriendly locals, and I was okay.

❋ ❋ ❋

On the eighth morning I kneeled in a stream in my one-piece bathing suit, which was now literally the suit that I bathed in—on the few occasions, that is, when I actually took a bath, with soap, as opposed to just opportunistically splashing myself. The stream came up to my waist and I scooped handfuls of the clear, chilly water over my head, rinsing out shampoo. I brushed my teeth and watched my soapy spit drift downstream, then dried myself with my blue and white batik sarong and began walking across the green grass back to our hut. I felt better than I had in days. I felt good. My legs were covered with sores, at least two of which looked infected, and I kept discovering new mosquito bites. But I was clean, we knew where we were on the map, my mind was clear, and my body had reached a turning point. Instead of getting more weak and sore and tired every day, it had stabilized.

As I arrived back to the house on stilts where we'd slept the night before, Patricia came to the door. "James is having a malaria relapse," she said.

✵ ✵ ✵

Malaria can kill swiftly, or it can lie low, incubating for months or years before returning to cause fever, delirium, and bone-jarring pain. This would be James's third bout since arriving in New Guinea five years before. He was gray-faced and incoherent, lying on his sleeping bag in the hut. We had to get him out of the jungle.

As we'd moved northward along the Kokoda Trail, the villages had become more touched by the outside world. We'd met an American missionary in one, and seen a few little churches and wide grassy slopes.

PNG has a terrible road network, but apparently you could hitchhike by airplane. This village where we had spent the night had an airstrip, and according to the headman, a bush pilot made deliveries from the outside world every few days. He suggested we ask for a ride.

Much as I thought I wanted some respite from the trail, I was surprised and let down to learn that the possibility of exit was so near at hand. I realized that I regretted having to leave. For one thing, I had the sense of a task undone. Though we'd spent more than a week in the forest, I felt like I was cheating on my plan to "do" the Kokoda Trail. But there was something else I would also really miss. All the focus on the physical world, on mending our sores and getting enough food and finding our way, had a satisfying simplicity. It took my life away from nuance and analysis and complicated relationships. Maybe this was why people went to sea. I felt more alive than ever.

So we put on our backpacks, said good-bye to our guides, and walked out to the airstrip. We let pale, clammy James lie down and erected a tarp over him, taking turns bringing him water. At mid-afternoon a small plane landed. The Australian pilot was reluctant at first, but when he saw James, he agreed to take our money and take us to the town of Kokoda.

In Kokoda we stayed the night in an abandoned school dormitory. The next morning, we rode in what passed for a bus—it was a flatbed truck with two benches and a canvas cover—from Kokoda to Popondetta. At least two dozen men sat on the benches, with more hanging on to bars and standing. James and Patricia rode with the driver in the cab, and Justin and I wedged into the back; when a space opened up on one of the benches we sat down, me in his lap. And there was his hard-on again, pressing against me, invisible and silent and enjoyed. PNG was, for us, "the exciting thing in exciting company," as Graham Greene once wrote, inviting his lover to come to an India roiled by postpartition slaughter. I watched a man who had gotten on with a bunch of bananas and was hanging out the back, standing on the bumper with one hand gripping the canvas cover. Without ever losing his balance, he proceeded to eat all of the bananas one by one, throwing the peels onto the receding roadway behind us.

❈ ❈ ❈

Patricia's boyfriend, Rupert, was a wise-cracking, voluble, balding Aussie. He met us on the airfield in Lae bearing chocolate-covered ice cream bars—he'd brought a cooler—which we lapped at like children. We piled into his car, where he blasted the air conditioner and Kurt Cobain, and he drove us to Patricia's home.

She shared a house with a roommate a short walk from her parents' place, though she said she used the connecting trail only in broad daylight when there had been no recent unrest. The house had what she called a "rape gate," an indoor floor-to-ceiling gate made of iron bars that could be locked to close off the bedroom wing from the living room, dining room, and kitchen; there was a telephone on the bedroom side so that the residents could retreat there and call for help.

Because it had the only double bed, Patricia gave us her bedroom. She went to sleep the first night at Rupert's, but on our second night in Lae she slept down the hall in her housemate's room. Our first night, as we were getting ready for bed, I looked at Justin and said, "She gave us her room." He looked at me and shrugged. It was cushy after the trail and the abandoned dormitory in Kokoda, with flowered sheets, extra pillows, even a boxspring mattress. As we drifted to sleep that night, Justin said, "You know when I was asking you to tell me a story?"

"Mm-hmm?"

"That was how I was telling you I loved you." It was the first time he'd said it, and I wasn't sure he needed to. One of the beautiful things about us, I thought, was the way in which we could feel things and know things without lathering them up in words. "Of course I love you," I said.

Justin and I spent a day with Patricia and Rupert on her family's motorboat, picnicking and snorkeling around rocky coves. The night before we were to leave, I washed my face at the bathroom sink and took out my contacts. I opened my glasses case, but it was empty. Everything was a blur, but I didn't want to go to the trouble of putting my contacts back in, so I went looking for Justin. He wasn't in our room, so I passed the rape gate and entered the living room. Patricia and Justin were sitting there in the dark, him in an easy chair and her opposite him, a few feet away, on the sofa.

"Hey, can you help me find my glasses?"

I heard Patricia sigh.

"Sure, one sec," Justin said, jumping up.

I stood there and reached out one hand to hold myself up against the wall.

"Sorry, I can't see a thing," I said. I felt rude. Patricia didn't say anything, and Justin moved toward me. Since we'd finished the hike Patricia had grown chillier toward me, as though, with survival no longer at stake, we had little to talk about. Her unspoken feelings for Justin, whatever they were, loomed so obviously to me that I found it remarkable that her boyfriend didn't seem to notice. I didn't think she was plotting a stealth seduction of Justin, but she wanted something—maybe just time alone with him.

"Good night," I said, with deliberate cheer, but she didn't answer.

Back in our—Patricia's—room, Justin found my glasses on a dresser right away.

"She was gearing up for a deep talk," he said. "She told me that she has a card I sent her on her desk at work. She rereads it all the time."

I felt bad for her. Maybe whatever romantic interest she had in Justin had been buried by material needs on the trail. Now that we were back in civilization, such as it was, and now that Justin was about to leave, her most turbulent emotions were reemerging. There'd been no opportunity on the trail to speak to Justin alone; then yesterday we'd spent with Rupert. This was her last chance. But for what? To express love?

The next morning, I was in the shower when Patricia left for work. When I came out Justin told me that she had told him, angrily, to just leave town already; she didn't want to speak to him again.

While Justin showered, the phone rang. I picked it up, and the person on the other end hung up with a click.

When it rang again, Justin answered; it was Patricia. Now she wanted us to stop by her office. A driver for her company would pick us up, take us to her office, and then take us to the station.

I sat in the car in the parking lot while Justin went in. After a few minutes the driver went somewhere too, and I was alone. I stared at the yellowing fiberglass of a boat sitting on a parked trailer, and at the hot pink bougainvillea dripping over it. Justin was gone about twenty minutes. For the first time, my feelings for Patricia shifted from curiosity and empathy toward irritation. He was mine.

Justin came back.

"She's furious with me," he said.

"She always seems so calm," I said, hearing myself sound sullen. "And she has a boyfriend."

"I told her that," he said. "She told me she loved me."

❋ ❋ ❋

With the road shortage, there was no easy land-based way to go straight west to Madang, so we were going up and inland to Goroka, provincial capital of the Eastern Highlands, then back down to the coast. Tribespeople from the surrounding mountains came down to Goroka to trade fruit and coffee and pigs, and I read in a guidebook that it was the "rape capital" of the country.

Just after dark we left our hotel room and walked down the main street to find something to eat, ending up at another hotel that had a restaurant.

We talked about the trek, and Patricia and Rupert, which led Justin to pontificate on our respective characters.

"You're as strong as a lion and as vulnerable as a lamb," he said.

This made me cringe and infuriated me. I didn't know where he got his vaguely biblical-sounding clichés—he'd also once told me that I had the legs of a gazelle—and the comment grated in ways I couldn't fully explain. But the animal vocabulary was the least of his offenses.

"I'm not vulnerable," I said.

"Of course you are," he said.

"No, I'm not. How dare you."

"I said you were as strong as a lion too! It's not bad to be vulnerable."

"Does it make you feel like a big hero to think that I'm vulnerable?"

"Beth, we're all vulnerable."

I knew I was picking a fight, but I felt wounded. I'd come through the jungle, for Christ's sake. I'd lived in Cairo and Karachi and a boat shed. Now he was poking holes in my hard-won confidence in my own strength. I would show him.

"I'm leaving," I said, and got up and marched out of the restaurant.

"Beth!" he called.

I stepped into the road, which was dark and deserted, suppressing the fear that threatened to rise up and send me back to the restaurant. *Rape capital, rape capital, rape capital,* I kept hearing in my head. What exactly did that mean, in practical terms? But I wouldn't go back. It was maybe a half a mile to the hotel, and I walked as fast as I could. I jiggled the hotel key chain in my pocket, then took the key and clamped it between two fingers and made a fist, so that the business end stuck out. Someone had told me how to do this in college; the idea was that if you punched someone, you would also gouge them with the key. Of course, I'd never actually tried this.

The street, lined with a few low hotels, the closed post office, and the silent and empty marketplace, was surreally deserted. Where was everybody? I couldn't decide if the underworldish quiet was good or bad for safety. There was only one street lamp along the route, and here and there a yellow flicker from a window. A man, stocky in a skirt and suit jacket, appeared out of a doorway and made me jump; I glared at him but he ignored me. *I have redefined stupidity,* I thought. Patricia's words. But if I went back now, it would only prove Justin's contention that I was vulnerable.

Finally, I passed our bored-looking hotel clerk, climbed the wooden stairs to our street-view room, and shakily unlocked the door. I locked it behind me and turned on the light. Never had a single bulb cast such a reassuring glow.

When Justin arrived back, I was sitting at the small desk writing a letter to Stu. One man to deflect another, so that I didn't need anyone too much. I wrote that we'd emerged from the jungle, and enclosed a piece of string tied in an approximation of a love knot, thinking he would get the reference: We'd both read the same novel that mentioned this sailors' symbol of true love. (In fact Stu, in his embrace of signs and symbols, would find the knot sinister.) I sealed the envelope; I'd mail it the next morning. I wasn't mad at Justin anymore, but I wasn't about to let him know that.

I propped my feet up on the table and looked out at the deserted street, thinking about the last fortnight. Before we learn to channel our emotions into the accepted routes, we see how messy they are. I hadn't loved Justin when I first met him; I'd wanted to keep him at arm's length. But then I grew comfortable, and trusting, and suddenly I desired him, and once I desired him I loved him. I also still loved Stu. Justin loved me. Patricia loved Justin. I was pretty sure that she didn't love Rupert, but maybe he loved her. Do people get married, I wondered, because all this volatility goes away, and they finally know, without a doubt, that they only love one person? Or do they get married out of hope that they can rise to the occasion, and then, if other feelings arise, tame them into submission?

Justin didn't hold grudges. He could be infuriatingly calm, but it also made me feel safe to know that he forgave all. I turned out the light and crawled into bed.

✳ ✳ ✳

Sweat- and dust-covered again, after another journey in the back of a truck, we arrived carrying our backpacks at the entrance to a dive resort outside the town of Madang. The main building was a luxurious take on a traditional longhouse, with a high thatched roof and a flagstone floor.

The resort offered an almost unbelievable level of comfort. In the past six months I'd slept in hostel dorm rooms, group houses, a metal boat shed, a sports utility vehicle, a hut, a tent, and as a guest in people's homes. I was about to gorge on hotel ease.

We had our own waterfront cabin to ourselves, raised on stilts in deference to the local aesthetic, but scrubbed to a gleam and endowed with crisp white sheets and curtains.

The next few days were as easy as the jungle had been hard. To go for a dive, I only had to wander from our cabin over to the dock, put on my gear, and climb into one of the outgoing boats. Or, if I felt like it, I could tumble right off the dock. There was a World War II bomber just a short swim offshore.

One evening Justin and I were on the bed in our room, clothed, with me sitting astride him. "Tell me a story," I said.

"There was a man, and there was a woman, and they'd known each other throughout all time," he said. As so often with him, I wanted both to cringe and to believe every word. I bent down and kissed his neck. "Go on," I said.

"They saw something in each other that they'd never seen in anyone else," he said. "Go on," I said, smiling into his neck.

"And they fell in love," he said. I kissed under his chin, the side of his stubbled jaw.

"Will you marry me?" he asked.

I froze. Were we still playing our game? Were we ourselves, or were we each pretending to be someone else? Part of me wanted to say yes, to give in to the desire to be swept away. But what if subsequently neither of us ever backed down, never ventured to suggest that it had all been a game? And what about Stu? We were broken up, but what a mess. I couldn't get engaged to Justin when I was barely unengaged from someone else. This whole trip, beginning with my flight from Seattle, had been a flight from marriage. I'd betray myself if I suddenly embraced that kind of commitment again. It would just be proof that I couldn't stand alone. And there was still so much of the world I hadn't seen.

"Beth?" Justin whispered.

I willed myself to be responsible. I felt glued to him. But then I sat up and climbed off with heavy regret. It was like refusing to go up in a hot air balloon. I said, quietly, "No."

We went to dinner, and he didn't bring it up again. Nor did we ever talk about whether he'd been serious or not.

✿ ✿ ✿

The next night we joined a group night dive on the wreck of a small cargo boat. "If we're lucky we'll see phosphorescents," the divemaster said.

Flashlights in hand, we took turns tumbling off the gunwales. At the divemaster's signal, we descended the anchor line into what might as well have been outer space.

Floating in the void, free of gravity, I made my way along the side of the ship. Justin floated somewhere near me, but darkness made the water doubly isolating. I listened to my own breaths. It was so dark, and I was so weightless, that I had to look for my bubbles to be sure which way was up. I swam backward a little, away from the boat and into outer space, and waved my arm through the water. Sure enough, the phosphorescents appeared, trailing my movement like the tail of a shooting star. I let myself tip upside down and floated there, watching the gentle snowstorm, marveling that a world of such strangeness existed here all the time, just under the surface.

✳ ✳ ✳

On December 5 we flew from Wewak to Port Moresby, and the same day caught our flight back to Brisbane. I had four more days until my flight to Auckland. At Justin's house in Coolum we did little but rest. The infected cuts stopped festering and began to heal, and the scabbed mosquito bites that covered my body in pointillist arcs began to fade. I stopped applying calamine lotion and began to feel strong again.

As my body healed, my heart grew apprehensive. I was flying from Justin, whom I undoubtedly loved, to Stu, whom I'd loved at least as much, but whom I'd wanted to run from. My heart was aching—literally—my chest hurt after Justin left me at the airport. Why did I have to go to Auckland? I wasn't sure; I just knew I did.

No one ever explained how to deal with this kind of pain. All the examples of what I was supposed to want were about channeling emotions, funneling them carefully into marriage or at least monogamy. What if I didn't work that way? I felt like I was trying to funnel a river delta after a hurricane into an irrigation ditch. The jungle, with its never-wavering pattern of life and death, its seasons and routines, its clarity about what would kill you, was a rational place compared to my own heart.

ON BEING FAR AWAY
chapter twenty-two

I *walked up Queen Street in* downtown Auckland, so slowly I almost came to a stop. I looked at people's faces, noticing them like I never had. I looked especially at the young women. I watched one come toward me and imagined her world: She's doing errands; she works in a shop. I shifted my gaze to a man in a suit, then a girl with matte black hair. They were at home. To me New Zealand *felt* far away. Familiarity made it strange. So much was similar to home, from the language to the Union Jack to the place names: Queen Street, Nelson, Stewart Island. It was just like my corner of Canada. Then something would jar me. A fern the size of a tree. Steam seeping from the ground. The other names of places: Waiheke, Wharariki, Whangarei.

All these tweaks made me feel more isolated and adrift than radical difference. I thought of the game I'd played as a child when I was too young to be afraid of much. We spent two weeks every summer on the Oregon Coast, in a house in a tiny beach town with the outsize name of Lincoln City. I spent hours every day in the surf, tossed around like a lost toy. The game was this: Ride in on a wave. Take a deep breath. Be pulled down underwater to the sand. Then ride the undertow back out, as far as it would take me, until I was running out of breath. Kick, surface, and repeat. Now, in Auckland,

I felt the undertow. I wondered if I'd let myself be pulled too far out. I wondered if I'd already closed doors.

I'd left Justin in the middle of love, tearing out the stitches of a seam. The threads were loose inside me, sickening me, like a shifting deck at sea. I was out of money. I'd let the time limit on my return ticket to Vancouver pass by. How many full moons back had that been? What had I been doing that day? It would cost more than a thousand dollars to get from here back to there. The place where I'd lost all momentum was on the far side of the world.

I stood on Queen Street wanting to be anyone else. I wondered how I could have screwed up so badly when I was only twenty-four. I had to step up to our house in Seattle, the ball and chain to which we'd shackled ourselves, and through which we were shackled to one another. Or we could let our house foreclose and go into bankruptcy in the United States and never return. I'd wanted to let my life be changed, but suddenly I was on the precipice of letting it all go too far. I saw various lives unspooling before me. In one I was free to build a career, move to a big city, be young and aspiring at the center of the world. In another I never left the southern hemisphere. I was overtaken by ease and beauty and let it hold me here.

You could adopt New Zealand and have it instantly be yours. You could shed off whatever skin you wore back home. You could make up a new self, maybe even shirk a debt or two. It was all temptingly easy. But then you would have cast a lot. You would have chosen a life far from the center. Antipodeans with high ambitions leave, for Los Angeles, London, New York. I could see already that the exotic stimulation of tree ferns and hot water beaches and black swans would become mundane, and then I would want to get back, and by then it might be too late. Back to where, and too late for what, I didn't know. I just knew that I was far from home.

I turned off of Queen Street and sat down at a café on a pedestrian passageway called Vulcan Lane. Of course it was, I thought. I was in outer space. The lane was brick-paved and charming and the waiters wore tight black aprons, as urbane as waiters anywhere. I began a letter to Kristin, who was still dating Jeremy and trying to get a job at a bank. She'd gone somewhere safe, whereas I'd gone into the deep end. I started to cry. For Justin, for the possibilities I feared I was closing off, and for the subtle way in which the quality of time had changed. I was still rich, could still spend my time without much thought. But I was watching it now, aware of it going by, sensing that I should put some aside. This trip had been a digging in of my heels against the passage of time. So much of my traveling—in Egypt and Yemen; New Guinea and Australia—had made me feel present in the moment. In fact, that feeling of being absorbed, not thinking of past or future, as consumed as I was when I was having sex, was part of the reason I loved being on the road. But now, instead of feeling present, I felt like I was missing out on something I was supposed to be doing somewhere else.

Quietly, as secretly as the bank account I'd hoarded in Seattle, a seed of ambition kicked in. I'd get to the place I was meant to be, even if I wasn't sure where that was.

❀ ❀ ❀

Stu had started over. He'd created a good life, maybe better than the one he'd had in Seattle. Being away from his family, from the endless projects on their houses and his own, had done him good. He worked at the Wooden Boat Workshop, where his coworkers welcomed and admired his talent. His skill had never been so appreciated. His Seattle coworkers, the carpenters and roofers and drywallers, had never seen what a craftsman he was. He might not have even realized it himself.

He'd rented the ground floor of a house with a roommate named Noah, a New Zealand–born, U.S.-raised kid, who was cheerful about his job as a cleaner at Stu's boat shop. He had also acquired a girlfriend in Auckland, a German blonde with a motorcycle and a scar like a scimitar on her left cheekbone. When I arrived he was easing her out of his life. He mentioned her name a few times, and I saw her picture, but I never met her; she just hovered like a shadow in the corner of my eye. Jealousy tightened my chest on the couple of occasions he went to see her, but I knew I had no right. In any case, I knew I just had to be patient a little while, and that the German girlfriend would be gone. It wasn't a competition for his affections; I was the one who compelled him. I knew, after a couple of weeks, that she was gone; felt it so completely that I figured she must have left town. I sensed that I had a scary kind of power over Stu, one that I was in danger of abusing. It made me feel responsible for his actions and feelings, and paradoxically hate that responsibility.

And so I moved into Stu's life. We slept on a mattress on the floor, awkward and asexual as siblings. I accidentally called him by Justin's name, repeatedly, then swore he was just a friend. That had been true, I rationalized, when I'd first planned to come to New Zealand. "Do you love me?" Stu asked. It was the most important thing, all that mattered. And I did. But if I hadn't loved him, I still would have had no choice. We had responsibilities that made us mutually dependent, and I thought that this tainted our bond. I was a love purist. When material need removed free will, the emotion was defiled. When I untangled it all, the situation came down to money, which meant that I was, in a way, selling myself, doing this to get that. I'd never compromised like this before.

Our house was on a street of bungalows, right where the road dipped into a shallow valley. Our backyard opened up onto a grassy park. We had a car: an unlicensed blue Datsun, rusting out in foot-wide patches all over the body, so worthless that a colleague of Stu's had given it away. He drove it over the hill and down to the harbor each morning. He helped me get my first job, as a hostess on the *Manu Moana,* an elegant new motor yacht that companies rented for parties. I served canapés made by a chef in the galley, and opened and poured bottles of champagne. My favorite times were when Patrick, the skipper, asked me to help him with something vaguely nautical, like pulling up the fenders, or tying off the lines when we got back to the dock. Sometimes after a party Stu and a few boat shop friends would join us on the top deck, and Patrick would serve us port.

Our plans were vague. I felt that my life was not as it should be, but Stu's was closer to the mark. He had respect. It wasn't even just a local respect—people from all over the world had yachts refurbished in Auckland. It was a sailing capital, a country where the boat-to-person ration was something like one to three. For Stu it was a center. It was a pit stop for cruisers, that flotilla of ordinary people who'd rejected normality back in Stockholm or Dallas or wherever, and put to sea. They followed a roughly similar global itinerary to one another, because of the trade winds and a desire for friendly faces in new ports. As well as big jobs, Stu's boat shop did small jobs, repairing a mast here and a tiller there.

We would go home at some point, maybe. Our plans were vague: We knew we had to go, but we put off talking about it the way some couples stay silent for years about commitment and marriage and children. At least it was easy enough to make money. I got an office job, and between the two of us we were able to wire money back to the United States every month to cover the mortgage. My brother, now a college student, was living in the house, ostensibly maintaining it, renting or loaning the basement to assorted friends. He didn't mind the tears in its fabric, the places where the insulation showed or a board covered a hole in the floor.

In December we traveled, to the hot water beaches of Lake Taupo and to Wellington, where on Christmas Day we woke up on the floor of a friend's van, parked in a marina. Somewhere around the time we were hitchhiking from Nelson to Picton, Stu and I became a couple again. His suspicion and anger dropped away, and my lust for him flickered back to life. In Taupo I folded my sarong in half and wore it short, so that he could easily hike it up. I could love two men at once but not desire them both, and now enough time had passed since Justin that I could want Stu again.

We returned to Auckland, where I got a job with a shipping company in a position that was almost exactly like my job in Seattle. I bought office clothes from a secondhand store and thought that I passed all right. I called Justin from the office, or had him call me there. He said he wanted to come down and drag me back to Australia by the scruff of my neck. On Tuesdays Stu and I went to the home of our new friends, Christine and Sam, to watch *The X-Files* on television, and on weekends we ordered enormous lattes on Ponsonby Road. Stu's coworker Abel had a house on Waiheke Island, and we went there with Noah, Abel, and Abel's wife, Laura.

Stu and his coworkers could always talk about woodwork or sailing; I didn't have much to say. I began to write, stories about my adventures, about Papua New Guinea and Lake Taupo. I wrote them by hand in my notebook, typed them at work, and mailed them to airline magazines. I was happy just to get back the rejection letters because they let me know I existed.

It dawned on me that there was a university in Auckland. Even when I was lonely on the road I'd never felt homesick, but now I realized that a university might be a comforting place. I'd grown up on and around the campus where my father taught. Vancouver and Auckland weren't such different places. They both had the feeling of being far-flung outposts, but universities connected them to something bigger, to the whole English-speaking world.

I didn't go to the campus just for comfort though. I went to its library one afternoon, and asked for the catalogs of graduate schools in the United States. The librarian directed me to a hefty volume, and I sat on the floor and leafed through. I looked for journalism and political science. I ran my finger over names: Baylor, American, Columbia. I wrote away for information.

The boat builders discovered that, across from their workplace, there was a gourmet produce company that supplied restaurants all over Auckland. At the end of the day the company discarded cartons of leftover food, almost undamaged, into the Dumpsters between the two sheds, so Stu and I began checking them every day. We dove for oyster mushrooms, champagne grapes, and tiny yellow tomatoes shaped like lightbulbs, thrilled with each find. I loved the silly, shameless ease of it, the way one could just get by so simply. We carried our treasures back home, invited friends, and made stir fries in our wok.

We'd re-created our Seattle life.

ON ESCAPE
chapter twenty-three

*E*rik *Weisz was born in* Budapest in 1874, and emigrated to America with his family in 1878. It was his first escape, into a land of reinvention, the America where any life was possible. He gave his first performances at the age of nine, calling himself "Ehrich, The Prince of Air." Later "Ehrich" turned into "Harry," and the great escapologist Harry Houdini was born. Throughout his career he created more and more elaborate situations from which to break free: handcuffed, padlocked into a trunk, hung upside down from a building. The point wasn't so much to *be* free as to *get* free. When you escape from something, you don't abscond into nothing—you escape from one place to another. The excitement is in the instant of deliverance itself, because that, not the final destination, is the only moment of being free. It's the moment of feeling most alive and most oneself, unburdened by the expectations on either side.

Adam Phillips, a psychoanalyst and the author of *Houdini's Box,* writes that "what one is escaping from is inextricable from, if not defined by, what one is escaping to." Likewise, my need to escape seemed to have an opposite pathology to go with it: I had, for the second time, created a home. I'd feathered a nest, hanging postcards on the wall and cooking up ragout. I'd have argued that this box had sucked me in, but it's as likely that I made it myself so that, like Houdini, I could perform an even greater escape.

ON GOING TO SEA
chapter twenty-four

I *ran up to Ponsonby Road* and down to the marina, where I paused to look at the bulletin board. Usually there was nothing of interest, just the day's menu at the Ponsonby Cruising Club, so I'd walk along and look at the sailboats, sizing up strengths and faults. Length, material, number of masts, width of beam. I composed a dream boat in my head: fifty feet long, low and narrow with teak decks. Normally I just looked, the way you might flirt with handsome men from the point of view of monogamy. This day, though, there was a sign: Crew wanted, sailing to Tonga. Call Ian and Helen, or stop by the *Copper Lady* on pier three. I would just stop by.

"Ian and Helen" had a nice, reassuring ring. You couldn't just throw yourself on any old boat, as Jess, a girl sailor I met in Auckland, had warned. She told me that the slang for girls who volunteered as crew on ocean crossings was "screw." Once you were out there, you were out there; there was no jumping out the door.

Ian and Helen were from Perth, and had sailed all the way around Australia and then New Zealand. He was brown-skinned, the product of an Indian mother and Scottish father. Helen was tall and lanky, barely tanned for so much time on the water, with long brown hair and bangs. They planned to follow the usual route: northeast to Tonga, then westward across the Pacific, on to Fiji, Vanuatu, and Nouvelle-Calédonie. I knew all the names, because they'd popped up as ports of call when I'd been at the shipping company in Seattle. Then as now, they'd sounded terribly romantic. It was almost June: The *Copper Lady* was leaving a little late in the season because they were waiting on repairs. Someone from the Wooden Boat Workshop was coming that day to install a new tiller.

We had tea in the cockpit. It shouldn't be too complicated a voyage, Ian said. Maybe five or six days, a week at the most. They just needed an extra set of hands and eyes, to handle the night watches.

In Auckland I'd once again developed outer and inner lives that didn't match. In my outer life I made love to my boyfriend, sat in cafés, and went to the office. I even once brought Stu to a company picnic. In my inner life I read graduate school brochures and walked up the road to call Justin. I had all the dialing codes memorized. He was my little escape hatch, giving me something to look forward to—I was sure we'd reunite—and lightening the feeling that I was getting mired down again.

Now, presented with an opportunity, my inner life reared its head.

The story I told Ian and Helen I made up as I went along. I'd sailed, I said. No blue water experience, but I'd been part of a delivery crew down the coast of Queensland and sailed in plenty of regattas. Depending on what you meant by "plenty." Then I told them that I was on my way home, and had planned all along to get there by sail.

"We'll sail from Whangarei in a week," Ian said. "We leave Auckland tomorrow."

"I can do that," was my automatic response. I'd commit now and then figure it out. My thoughts shuttled between my job and Stu. How quickly could I shut down my life? I thought of a plan.

"Can I meet you in Whangarei?"

They said sure. Helen asked if I would like more tea, and with that I saw Stu coming along the pier with his coworker Abel, tiller in hand. I knew I had to think things through quickly, to get my story straight, but my mind got tangled in the contradictions, and I still had nothing to say when he got to the boat. I was being caught. My two narratives were about to collide.

"Oh, we know each other," I said to Ian when we were about to be introduced. Somehow the word *boyfriend* didn't make it out of my mouth. I felt furtive and guilty. I told myself I hadn't done anything wrong. Tonga was a lark, a trip; I could go and just come back.

Then I thought maybe I'd done something wrong after all. The sure sign was that I couldn't give everyone the same story. I couldn't yet tell Stu what I'd just told Ian and Helen. I'd been snared before I'd been able to talk about it first with him, at home, to gently broach the subject, make it a discussion.

But there was no way around it; everyone was in earshot.

"I'm going to Tonga," I told Stu.

"You're going to Tonga," he said. He was calm. Unnaturally calm. Abel looked from Stu to me and back. Helen offered them tea.

✹ ✹ ✹

When we talked that night, we decided we'd move back to Seattle sooner rather than later. Stu helped me disassemble my life at top speed so that I could leave in just a week. He'd give notice at the boat shop and meet me in Tonga. We bought sailing boots, pants, and a jacket for me, anticipating that it would be cold and wet for my first few days at sea.

There was my job to consider, doing customer service for the shipping firm. I had been there only five months, and my boss liked me. I couldn't even give a full week's notice because I had to get ready to leave. This seemed to be the real impossibility of my situation. I never played hooky; I was the A student, the model employee. I was about to breach a personal code of responsibility, and it made me feel like I was about to do something illegal. I'm not sure if I felt guilty or just feared getting caught, but I anticipated consequences. Out-of-proportion consequences.

There won't be any consequences, I argued back to myself. Maybe I'd be too mortified to ever come back to New Zealand, but that would be okay. If you had to pick a country to close the door on, this buoy in the South Seas would do.

After Monday I didn't show up to work. I refused to answer our mobile phone. My boss left messages. He started calling a colleague of mine, Antony, with whom he knew Stu and I were friendly. Antony was forced to come over since we weren't answering the phone.

"What should I tell him?" he asked.

I made up a story. I finally called my boss and told him that my best friend back home had been diagnosed with a terrible disease. Hodgkin's lymphoma, I said. I wasn't even sure what that was, but it sounded bad. I was going home to be with her. I pictured Kristin with a terrible disease, and for a moment believed my story and felt sad.

I wondered why I thought I had to make something up, when I was abandoning the place either way. I'd never see my boss again. But even in the midst of bad behavior I wanted to be seen as good. To my horror, my boss told me that he understood, and then I felt guiltier. But I had to come in and talk to him about it, he said. We had to say good-bye.

I didn't think I could keep up my lie face-to-face, and in any case hated to say good-bye. I told him I would come in the next Monday, by which time I knew that I would be at sea.

Stu drove me to the bus that would take me up to Whangarei, where the thumb of the North Island points to the equator. I'd
mailed some boxes and reduced the rest of my life to a backpack. It
was amazing how life could just expand and contract like that. We
accrue things, and it gives us the illusion of having an anchorage.
Laura and Abel came over to say good-bye, as did our two *X-Files*
friends. They all planned to go abroad, and no doubt would; they
said they'd see me again. I knew it was unlikely, but I assured them
it would happen.

The bus dropped me off in Whangarei, and I shouldered my
backpack and looked around the well-protected bay. Everything was
neatly landscaped, trimmed and aligned in that way that tells you
the English were here. The grass was bright green, the footpaths
paved, the dock as yet unsplintered. Vacationing families sat in the
sun at the outdoor cafés, parents daubing ice cream from their toddlers' mouths. They'd sit on the beach and go placidly back to their
bed-and-breakfasts; they'd drive their cars back to Auckland. *All this
normality could be yours,* I reminded myself. But once I was on the
boat, I was on the boat. I could run now, take the bus back to Stu.
I didn't have to go. But I did. It wasn't so much that I didn't want
to admit fear to Stu or anyone else. I didn't want to admit fear to
myself. Just a few white puffs marred the sky.

The *Copper Lady* was a thirty-four-foot cutter-rigged vessel with
dark green sail covers and trim. The cockpit was deep and protected,
with benches all around and lockers under each one. I found Ian and
Helen detaching everything that couldn't be secured from the deck.
They stowed all the creature comforts—seat cushions and *bimini* and
tea towels that had been drying on the rail—in the cabin.

We ate an early dinner on deck, and Ian went over the plan
while we had oranges for dessert. We would do six-hour watches.

The main task of the person on watch was just to be a lookout. We had an autopilot to help keep us on course, and the reaches would be so long that we wouldn't have to tack very often. The scariest thing to look out for was container ships, the kind for which I was so recently making bookings. The ocean seemed incomprehensibly huge, and yet every cruiser knew a story about a sailboat run over by a ship. They came so fast and the crews couldn't see the water below, and couldn't stop their leviathans in any case. The only thing to do was to spot them from afar and steer clear. Other than big ships, there weren't many foreign objects at sea, but sometimes a container fell into the ocean and bobbed along, and a collision with one of them could sink us. Closer to land, logs and tangled fishing nets were a possibility. As for sea creatures, the only hazards might be whales. The main thing was to stay alert.

We were using a service in Auckland to let friends and family monitor our progress. We would radio every day, Ian said, to report our whereabouts and conditions. Anyone could call the service and find out where we were. I'd given the phone number to Stu and given Stu's number to my parents.

We motored out of the marina at dusk, yellow and orange rays piercing through the building clouds above. "Raise the mainsail," Ian called, and I pulled hard on the halyard, watching the sail ribbon up and finally grow taut. While I was doing that, Helen unfurled the jib, and it instantly filled out like a vertical blimp. We expected winds from the northwest, but when we got out of the marina they were coming from the northeast. We wanted to go north by northeast, which meant we'd have to sail pretty close hauled, not the fastest point of sail but not a big deal. I zipped and Velcroed myself into my fleece-lined waterproof jacket, which gave me an instant feeling of safety and warmth.

In another half hour, as the sky drew shut like a sack, I was getting cold again. My legs were slick from the waves, and I went below to dry off and get into my waterproof pants. I was sitting on the steps below the hatch when a swell lifted and then dropped the boat, making me stumble. I quelled my alarm by reminding myself that this was open water. Big swells were normal, new to me but not dangerous, and sailboats were designed to ride them out.

The wind picked up and the rain came down. We'd planned to start our watches by now, but instead we crowded the cockpit, Ian standing at the tiller, brow furrowed at the invisible horizon, and Helen and I sitting alert. We each wore a harness and a long, loose line that allowed movement while keeping us attached to the boat. The procedure was that if you had to go forward, you did so with your line attached to the rail.

I was taking my cues from Helen, who'd no doubt seen this all before. The wind rose to thirty, forty, then fifty knots. The sound of one discrete wave at a time rose to a unified bawl, punctuated by whistles and clangs as the wind and water hit the boat. We rode up the face of a wave then down the other side; the first ten or fifteen times the bow pointed down to the bottom of the sea, my throat tightened and I braced my limbs against whatever they could find.

Swells were normal, I kept telling myself. We went up after we went down. What was it Stu had told me? If the distance between the peaks was the same length as the boat, that meant that . . . what? Something bad. I tried to assess the distance. I wanted to go below deck, because now I was afraid. But I'd filled my spot in the cockpit like cement hardening into a mold. Movement seemed hazardous, if not impossible. And I was mesmerized by the sight of the waves and their foamy peaks, each one like the teeth of a maw. I stared as though I could be sure we were safe only by keeping an eye on them. They billowed above us like dark satin sheets.

As it turned out, this wasn't normal at all. The wind shifted by fifteen degrees so that now we had to sail even closer. Ian shouted directions. I dislodged myself from the cockpit to reef the mainsail a second time, giving us the smallest possible triangle so that the high winds didn't spin us out of control. Having a task on which to focus made me less scared. The mind finds new reserves of discipline when it has to. Onshore, lying in bed at night, you can imaginatively explore the depths of your fear. Here you couldn't go there.

Waves washed over the deck. I thought we were so tiny and weak against the ocean that we might as well have been a cork.

There came a point when there wasn't much more we could do. The sails were reefed, the tiller secured in place, the outboard motor switched on for extra power. "I think we're going to have to change course," Ian shouted. I didn't like the "I think"—the captain had to know. He had to at least appear to know. I'd rather have felt safe than informed.

We had to fall off a little from the wind, because we were getting beat up and could barely move forward. But changing course by even a few degrees would, over distance, put us far from where we wanted to go. An inch between radians here became a thousand miles over there. Ian decided we would wait and see. He told us we should start our watches now, and that he would take the first one.

Helen climbed down to the cabin and I followed her. As soon as I shimmied into the hatch my nausea rose, and I pointed myself at the galley sink just in time. I was too battered to be embarrassed. Lurching and bracing, Helen procured a bucket, and bungeed it into place below the hatch. Ian was the next to puke, as though in solidarity.

I was sitting and Helen was standing when the big wave came.

It came from the stern, which was all wrong. Storms were supposed to go in one direction, but this one was just churning, crashing violently against itself. The wave came straight through the hatch and into the cabin, and suddenly we were horizontal to the planet. The mast kissed the sea, and I wondered if it would come back up.

At that moment Helen screamed. I sat immobilized against the bunk. There was nothing to do, nowhere to climb to, no way out. I'd been watching Helen for reassurance, and now she was afraid. I pictured the boat from the sky. I imagined how tiny we were in the ocean, how irrelevant, how lost.

"Shut up, shut up," Ian screamed at Helen from the cockpit, and she did. "Get up here," he screamed, and we did. The boat righted.

We'd lost three things: the ladder and lifesaver that had been secured to the stern rail—and our radio. During the screaming and crashing, it had fizzed and gone dark. Our link to the world was gone and we were alone.

How likely was this, I wondered. People sailed for years and never hit this kind of storm. I'd gambled and lost. I'd been in close calls in cars a couple of times, but everything had happened so quickly that there was no chance to contemplate death. Now that the drama of the rogue wave had passed, I had time to think. Death loomed as a real possibility for the first time in my life. How long would I survive, floating on a scrap on the seething sea? I feared my fear. Clinging to a board, my terror could go on for days, which would be too awful. I thought I'd rather die quickly. What a shame that would be, I thought, especially considering that I didn't have to be here in the first place.

I stretched out on the leeward side bunk, strapped myself in, and closed my eyes. The boat rose and fell, rose and fell, rocking me into a trance. There was nothing I could do but abdicate. Worry would make no difference.

When Helen woke me, I zipped into my red, white, and blue rain gear, reeling a little, and climbed up. I clipped in and sat up on the bench on the windward side of the cockpit, feet braced below. You had to be up this high to see past the bow. The horizon was close and dark; if there was anything ahead I'd see it only as we rode down a wave. The storm didn't abate. Even though the boat's weak beams were the only light, the sheen of the waves looked almost bright, as though the ocean glowed from within.

The direction of the wind shifted a few more degrees, and Tonga became officially hopeless. We couldn't sail straight upwind. Instead we'd go due north to Fiji, taking advantage of the storm to drive us forward. Fiji was hundreds of miles from Tonga, and I wondered how I would find Stu, but there was nothing we could do. I felt chagrined for him since we'd never even been able to radio Auckland. I hoped he was protecting my parents.

The mind isn't cut out to remain frightened and panicked for long periods, even when the frightening conditions go on. At some point you adjust, the conditions become the new normal, and the fear recedes. It was like this with the storm. It didn't subside, but we calmed down.

We shortened our watches to four hours from six to stave off exhaustion. I slept most of the time I was off, and sometimes read in my bunk. A small library was bungeed into the shelf above, and I plucked out a book about Provence. I let it take me away to a safe, bucolic, landlocked place, escaping from my escape.

Whenever it was my turn, I drank a little seltzer, tucked a bag of Saltines into my jacket, and climbed on deck. We were eating almost nothing. I watched the horizon as best I could, but our whole world was enclosed by waves. After the first ten minutes or so on deck I usually threw up, which was now so routine that I felt it coming and leaned toward the rail, letting it be washed away. I huddled into my coat, tempted to crawl down to the floor of the cockpit, but this was forbidden, as I had to look ahead.

The days beat on. I had no idea how many went by. Once, at the top of a swell, I saw lights on the horizon, probably a ship, and then they were gone again as we dove into the trough. As often happens when sailing, there was too much time to think. I explored, massaged, and embellished my guilt over bolting from my job. I pondered the Tonga–Fiji dilemma. I wondered if my travels would end in an oceanic whirlpool.

And then I came on deck for my shift and saw that the distance between swells had lengthened and their white crowns disappeared. The gray ocean had taken on color, and the sky was pale. I stood in the cockpit and crinkled back my hood, and watched the horizon roll away.

A half day later we were in the sun. I'd lost track of time, but Ian hadn't: We'd been in the storm for seven days. We unreefed the mainsail and unfurled the jib. The breeze was ideal, fifteen to twenty knots. Now, when it wasn't my turn on watch, I moved around the deck. I sat on the bow, just because I could, watching the sky turn blue and white. Harnesses on, we took turns jumping into the ocean off the stern for our first baths, and then rinsed with a little fresh water from the tank. Ian cooked *dal,* filling the cabin with scent of cumin and onion, and we had our first real meal. For our second meal, we trailed a fishing line behind the boat and caught a fat, iridescent tuna. Ian clubbed it dead, bloodying the deck, and we ate thin slices of sashimi dribbled with lemon.

We were now about three days out from Fiji. In better conditions the whole trip should have taken only a week. The time ahead of us before we hit land seemed to expand and contract; I couldn't decide if it was long or short. Ian and Helen, now liberated to blow off steam, squabbled in the cockpit, and I closed my eyes and lay on the deck. I craved land and other people; I thought this was going to take an eternity. But as the sun warmed me up, I thought our cruise couldn't last long enough. I was a little afraid of land. If traveling is a hiatus from life, cruising was one hiatus beyond. A complete checking out from the world. I didn't know if that was noble or cowardly. In Australia and even Papua New Guinea, news had filtered my way after the fact. Jerry Garcia, O. J. Simpson, Yitzhak Rabin. Now I was completely cut off.

Are we obligated to know the important events of our time? Or is the whole project of knowing, of being part of a society, neither moral nor immoral, but just a way to pass the time? Is it enough to do no harm to the world, or do you have to contribute too? I wanted to go toward the man-made heat and light, the cultural center, the heart of civilization. At the same time, I didn't want to get off the boat.

In movies and books, sailors spot land and the next thing you know they're onshore. But in fact when land first appears, it's a line drawn with the smallest nib. It grows so slowly that you can't watch. You have to just ignore it and let it sneak up, so that when you look back a few hours later it might have been drawn with a felt-tip pen. From the time we first noticed the line and thought maybe it was a mirage, it took a day and a night for Fiji to take on dimension.

We eased into Suva one bright afternoon, anchored sailboats bobbing all around. When I finally stepped off the boat onto the marina dock, my legs buckled underneath.

ON TEMPTATION
chapter twenty-five

*B*eing on land meant responsibility and choices. It meant all the options were back on the table, each with its own consequence.

I tried to phone Stu, but our old mobile phone had been disconnected. According to our original plan he would be arriving in Tonga. I thought of trying to contact him there, but how was that going to work? Would I call some marina and ask if they'd seen a tall blond man? I decided to sit tight and let things work themselves out. I took a pink-striped bus into the city and wandered around. I took pictures of the rainbow-frosted Hindu temples, then came back to the yacht club and sat in the open-air bar. Pacific Ocean travelers washed in like old fishing nets. On the bulletin board there were numerous crew-wanted signs, and each one was a temptation. Vanuatu, Tahiti, Ambon. Maybe I didn't have to go home. I didn't want to go to Seattle.

But Seattle was my only springboard back to real life. Or maybe not "back to," since I'd shirked real life so far. My existence had been all prep, pretense, and peregrination. When I got to real life, I thought, I'd know that I was in the right place at the right time. I wouldn't feel like I had to leave. To get there I had to do the right thing, which meant not sailing back across the

Pacific. It occurred to me that if I'd stayed at sea, I wouldn't have had to think about all this.

There were old salts and young salts at the bar. One was Leo, a compact Englishman with a blond swish across his forehead. He had a degree in marine biology and was a photographer; he had an elegant wooden sloop. He took underwater pictures of whales and sharks for magazines. He showed me the light table he had in his cabin for looking at slides, and told me he was going to Tahiti to shoot the whales. He was perfect, some man I would have molded out of clay.

I noticed that he'd put up a sign on the bulletin board: First mate wanted, only women need apply. I was amazed at the baldness of his search. Could you even do that? Put a sign up for an ocean-going hired girlfriend? Couldn't he have just found a girlfriend? He was charming enough.

His terms confused me. He wasn't offering money. He was offering something I wanted so much more—adventure. I'd thought that my specific desires made me special. *I* wasn't materialistic. And yet Leo had reduced what I wanted to trade. He knew a certain kind of woman would put up with a lot to swim with the whales. I knew he'd find someone to go. He wouldn't even have to mention the sex until fifty miles offshore. By which time his first mate would be dependent and cut off. Crew, screw.

❀ ❀ ❀

When Stu found me in the yacht club bar, I ran to him the way I hadn't when I arrived in New Zealand, and he cradled me up in his anvil embrace. I was breathless and wide-eyed; I had to tell him all about my trip right now. I felt like I'd been lost and then found, and he felt like he'd lost me and found me. He'd flown to Tonga, figured out from other sailors what must have happened, and then flown here.

That night we checked in to the colonnaded Hotel Metropole, in a seedy room above the bar. We ate greasy fried rice in a Chinese restaurant and tried to decide what to do next. The prospect of going home still seemed surreal. It had been nine months for him, fourteen for me.

The next day we went back to the yacht club to say good-bye to Helen and Ian. Stu examined the tiller he'd installed in Auckland, which had come through the beating in good shape. I looked idly at the bulletin board, just for kicks, and saw that a South African family with a sixty-foot catamaran had put up a sign. Two of them were in the bar, and I went to talk to them.

Liam and Donna, the owners, were a couple in their fifties and were traveling with their son and his wife, who was eight months' pregnant. They wanted to get to Brisbane in a hurry so that she could deliver there. At "Brisbane" my synapses fired for Justin. A boat like theirs could cross the seventeen hundred miles in a few days, but they needed experienced help. Their state-of-the-art boat was an engineering feat, with carbon fiber parts and the latest navigation tools. "I just sailed from New Zealand," I offered, but they had no interest in me.

I pointed down to the dock. "That's my boyfriend," I said. "He's blue water. And he's a boat builder." They could see the Michelangelo shoulders, the Popeye arms. "We could take the both of you," Liam offered. If they could have him on deck, I could lounge in a queen-size cabin for three days, then find myself in Australia again. I introduced Stu, and Liam repeated his offer.

I knew it was a fulcrum in time. If the balance swung one way, we started the trip all over again. Back to the ups and downs of a future unknown. I could travel north and west across Australia, sail from Darwin to Bali.

If I went back to America, I knew what was next. We faced the house and the debt. I faced the uphill climb of getting out of it all, which, from the dock in Fiji, looked Sisyphean.

But maybe, I told myself, it would just be a slog. I'd climbed over all those ridges in Papua New Guinea, even when I thought I couldn't make it. I'd extricated myself from Seattle once, and I could do it again, this time in a final way. This time organization would take the place of headlong flight. I'd apply to graduate school; I'd get on track. I saw my love for Stu as now thoroughly tarnished, not because we'd hurt each other or slept with other people or spent time apart—all those usual suspects made no difference. It was tarnished because now it was wrapped up in obligation. Obligation, of course, is what binds marriages all over the world. You get into financial dependence, kids, intertwined lives, and you can't get out. Mutual obligation is the norm, the glue. Loss of freedom is the point, the thing that evens out the vagaries of the heart. I didn't understand any of that.

Stu and I conferred at a table in the back of the bar. I knew I could convince him to hop the catamaran. This decision was on me. The impulse to go back to sea was as strong as any of those momentary flashes that had sent me on other trips. But I fought it this time. Just as Stu was thinking seriously about the possibility, I smiled to show it was all a flight of fancy, a joke. I let go of wanderlust. I didn't have to do a thing just because it was there. "We'd better go home," I said.

❋ ❋ ❋

We bought plane tickets to Seattle via Honolulu and left Fiji on July fifth. Because of the international date line, though, we landed in Honolulu at 11:00 PM on the fourth. I tried to work out that distortion, but it was pure magic to me, the hole through which

I'd wriggled back out of my mirror world. A television blared in the airport lounge, with snippets of all the day's parties. Fireworks over Chicago. A parade with confetti and floats down a small-town street. The ball dropping over Times Square in New York. I felt like I was arriving in a foreign land, observing its quaint rituals for the first time.

That feeling had dissipated by the time we got back to Seattle. The place was dauntingly familiar. As I walked through our house and back to the ramshackle deck, I felt like I was watching my own life again, just as I had when I arrived in Malaysia, riding through green fields to the coast. I was experiencing reverse culture shock, waiting for my mind to catch up to my physical presence.

I didn't feel sad or entrapped, though. I felt optimistic. I began planning to leave Seattle as soon as I got back.

MOMENTUM

. . . everybody hates a tourist
especially one who thinks
it's all such a laugh
and the chip stain's grease
will come out in the bath.

—Pulp,
"Common People"

PART THREE

ON THE HEART OF CIVILIZATION
chapter twenty-six

*T*he *lights streak by, bright* and beautiful as fireworks. Shop windows pulse like stars. We're cruising, frictionless, four in a taxi, night-sailing up the Avenue of the Americas. We were so far downtown, and we live so far up. I hope that we'll cut through Times Square, because when your vision is blurred and it's four in the morning, it's like flying to the heart of the sun.

The ride from Houston Street to the hundreds is the end to more and more of our nights. We don't yet understand what a deal we're getting on our apartments. We blow our meager funds on alcohol and taxis, but we know that everything will turn out. We'll get jobs someday, good ones. It's 1997 and we're twenty-seven, and we know beyond doubt that this *is* the right place at the right time. Those shy hopes that we're special, chosen, lucky, are coming to fruition. We think we're smarter than everyone else. We expect our careers to be glamorous, not fashion-glamorous or music-glamorous, but the running-the-world kind. Uptown in the classrooms or downtown at night, I'm never bored but happily consumed. We've found each other, pulled like asteroids from Barcelona, Cote d'Ivoire, the South Seas. These are my people.

We're all the more ardent and wide-eyed because we were late to the party. We didn't come to New York after college. Instead we went away, on what we now choose to describe as personal odysseys, even if we were bored out of our skulls in some impoverished hinterland, or jobless and ten-to-a-flat in the wrong part of Europe. It turns out that the road in all cases led to this modern Rome. And if you'd lived at the time of the Roman Empire, wouldn't you have wanted, at least once, to live in Rome? At four in the morning especially, it's a playground made just for us. With the zeal of the converted, we literally dance on bars. We borrow limousines. We look for the gayest clubs, the grimiest dives. Cabs appear—I can't get over this—right when we want them, at whatever time of night. And our New York is just a tiny sliver. The city spreads away forever, rings coddling the core, every layer a core itself, Bengali or Korean or Greek. It's a whole cosmos; you could explore it your entire life. It's the center of the world, and it's ours. The taxi turns into Times Square, and the waterfalls of light rise above.

❋ ❋ ❋

My surreptitious visit to the library stacks in Auckland eventually led me here. Columbia's School of International and Public Affairs, SIPA for short. Like my first degree, this one is intended, in part, to lay a veneer of respectability over my desire to travel. It's the final coat. We take classes in history and economics, but I suspect that many of my classmates ended up here for the same reason I did. Insatiable wanderlust met the need to get a real job. My new friends will vie for positions at the UN, the State Department, the international banks. But first we have two years to spend like this, in the cycle of papers, exams, and internships, interspersed with the discovery of New York.

Early in the New Year I get a boyfriend, a fellow student. He's studying finance, and he's very good with logic and numbers, and he helps me get through economics. First we take macro: inflation, unemployment, GDP. The inner workings of the world. Then micro: supply and demand.

I'd stitched together a vague fantasy of my life in New York before I came, of how it would be. It was mainly this one static image: looking out a floor-to-ceiling window on a cold morning, still undressed, and seeing the glinting cityscape. There's a man in the background, someone fascinating and successful. This sophisticated apartment is not mine but his: My fantasy of myself is as a visitor.

Paul is tall, blue-eyed, from the outskirts of Boston. I like him partly because he's smart, one of the smartest people I've met. It's not just economics; he's also widely and deeply read. He studies Japanese and aces history.

He's the only Republican among just about everyone we know at graduate school, and I suspect sometimes that he just wants to be contrarian. He likes to spar over politics, and we do. (I think of my own politics, which are still evolving, as unconventional, not really fitting in to the American spectrum, with its arbitrary alliance between social conservatives and economic liberals.) I know sometimes he's just trying to provoke me, like when he tells me to watch an interview with a young, female conservative star, who argues that women belong at home. I let myself be provoked. We wrangle over whether the IMF should bail out Thailand, and over Bill Clinton and Monica Lewinsky and Kenneth Starr—I don't give a damn about the blowjobs, and he'd like to see Clinton disgraced—and it's partly just because we like the fight. His girlfriends have never pushed back enough, and he wants it. I like that he can be overbearing, because it's like giving me a hill to climb.

He likes that I'm feminine and also not, and I like that he likes this about me. I remember that in my late teens I thought there was something inherently male about me, some way in which I didn't fit in with girls. It was such an ingrained and inarticulate thought that I'd never wondered where it came from. I wasn't a tomboy; I looked girlish; I loved makeup and short skirts. I just instinctively knew that an emotional component was missing. I never had the wedding fantasies I'd always heard about. When I was dating a boy, I always felt like a timer went off inside me, after which I was done, just done. I thought sentimentality was cloying and domesticity suspect. Without knowing why, I'd internalized the idea that these traits were male. But when I said to a friend that I was unfeminine, he asked me what on earth I was talking about. He said I was one of the most feminine girls he'd known. And I saw that the way I was seen wasn't necessarily the way I felt inside.

Paul sees both sides, and one of the things we want from a lover, always, is to feel like we're known. He likes the outward femininity in an uncomplicated way, but he also sees my cocksure side, and he falls for me, in part, because of it. It's as though there's something he can't get to or break through, and the challenge goads him on. He gets under my skin too, an itch that can't quite be scratched.

He also falls for me because I have something he doesn't. For all his brilliance, Paul doesn't have a passion. As my ambitions come into focus, I'm driven. Writers write because we have to. My other grad school friends are likewise motivated; their nascent careers are their callings. Paul, on the other hand, gets A's without much effort, but isn't impelled to do anything in particular. So he falls for people who are driven to create.

Paul went to a private school and then Princeton, where he belonged to an eating club and rowed crew. Here in New York he has a dozen childhood and college friends, for which I envy him. They didn't fish in Alaska or get married, but came here, apparently with a sense of direction, to start careers. Their parents may have bought them apartments. If the boys sometimes mention ownership of a tool belt, it's to make themselves stand out. The girls have picked jobs in philanthropy or PR. I have the feeling that Paul belongs to a world I've only heard about in novels, of Northeasterners at the top of the American food chain. He's the quintessential WASP. And yet he's done something that no one of his class does anymore: Before graduate school he went and joined the Marine Corps, and I respect this deviation from the norm. I'm drawn to both sides of him, the irrefutable physicality of his military service, and the way he belongs to a certain slice of New York. He's not in student housing but shares a spacious apartment, with real non-Ikea furniture and saturated colors on the walls. The windows are not floor-to-ceiling, but I do sometimes look out them on cold mornings, at the silhouettes of the rooftop water towers against the pale winter light, thinking about brunch or going back to bed, and telling myself a metanarrative of my own life, about how looking out at the city and pondering these options make me finally feel like I've arrived. Your first months, or maybe years, in New York, you can't help thinking, *I'm in New York.*

Once again I feel like I've come from nowhere, and arrived on the scene as a blank slate.

The damp woods of Vancouver, my Home Depot days, my Middle Eastern and Australasian years, are all irrelevant now, more parts of me to be cut off as I move into this new milieu. Especially Seattle, from which I feel like I made a narrow escape. Slowly, over the year between New Zealand and New York, I convinced Stu to buy me out of the house, and we said good-bye. New York is full of moths to the flame, and there is a kind of solidarity in our erased pasts. Like all twentysomething arrivals to New York, I am, without even realizing it, animated and energized by the fear of being sucked back whence I came. Paul helps to anchor me, to make me feel like I belong here.

I don't fit into Paul's world, but I think that with a little study I could. The way I dress is still too provincial, too Gap-based. The sarongs and waitress uniforms and hiking boots left me with no urban style. I wear too-tight T-shirts to restaurants; my idea of pretty is sexy, and my idea of sexy is cheap. But I can figure this out, the way I learned to wrap myself up in the Middle East, or broaden my vowels into an Australian drawl. There's a scene in the Woody Allen film *Annie Hall* where Alvy Singer takes one look at a woman he's just met and then runs down his list of assumptions about her— Central Park West, Brandeis University—to which she sarcastically replies, "No, that was wonderful. I love being reduced to a cultural stereotype." I *want* people to look at me and reduce me to a cultural stereotype, one specific to New York, because it will mean I've successfully passed. When we graduate, Paul's parents will give me a bracelet from Tiffany's, and this small nod to the fetishized jewelry store, the go-to cliché of girlish romantic achievement, will signal to me that I've arrived.

❋ ❋ ❋

For a career path I choose journalism so that I'll finally be able to get paid to write. During the summer between our first and second years, everyone is supposed to get an internship, and I get a position reporting for Reuters in Jerusalem, a city I visited during the year I studied in Egypt. That time I came via Jordan, over the Allenby Bridge and through the West Bank. This time I'll fly to Tel Aviv. Now, finally, something starts to make sense. I see continuity in my life. That year, all that time studying Arabic, is leading me back to the same place, making it real again. The last time around may not have been a fling after all, but something more like a building block.

When I'm offered the position, Paul buys me a dozen red roses. He's good at observing the rituals of romance, better than I am, but I guess that's more imperative on the guy. He's been trained in traditions I don't well know; he's dated girls who expect them. Graham once gave me a fully stocked toolbox, with each implement separately wrapped. Justin gave me a sleeping bag, and Stu bought me a plane ticket and sailing clothes. But Paul gives me flowers. When we'd barely started dating, he mailed me a postcard to ask me to Valentine's Day dinner.

Paul accompanies me to the airport, and we sit holding hands near the security gate, and he promises to come see me at the end of the summer. He'll be coming across the world from Hong Kong, where he's landed his own summer job. This is getting to be familiar. Travel equals longing equals love.

ON DOUBLE LIVES
chapter twenty-seven

*I*n *between grad school and a job* I've been offered in London, I do what I do best. I fly to Lima, Peru, and then up to the mountain city of Cusco. I've urged Paul to come with me, but he's declined, saying he needs to look for a job. Our friend Mike is spending part of the summer studying in Cusco, but he's leaving to go down to Lima several days after my arrival, so he shows me around, introduces me to some people he's met, and leaves me on my own. I feel primed for something to happen, and the tension of anticipation makes up for the self-consciousness of being alone. In the evenings I buy cornhusk-wrapped tamales from one of the street vendors, and take them up to my room to eat alone, but in the mornings I have granola on the balcony of a café, overlooking the main square.

Cusco is a Spanish colonial city built atop the capital of the Inca Empire. The fountain at the center of the Plaza de Armas is baroque, with curling friezes and horn-blowing statues, but the vast gray stones that line the side streets are pre-European; their proportions violate the Mediterranean eye and the weight of each one bespeaks forced labor. From the northeast side of the plaza the city sprawls steeply up, and the streets become too narrow and inaccessible for cars, so that to reach the little hotels and hostels you have to climb on foot. In my first few days I'm light-headed from the altitude; Cusco sits above eleven thousand feet.

I go on hikes by myself, first up to Sacsayhuaman, a megalithic complex built by pre-Incan people called the Killke, whom I've never heard of before. It's one of those places, like the Egyptian and Mayan pyramids, that fanciful minds have declared suspiciously alien, and Europeans and Japanese are arrayed around a high ceremonial platform, testing the possibilities for spiritual solace. I go higher, winding through the hills above Cusco. I've rarely hiked alone, and it makes me feel self-reliant. On my way back down to Cusco I think I feel my lungs expand. Together the inrush of oxygen and my sense of accomplishment make me elated.

Friends of Mike's—two Britons trying to start a newspaper, or open an Irish restaurant, or, in any case, not go home—invite me to one of the nightclubs on the main square. The city is constantly cold and dry, and Peruvians and foreigners alike wear jeans everywhere. In the club we strip down to tank tops and T-shirts, piling Gor-Tex and fleece on a chair. A boy with messy sun-bleached hair bobs his head and watches me, and so I say *"hola,"* and he says *"hola."* We're both obviously not locals. *"Cuál es tu lengua materna?"* I ask. What's your first language? For that one suspended moment, neither of us is from anywhere. We could say anything, make something up right on the spot about who we are. When he tells me his language is French, I tell him, in mangled French, that I speak it too. I don't yet tell him where I'm from, because I want to draw out this moment of cultural anonymity. I free-float, enjoying the sense that I could be anyone, and it's like dreaming about flying. I look down on all the possible identities I could choose, before finally telling him who I am. It turns out that Raphael is from Paris, and we settle into a mishmash of Spanish, French, and English, one of those in-between languages made up on the road.

He's on a bicycle ride, he says. From Ushuaia, at the southern tip of South America, to Alaska. I could love him just for that. Raphael, then, is the thing for which I've been on high alert. He suddenly puts me in a world where no one cares about banking careers or Ivy League schools, bringing me back to my traveler self. And what's the harm? I'm just taking a break between one real-life thing and another. Pretty soon I'll be at my job in London.

I let him chase me for a few days, during which we make little dates to meet for coffee on the Plaza. He leaves me handwritten notes at my hotel. He's superlatively fit and also chain smokes, which I would normally mind but don't in this case, because I know it isn't a serious thing. One night I invite him to my cold room—it's a high dry southern winter, and these little hotels don't spring for heating. I let him kiss me, then let him into my bed. I don't think of Paul, because this feels like another world.

Raphael, who is twenty-six, is cycling with two teammates, another Frenchman and a Quebecois. They're radio journalists, recording stories along the way. Usually they ride every day, but they've stopped in Cusco for a few weeks to make repairs and receive a visit from Raphael's mother, Elodie. She arrives a few days after I meet him, bearing paté and other gifts. She's prone to crying jags brought on by her recent divorce from Raphael's dad. Raphael is preoccupied with caring for her, trying to make sure she's comfortable in the windowless stone room that he's rented on his minimal budget. He listens patiently for hours, the two of them smoking, while she repeats her miseries, and together they tell me about when their family was intact and living in Oman. When I insist that Raphael get lip balm, because his lower lip is so chapped it looks cut, he tells me he's touched that I'm caring for him.

We travel together to the remote village of Paucartambo, where a multiday festival celebrates the Virgin Mary and murkier pre-Spanish beliefs. Thousands have come. Groups of devotees, who've spent a year preparing and stitching costumes, dress up as characters, so that the streets are filled with masked buffoons, feathered warriors, and devils. One group wears satin stripes in green, yellow, blue, and red, with trousers spiraled like barbershop poles. Another wears nurse and doctor uniforms, and carries grotesque yellow masks. One of the masks is skull-shaped and gushing blood, some have head wounds, and one has a nose that looks for all the world like a dildo. The players heap the masks onto the graves, acting out a drama I don't understand.

Every street and square is crowded with people, all day and all night, and the disguised men prowl around among us, putting on shows between fireworks displays and marching bands. We stand in a square looking up at masked men leaping from balcony to parapet, reenacting a battle. It's hard to tell who anyone is behind their headdresses and trains and masks; neighbor might not even know neighbor. If I had a masked ball to go to every year, during which I could play a warrior or a devil, I wonder if, with that outlet at hand, I'd be more able to settle into my own time and place. I think of the carnivals in Brazil and the Caribbean, and the ecstatic dancers I saw during Ashura in Pakistan, bloodying themselves into another state of mind. I have no ritual to take me away. Halloween is a dull and distant cousin.

After the festival we camp on a promontory above the clouds. Down there is Amazonia, Raphael says. He'll be riding that way soon. We talk about hiking down into the clouds, and Elodie asks us what we're supposed to live on. *"D'amour et d'eau fraîche,"* Raphael says. And I want to do that more than anything. I want to climb down into the clouds and live on love and water, and not go to London or back to New York. I want to drop away from civilization again.

Instead we get a bus back to Cusco, where I grow morose and

frustrated on my last day, and Raphael consoles me by fucking me all night in our little red room with dripping candle wax beside the bed. Refracted through my impending departure, every sensation becomes acute. Every thrust is the last of its kind, and I begin to long for him even while he's inside of me.

The intensity of the night ebbs into affectionate resignation the next morning. I've become attached to him, and it's not just because I tend to love in the safety of impending separation, but because I love his wandering nature. He comes with me to the airport, and has a cigarette and an espresso while we wait. We know better than to make promises. It would be absurd, I can see that, even though a little part of me wishes that we would. We exchange email addresses and go on our way.

✻ ✻ ✻

In New York the logistics seem bottomless, so much more complicated than they were in Peru. I'm no longer just dependent on a backpack. My employer is paying to ship my stuff to London, and it hardly seems worthwhile, but movers come to take my eight boxes and my futon. I'm going on vacation with Paul's family in Idaho, which requires a suitcase with outdoor gear, and then I'll fly straight to London, which requires a suitcase full of office clothes. I don't tell Paul about Raphael. I feel vaguely pleased with myself that I can be with these two very different kinds of men, whose paths would never cross, who would be unsympathetic to one another's worldview.

I go out for lunch with my friend Chelsea, who graduated from SIPA at the same time as me. She also has a job as a reporter, but hers is in New York, and she's found a new place with a roommate in the West Village. I tell her about Raphael, and she asks me what he does. "He's, uh, riding his bike from Argentina to Alaska," I say, and she cracks up. She knows enough about my past to think that

Raphael sounds like my type: away on some romantic voyage, not remotely available in the here and now. When she laughs it's my first inkling that *I'm* becoming a type. I'm the gypsy eccentric who can't find pleasure in quotidian life, who'd rather pursue adventure and adventurers than stability in New York. When I was offered the job in London, it didn't even occur to me to say no, but now I see that another sort of person might have considered the choice.

❀ ❀ ❀

Paul and I do make promises. We've been together now for a year and a half, and he plans to stay in New York. Once or twice I suggest that he look for a position in London and come join me. He doesn't consider this idea seriously, nor do I really expect him to. I suggest it in part to confirm my suspicion that he won't do it, that he's too staid to follow a girl that far.

Neither of us suggests breaking up. We plan to see each other on holidays and weekends. But I'm not twenty-one anymore, I'm twenty-eight, and long-distance relationships are different. Now we have email and cell phones, and we can afford to phone or fly. Reality intrudes on the perfection of the distant image. It's no longer possible to think of someone across the world the way I thought about Graham, longing for his perfect looks, his perfect loyalty, his perfect love for me, and burnishing my longing until it became a thing of beauty itself. In a long-distance relationship, you're always living with anticipation, which never disappoints, the expectation of pleasure being a pleasure in itself. But now technology and money have made long-distance romance mundane. Time and age have also done their part. The implicit permission to do anything no longer flies. Monogamy is part of the boyfriend-girlfriend deal, and forgiveness isn't assumed.

Paul, though, has become the line attaching me to New York.

I don't want to give it up, I want it and London both. I've loved New York, I've made friends here, it's a better fit than anywhere I've lived. I was never going to be the best skier or sailor or homemaker, in Vancouver or Auckland or Seattle, but here, other things count. In not breaking up with Paul, I'm holding on to New York.

In one of his romantic moments, Paul compared himself to a kite-flyer and me to a kite. He meant that a grounding force needed a freewheeling one, and vice versa. But I think of the metaphor again as I leave for London. I need to be connected to him, because some part of me is afraid of being too free.

❀ ❀ ❀

London feels like the capital of Europe. My neighborhood is called Clerkenwell, which I never learn to pronounce quite right. It's on the edge of the City, which is what they call the one-square-mile financial district, and is packed with financiers from around the continent. I work in a sleek white-glass office building on Gray's Inn Road. My company also has a building on Fleet Street, next to St. Bride's Church, so I sometimes go down there. All the big newspapers have moved out to the suburbs, but a bookstore obligingly sells me a copy of *Scoop,* Evelyn Waugh's great satire of the foreign correspondent's life. One of the old editors tells me how in the printing presses of yore, you could smell the ink coming out of the brick walls. I stand on the Fleet Street sidewalk and imagine that I can smell it too.

The apartment is in a brand-new building, with floor-to-ceiling windows and wall-to-wall carpet, on the incongruously named street Herbal Hill. My flat mate is Indian, and his girlfriend comes from Germany. We have friends from Holland and Israel come stay with us, and our apartment feels like an upscale youth hostel.

I get a Swedish boyfriend named Stefan. He's twenty-four,

works in animation, and has a trendily asymmetric haircut. We don't have a sustainable well of things to talk about, but he's sweet and there's a pull between us. I'm fond of him but I don't feel compelled; I know that he, Stefan, the individual, isn't essential to my life. I'm still seeing Paul, flying back and forth on Virgin or BA.

Raphael and Peru were otherworldly, but London feels like an extension of life in New York. It's magnetic like New York, a full cornucopia of finance and fashion and everything else, and my colleagues here could be my colleagues there. There's an ocean separating me from Paul, but we're running in the same cosmopolitan world. And maybe that—the sense of cheating on home turf, with no obvious end in sight—is what makes me start to interrogate myself about just what the hell I'm doing.

In the wake of an infidelity, someone always asks, why didn't you just break up? It seems like the sensible solution amid all of our modern free-will arrangements. If I were married, wouldn't it make sense to inflict the (possibly) lesser pain of walking out, before creating the (possibly) greater pain of deception and jealousy? And I'm not married; I've been in a relationship with no children, no shared home, no greater joint obligation, really, than a favorite brunch spot and a Sunday talk show. So why do I bother with deception at all? Why did I create a relationship based on an understanding of fidelity, then undermine it? And what does it say, anyway, that with no marriage in sight, I'm pondering how to handle my own infidelity if I enter one?

No one forced me to be in any of these relationships. All I have to do is be true to my word. It's not like I'm some Yemeni girl sold into a bigamous marriage. It's not like I live in 1750, 1850, or even 1950, struggling under the burden of social mores, having to lie to keep myself sane. All you have to do in relationships anymore is what you said you would. That's the only rule left.

I know it's not strictly sex that accounts for my straying, the motive usually attributed to men. I think it's just too tempting to have two lives rather than one. Some people think that too much travel begets infidelity: Separation and opportunity test the bonds of love. I think it's more likely that people who hate to make choices, to settle on one thing or another, are attracted to travel. Travel doesn't beget a double life. The appeal of the double life begets travel.

With two lives, you're always escaping back and forth. Why did Houdini keep building more and more elaborate confinements? He could have just stuck with a few ropes, but he had to escalate to a trunk wrapped in chains. Deep down, I know that it's not some unforeseen circumstance that causes Paul and Stefan to overlap. It's not that my emotions are confused. When Stefan leaves in the morning, and I stuff the cream sheet into the hamper and snap the purple one across the bed, knowing Paul will be here when I get back from work, I'm not in turmoil. I *like* it. I'm turned on by this moment in between, almost more than I am by either of the guys. Maybe this is why I wanted Stefan in the first place, so that I could have two men, two possibilities, instead of one. I like that I have to be careful, especially with Paul, with whom there's more at stake—with whom I still imagine a possible life in New York. Stefan could have left a sock in my room, or we could see him in the street. Paul could ask me where I got the rock climbing book Stefan gave me, which I happen to leave lying around, as though courting disaster. I have to be careful not to say the wrong thing, and then when Paul leaves I can let down my guard again. In between the two men, I'm not presenting myself for either one. I'm not talking about art with Stefan or politics with Paul. It's getting into and out of these different selves that gives me a kick, more than actually being in one or the other.

I don't trust Paul, and I can see that this is one of the paybacks of infidelity: Being untrustworthy makes me suspicious that others are too. I start to lose respect for him, because I've outsmarted him too much now, which wasn't possible during our old feisty debates. I get lazy about the relationship, and when I utterly fail to plan a getaway to Bath, which I forgot that I said I'd arrange, he's so angry that I think he must feel more than he knows. We fight as we walk around the ancient city, knocking on the doors of fullybooked hotels.

But whatever I may think of him, I start to not want to be a person who treats people like this. I resolve to break up with Stefan and Paul at the same time, to wipe the slate clean. I do break up with Stefan, but I lose my resolve when it comes to Paul, and we keep flying back and forth.

✿ ✿ ✿

And then things happen with the Englishman. He's my age and my colleague. I was attracted to him from my first day of work, six months back. I'm drawn to his rugby-trained body and curiously high forehead, and he makes me laugh when he anthropomorphizes, attributing free will to notebooks and dogs. Our company is experimenting with hiring non-Oxbridge graduates, and the Englishman, who's from outside of Sheffield, comes via the University of Glasgow. He's also studied in Russia.

For months we went out in groups, to the dim, brass-trimmed pub that our bosses liked, or to movies and night clubs in the West End. We talked about our roommates, our colleagues, and the minutiae of work—my trips to the Bank of England, and his to the commodities exchange. We talked about books; both of us were in a Martin Amis phase. I discovered that, like me, he saw the wire service as a springboard to something else. It was a way to get around the world, a place to learn how to interview people and organize words.

We first kiss while waiting for our respective night buses on Charing Cross Road, and I see that the months leading up to the moment were one long run of anticipation. We try to keep it under wraps at the office, but we arrange to meet outside at lunch, and usually end up making out on a park bench. We're big on public displays of affection, not really by intention, but because we can't keep our bodies apart. He makes me feel like I have a thousand extra sensors per square inch of skin.

Now I have to break up with Paul, because I'm free-falling into love. I'm consumed by the Englishman, and it's stronger than any thrill I was getting from my own duplicity.

My decision is made. And when I look back I see all the evidence that I should have done it much sooner. With the way I was acting—the way I evidently wanted to act—how could I have thought the relationship with Paul might work? The need to break up becomes so madly urgent that I do it on the phone, right before Paul and I are supposed to go on a trip to Morocco. The fact that we've been planning the trip makes it all the more bizarre to him that I'm doing this now, and so there's incomprehension in his anguish. I'm anguished too, because while I'm resolved, I know that I'm letting go not only of a person who understood me, but also of a possible life I'd entertained. I'm shutting that door and jumping into the Englishman's arms, with all of its unknowns. After Paul and I have cried, I know that I've been callous. But I also feel purified.

When the deed is done I still have the week of vacation I'd booked. The Englishman and I go to Sicily.

ON DESIRE
chapter twenty-eight

*W*ith *the Englishman it's different.* I haven't felt this physical magnetism in a long time, at least not since Justin, whom I think maybe I can finally stop thinking about. The Englishman and I read the papers together for an hour or two on Sunday mornings, and sometimes we read poetry out loud. He loves Ted Hughes, with all his birds and wolves, which I think must remind him of an imaginary Yorkshire, his own having been suburban. He says he wants a dog, and then says the thing that travelers say when asked about pets, which is that our lifestyles don't permit them. Maybe we don't really want them all that much.

A separation hangs over us. After twelve months in London, the Englishman is supposed to be sent to Russia and I'm supposed to go back to the United States. I don't give much thought to what this might mean, since long-distance love has become my norm. I don't consider not choosing it. I don't believe that love is a choice. It doesn't occur to me that that our pending division might be one of the things that makes me want him so much. Maybe after being bogged down in Seattle, I'm afraid to love anyone who might stick around.

In the meantime, while still based in London, we take vacations. It's the dawn of the budget airline era, and we can get cheap tickets to anywhere in Europe. After Sicily we go to Croatia, and late in the summer we cycle around Scotland. Our first six months together are a blur of food and sex and travel. After antipasto and prosecco in Taormina, he feels me up on the train until my shorts are soaked. Somewhere near Loch Lomond, after a full Scottish breakfast of sausage, eggs, bacon, beans, mushrooms, black pudding, and tomato, the proprietress has to kick us out, because it's 11:00 AM and we had to use the bed one last time. In London after ravioli, in a deserted lane just minutes from my flat, we push and pull each other into a doorway and I suck him off. Once the floodgates are open, neither of us ever wants to stop. It's my kind of sex, our kind of sex. We don't race to the finish but just go on and on, because we both understand that anticipation can never disappoint; it just gets better and better. And when we finally come because we can't go on another second, as well as the physical release there's the mental release of compulsion, of having been made to do something against our will.

I crave him in my body and heart. I don't think I can bear detachment. But we separate because work is taking us in different directions; he doesn't question going to Russia any more than I question going to the States. After that things just speed up: more countries, more food, more sex. We meet in Barcelona and Ireland. We visit each other in Moscow and Seattle. After we've both quit the wire service, we decide to spend two months in Mexico.

Staying on the Sea of Cortez, neither of us really has a plan. Writing, travel, love: These seem to be the most important things in life. I'm finishing my first book, and my idea for what to do after that is to write more. That's as concrete as it gets. The Englishman is studying Spanish, which will be his third language after Russian, and he's working on a novel, that first messy, unreadable, necessary attempt. While I'm waiting on edits, I work on an unreadable novel too. We're here but not really "living" here, and I don't know where we'll go next. It's time between time. We wake up to blue sky and undulating white curtains. We eat tortillas, chorizo, and avocados, and maybe some fresh squeezed juice. We swim then write, or we write then swim. We fuck at midday, maybe in the red-tiled kitchen, then read in the afternoon, cracking all those classics we never got around to before—Herodotus, John Steinbeck. Then we eat from the same basic ingredient list as breakfast, have sex in bed, and maybe read some more. We see few other people. We've checked out of the real world, and I think I could probably live like this for a very long time.

As for what to do next, we're like two people going on a date, saying back and forth, "What do you want to do?" "I don't know; what do you want to do?" Except that it's more than a date; it's a life plan. When you're two people living in the same city, you're not forced into this kind of decision, because you've each built up a life where you are. You'll stay put with or without the other. But when you've come together in a foreign country, from homes far away— not that either of us could have told you where home was—the decision carries more weight. The practical implications alone are huge. Buy plane tickets, rent a home, move furniture across the world? Settle down in a foreign land? Settle down at all?

The Englishman wants to study Spanish in Cuba, and I say I'll probably go with him, but after that we have no scheme at all, together or alone. So I think back to the place that felt the most right: New York. It's just been attacked in an act of war, with thousands killed—that's the reality from which we've checked out. We're startled when the gardener says *"la caída"* because we think he's said "Al Qaeda," but then we realize he's only talking about "the fall," the stairs where the bougainvillea tumbles down to the beach. I have the same thought I did while sailing across the Pacific: Are we obligated to do something useful in the world, or just not mess it up? I want to run to New York, like it's my lover wounded in battle. I make a decision: I'm going to move back there. I suggest to the Englishman that he come with me.

I still want him so much. I want to touch him, feed him, fuck him, and talk all day about the writers we love. I've never wanted someone so much for so long. In my most serious relationships, with Stu and Paul, both times the sharp edge of love went blunt. (That never happened with Graham, but I don't think to wonder why, or whether it had anything to do with all that time apart.) The loss was okay—I still felt safe and companionable. I saw that there were other important things. I knew in theory that a grown-up chooses to leave her highs behind, in favor of a stable life. But I missed my desire. I missed my thirst. I tried to heighten what was left of them, hoping to feel the way I had before. I took off across the world, I cheated, and—this possibility came like a revelation—realized that you could play games in bed. You could become the stripper, the slave, the teacher's pet. Sex became a portal to another place.

But with the Englishman so little of this is even necessary. I've finally found the man with whom I'll never get bored. It's been almost two years, and I still want him like I did when our forearms first brushed at the office. I have everything in the Englishman: a travel companion, an intellectual partner, and lust.

I'm anxious while I wait for him to answer me about New York. I fear that he won't want to come. It's a huge decision, and I practically feel like I've asked him to marry me. I convince myself that he's going to say no, trying to prepare myself for the worst. I want him more than ever.

One night we're in the big white bed with the reading lamps

on, our books lying all around. The rhythmic sound of the night sea floats in through the window screens. We're calm and friendly, getting ready to sleep. "I'm going to do it," he says. "After Cuba, I'm going to come to New York."

"That's great," I say. It hasn't quite sunk in yet, and I don't know how to react. When I've had a moment to absorb it, I crawl over and tickle him and say, "Yay." We laugh together in surprise.

Then a strange thing happens. We turn off the lights and I face away. I stare at a moonlit square of white wall, which frames the black silhouette of a gecko. While I'm watching the reptile, I know suddenly that the feeling is gone. The sweet, painful, overwhelming desire that I've carried these last many months has been snuffed out. There's a caring companion beside me. But that sharp craving, which I need to have so that it can be fulfilled and I can feel ecstatic, has disappeared.

I'm so disappointed I could cry. Not just because I miss the desire itself. I'm also sad because I was wrong about my feelings for the Englishman. I thought he was the one who could stop my wandering heart. I thought that this relationship was different, that I could go on loving him the way I had so far. I thought I could be happy with just one man. I'm sad because I see now that I'm the problem. I'm perverse. I wanted him until I knew that I could have him, and as soon as he made me a promise, my want went away. I'm sad because this might mean that I'll never be satisfied. I can be satisfied for a moment, or even a few months. The Englishman satisfied like crazy. But it can't last. Nothing, with me, can last. I mourn for all the things that can't last, and I mourn for what I've discovered about myself. I can seek bigger and better thrills, but in the end I'm bound by the same thing that binds everyone else. Love is only a moment passed through, not somewhere you can go and live. That's why people build those scaffolds I've so disdained. They make homes, families, networks of colleagues and friends. They're infrastructure projects unto themselves, connected to others by rods and beams. They know they can't stay on the crest of a wave. They build their worlds to get through all the rest. Maybe I should do that too.

ON MAKING THE SENSIBLE CHOICE
chapter twenty-nine

I *run into Central Park and up* to the reservoir, a wide shining pool with a path on its rim. In the middle distance on the east and west sides, the crenellated tops of buildings rise in two-mile-long rows, anchorless above the trees, as if they're going to float up and away. The painstakingly carved balconies and turrets are like castles in the sky, more impressive than any of the ruins I've ever seen—Roman, Sabaean, Indus Valley—because they still hum with life. I wonder if, in half a millennium, they'll be empty and crumbling too, artifacts for the archaeologists to read. For now I feel once again like the city is my playground. I've reunited with friends from graduate school and go out almost every night. It's seven months after 9/11, but there's a vigor in the recovery, a grand fuck-you to the world.

The exertion clears my head, but when I get back to my studio sublet I start thinking about the Englishman again. I'm both ambivalent and impatient pending his arrival. Even after that moment in Mexico, of realizing that desire had ebbed like it always does, I've hung on to the belief that he's different. He's my best-ever shot at long-term love, maybe even marriage. Not in the sense that I know he wants those things, but insofar as I, for once, think that I do. I've seen how different I can be with him. I could commit. I could say okay to a lifetime. I think. I waffle back and forth on the subject to close friends. Only part of my ambivalence comes from thinking about these lifetime plans. I'm also afraid that he'll change his mind and I'll lose him, and I'm trying to shelter myself in advance.

The Englishman, after equivocating on dates—first it's one Monday, then it's the next Monday, then it's Saturday afternoon—arrives on my doorstep five weeks after I do. He's nearly finished writing his novel, and when he's done, I press him. What are we doing? What's next? Is he staying in New York? I can't believe I've become a woman who asks these questions. Who asks for that dreaded and amorphous thing, commitment. I can't even tell if I want it, or just think I'm supposed to want it. I can't envision exactly what I want. But still I press ahead.

My ambivalence doesn't protect me from being devastated when, a month after his arrival, he leaves. I asked him to choose a particular life, and he said no. I think about how bad I've always been at choosing. I think about how he was a very safe person for me to want, because, like me, he was always going away.

These thoughts are buried in tears, because I'm crushed like I've never been before. I'm thirty and it's late in life to be left for the first time, but I know it's not because I've been more wanted than anyone else. It's just because I've protected myself by always exiting first.

Some days I feel like I can't breathe. I have no idea how to handle this, so I try to suppress my sorrow the way I try to stop heartburn on the running trail: I suck in my solar plexus as hard as I can, squeezing the pain away. The problem is that as soon as I let go, the pain comes back.

❋ ❋ ❋

It's around this time that I meet Dominic. Remeet, actually; we were acquaintances in graduate school. The second time I see him, he's heard about my breakup, and he tells me that if I need someone to talk to, he's there and he cares. Over time I'll learn that he's shy, and that he was being bold when he said that. I know it's way too soon, that I have no capacity to make judgments. I know that I'm trying to erase one man with another. But I can't stop myself. I don't know how else to get by. I'm falling and he reaches out to catch me.

I'm emotionally numb when I enter our relationship, repeating some dimly recollected pattern, this time underwater. I'm grateful that he's the kind of person who, being undemonstrative himself, doesn't seem to notice. As best I can, I close off the subterranean caverns where the Englishman dwells, and while I don't convince myself that I'm okay, I'm able to convince others that I'm okay. I rarely talk about the Englishman, because to even open my mouth would let grief come pouring forth. I will myself to become okay, which will take a very long time.

Not that that's all there is to it. There's a spark with Dominic, weaker in degree than some other sparks I've felt, but genuine; I think maybe I can fan it into a fire. Our attraction flares at a Swedish bar in a former Chinese restaurant, after they push tables out of the way and the DJ starts. It continues at a nightclub called the Bulgarian, where they play gypsy punk and always exceed the fire code. I'm smitten at first with the fact that he can dance; it's been a long time since I've been with someone who would. I like his taste, the way he mixes vintage everything with an unabashed pursuit of the cutting edge. He ferrets out new music, clothes, and neighborhoods, then feels vindicated and annoyed when they come into fashion. I don't feel very cool, but I think that he thinks I am.

Early on, after we've been out all night, he's driving me uptown on his motorcycle, when it breaks down under the old raised railway on the West Side. I sit down on a curb and watch him try to affix a bolt, which takes a while. A couple of skinny boys in tight T-shirts walk briskly by, heads bopping. Daylight begins to spread, slanting down under the obsolete tracks, bouncing off the Hudson that flows just beyond my sight. Later Dominic will tell me that at this moment he thought our relationship wouldn't survive. Women are irritated by this sort of thing, he'll say—falling ceiling tiles, hand-to-mouth budgets, broken bikes. I'll tell him that I'm not like that. I try to be in love with Dominic, and I think it starts to work. It's like that moment when you've taken a drug of dubious quality, and you keep asking yourself if the high is coming on. There are different kinds of love, I tell myself, and this one is calmer, quieter, reserved—but maybe much more steady.

When we begin dating, he's trying to get into the State Department. He scores high on the exams, but that only gets you on a list. He enters the long, uncertain waiting period before you're assigned to a training class. I think of my State Department internship a decade earlier. I think even further back, to my college year in Egypt. Dominic also studied Arabic and worked in the Middle East; if he's accepted he'll eventually be sent to the region. I think of how I could have taken Dominic's path. When you're twenty-one, all possible lives are still ahead. Dominic and I even have the same graduate degree, in international affairs, another whisper that in an alternate universe, I might have been able to go his way. But by now I've cast my lot as a writer. I've closed doors. Not least of all, I wouldn't pass the State Department's security clearance. But being with someone who's taken the other route will let me experience it by proxy.

I'm a sort of proxy for him too. He can't face the twin risks of chaos and poverty that inform a writer's life; his childhood was unstable enough, and he still helps out his sister and mother back home. He's a talented writer, but writing will only ever be a hobby for him. Through me he'll be in touch with a life he can't live.

✻ ✻ ✻

My sublet expires when the owners come back from France. I move
to a shared apartment in Fort Greene, Brooklyn, where my unhinged
roommate hurls verbal abuse. I leave in the night to stay at Dominic's apartment in the East Village; then to a place on West 103rd,
emptied by a friend who's gone to Holland; then to a sublet in Astoria, Queens, belonging to a friend who's in Senegal. In the small
community I've formed in New York, someone is always going off
somewhere. Pinging around from place to place, I feel as though I
can't stop the momentum, and I become exhausted. I'm also impoverished, having overestimated what I can earn from freelancing, and
underestimated the cost of living in this town.

My credit card debt mounts. Every month I lay out my bills
in the kitchen, and hope that some overlooked asset will magically
appear. Three hundred dollars seems like a good fee for a story,
then I do the math and it doesn't. I shelve my passion projects—
that unreadable novel, a magazine pitch—sunk by the imperatives
of working to live. I do legal research and work as an usher, and
the math still doesn't work out. I try to open an account at a new
bank, and it turns me down. In Astoria, each of several blizzards
traps me far from anyone I know. My apartment trembles when the
elevated train goes by. My coat is only wool, not down. When I have
to go outdoors, which is all the time, I wear tights under my jeans
and layers of intermediate sweaters. Aside from a few stellar Greek
restaurants, Astoria is inconvenient to everywhere I want to go. It's
convenient, though, to La Guardia Airport, which lies a quick shot
away on the bus. Seeing the M60 plow through the slush gives me a
little trill of warmth. The airport could be a way to escape the piles
of bills and the shaking flat. Escape is my usual path, though, and

I'm determined not to do it this time. Yet stuck in place, I start to feel desperate. My love for New York has gone from the flush of reunion to sick dependence, but I beat against the city like a moth on a bulb.

As my career and finances become more and more tenuous, I start to think of Dominic as a lifeline. I have nothing else solid. When we first got together, I made a few efforts to maintain my independence. I refrained from inviting him to a friend's wedding, and when I was routed from one apartment after another, I never suggested we move in, the way so many New York couples resolve their real estate woes. But by the winter I've given up. I'm pushing the relationship into tighter, more intertwined territory, more like the one I had with Stu. Dominic seems okay with this. He's a rescueman, the kind of guy who responds to need. We fly to visit each other's families. I spend more nights in the East Village, and he spends more nights in Queens.

I suspect that I've misused my freedom. My friends from graduate school have incomes and jobs, some of them very good, the very ones we predicted for ourselves. They're advising on where in the world to plunk a million bucks, or campaigning for human rights, or running for office. Even the journalists are on their way, producing television that people watch, and writing things that people read. They're flying first class. I, on the other hand, have screwed up.

The State Department finally confirms Dominic's acceptance; it's March now and he's supposed to start training in May. We've been together for a little less than a year. I tell him that I don't want another long-distance relationship, and that I don't want to break up. Does he agree? He does. We decide that I should follow him to Washington.

We begin planning the logistics. I talk to my landlord and friend, who says that he's coming home from Senegal soon. In the meantime his girlfriend will move in. Many of us went away after finishing our degrees, but now the ones who want to live in New York are coming back and settling down. "Settling down." I'm not sure what it means, and I didn't used to think it was something I wanted. I went to almost violent lengths to reject it. But now, going away makes me uneasy. I don't feel the thrill of escape. For the first time I wonder if I hadn't better put down roots. But I can't. I feel like Dominic is all I have, and he's moving away.

I tell myself and others that this is all just fine. A diplomat plus a writer make a perfect pair. I need no fixed location, so together we can go off and explore the world. It sounds romantic and glamorous. We'll be like Dick and Nicole Diver, with all the glamour but none of the crazy. The story I tell makes sense. But the truth is that New York has chewed me up and spat me out.

ON IMAGINARY LOVERS
chapter thirty

There's always a parallel story. The paths not taken go on in our heads. It's just like when my grandmother died, and I heard about it from a phone booth in Malaysia, she never really died for me, but lived on as an idea.

Justin and I stayed in touch. I talked to him on the phone from New Zealand, then from Seattle. We discussed how and when we would reunite. By the time I moved to New York for the first time, in 1997, it was almost two years after he drove me to the airport. I'd unloosed myself from Seattle, and felt triumphant and free. Before, my relationship with Justin had been overshadowed by my connection to Stu, but now we could finally be together without any encumbrance.

In my first weeks in New York, I had fantasies of what it would be like when Justin came. I imagined what I would be wearing (tartan miniskirt) when he walked up the steps of Columbia. "So?" I asked him when we spoke on the phone that fall. Soon, he said. He had to finish up some work.

In December I called his family's home and reached his brother. "Have you heard the news?" his brother asked. "Justin's gotten engaged." I noticed the way he drawled out the "a," but I couldn't make sense of what I was hearing. It had to be a joke. Or a misunderstanding. In our phone calls we never pretended to be beholden to each another; I talked to him about Stu and he told me about other girls. Surely he would have said something if he were heading toward marriage.

"Can you have him call me?" I managed to ask, and hung up the phone. I put it out of my mind. The absurdity of the news made it hard to take seriously, and I had plenty of distractions. I had classes every day, new friends, stacks of homework. The days turned from crisp to bitingly cold, and I took the bright, screeching, grimy subway down to Soho to shop for a real winter coat. Queensland seemed unreal, like a place I once read about in a magazine.

When Justin called a few days later, he told me that it was true. "How did I not hear about this?" I asked, straining to sound lighthearted. "It happened really quickly," he said. A whirlwind romance. I thought of our own whirlwind, of how quickly it had turned into love, and his strange proposal of marriage. Now it was early December again, the same time of year we were in New Guinea. I still didn't have a watch, but I no longer marked time by the full moon. Even if I were in the southern hemisphere, I could no longer have told you how to find and use the Southern Cross. "I've never spent Christmas with someone before," he said. Only later would I remember the plaintive note in his voice, and feel sympathy for his desire to bring a girl home. When he said it, though, I just felt angry. I was supposed to be the girl, the one. He'd promised to come. How could he do this?

There was a series of phone calls, more frequent than usual, almost daily. He told me contradictory things, and with each new statement I became more alarmed. It hadn't occurred to me, before now, to doubt his word. But I had no choice. I longed for his calls because he always told me something I wanted to believe. I dreaded his calls because they gave me more evidence of duplicity. I wasn't the only one addicted to the double life.

He told me he would still come to New York. He would come before his wedding, or maybe after. His wedding would be very soon, or many months away. He'd told his bride-to-be about me, he said, but told her that I was a lesbian, and ugly. He praised her— she was smart, beautiful, kind. An environmental lawyer. He complained about her. She didn't understand him the way I did, he said. I wanted to lap up his praise for me and disparagement of her, but I knew that something was very wrong. The Justin I imagined didn't do this, didn't get engaged to someone and then complain about her to his ex-girlfriend in the United States. I was chagrined on her behalf as well as my own. I remembered Patricia and how besotted she was with Justin even when he was with me. I remembered his stories of how she'd flown to see him and declared her love. I remembered how powerful and confident I felt then, and sorry for Patricia. I didn't want to be Patricia.

I knew nothing about Justin's new girlfriend—fiancée—except for what he told me. They could, for all I knew, already be married, or she could, for all I knew, not exist. My attachment to Justin over the last two years had been nurtured with the droplets he'd chosen to present. That was all I'd had. Now I understood that what he'd said might have deviated wildly from the full picture, and it made me feel dizzy.

One day Justin confirmed my fear: They were already married. I hung up the phone on him, enraged by the marriage itself, and by our running conversation of shadows and feints. It felt like a breakup. I cried all night, mourning his disappearance from my life. I wondered if real-life adultery was easier to deal with. In that situation everything was tangible. There was a firestorm, but then it was over.

Then I tried to bury my pain under study. I didn't talk about the rift to anyone, because there was no version of the story in which

I didn't sound like a fool. There was no way to explain my sense of loss, since I hadn't seen the guy in two years. He was my inexplicable secret. Even though the relationship felt real to me, I could see how it might look like I mostly dreamed it up. So much of it must have been my own invention. I djinned up a Justin who would join me in New York, fantasized about him coming into my new life. He gave me encouragement, to be sure, but I'd needed very little. Now I hadn't been widowed or divorced or even broken up with a boyfriend. All I'd lost was an idea. I was crushed, but I thought no one would understand.

❋ ❋ ❋

After several months, my anger at Justin dissipated, and other memories buoyed up. Recollections of pleasure and excitement, so much preferable to our weird end game, made me forget why I was mad. My thoughts of him abated, so that soon I was thinking of him only once a day, then only every few days. I never stopped thinking of him entirely. If we'd had a chance to settle down and become irritated by each other's idiosyncrasies, maybe things would have been different. But we separated at the precise moment of falling in love, and now those feelings seemed to have frozen into a solid, permanent thing.

What did I call this? What did I do with it? It didn't count as a relationship. I could never have brought him to meet my family or friends, and if I were honest with myself, he wouldn't have fit in in New York anyway. He wasn't malleable and wandering like me; he belonged to his beaches, his business, his mom. I had nothing to show in my day-to-day life for the mental space he took up. There was nothing that anyone besides me could see. He should just have been an old story, someone I once met. (I thought of how often, when we were together and later on the phone, he would ask me to tell him a story.)

And yet . . . Was a thing unreal, just because it existed only in the mind? Weren't our imaginations part of our lives too? If I spent years thinking about someone, wasn't he a part of my world?

I liked to imagine him watching over me. A change in environment could set me off thinking about him more than usual, and when I moved to London, he entered my mind at the same time every day. It was always in the same stretch of my walk from my apartment to work: heading up Clerkenwell, past St. Peter's Italian church and the Italian grocery store, before turning onto Gray's Inn. Why right there? Maybe something reminded me of him one day, then the next day made me think of how I'd thought of him the day before, and then I just fell into the habit. My memories of memories became as real as my memories of actual events.

Three years after I hang up on Justin and five years after I've seen him, I decide to send a Christmas card. In response he calls in the middle of my night, I pick up the phone, and he says, "Beth." He's the only boyfriend who's ever called me that, and instantly I'm on the floor of a tent in Papua New Guinea, insides molten, wet as the jungle. I'm affected, and it's real. Suddenly we're talking all the time again.

When we met no one used email; now we do. We're flirtatious, casual, friendly. He talks a little about his wife, not in glowing or disparaging terms but in a matter-of-fact way; I find myself not caring as much about the subject as I once did. It's as though I've acquiesced to seeing our relationship in a new way: It's *supposed* to be fantasy, detached from any reality that includes wives or boyfriends. I hadn't gotten it before. I hadn't distinguished my actual life from this man on the phone. Justin flirts with me and flatters me, boosting my ego, and needs only the same in return. There's no downside. It's like hearing from an old friend, with the added frisson of desiring and being desired, but with no consequences. It's the safest sex there is.

He says he'll visit me and doesn't. We say we'll reunite in the Pacific—Hawaii, Vanuatu—and don't. Once I call him from Heathrow and, to tease and test him, begin by saying, "I'm at the airport." There's a long, serious silence on the line—he's still married—and then he asks, suspecting my prank, "Which airport?" Whenever we speak, the world around me dims, and I feel high with the thrill of anticipation.

He has a wife. He has nicknames for my boyfriends. Paul is "the Marine," and the Englishman becomes "the Yorkshireman." It's not like we hide much, as far as I can tell. It's not like we pretend that we're single when we're not. We're just playing out a drama in our heads.

The time when Justin seems most serious about visiting me is when things are just beginning with Dominic. Since I left Australia, Justin's business has evolved from a one-man gardening outfit into an environmental consulting firm, and he has upcoming meetings in the United States. He gives me a date.

He's backed down from our bluff before, but this time I'm the one who has to ask him not to come. I'm not sure if it was a bluff or not. We go quiet for a while.

❋ ❋ ❋

I burnish a desire to reunite with Justin, but I'm not completely irrational. I recognize that this man isn't really part of my life. I know that I don't know him anymore, that my idea of him is just an idea. I've taken a brief time with a real, sweating, crying person, and embellished it over the years. I've stitched memory with beliefs: that he shares my sensibilities, has a certain kind of intelligence, is an honest man. I know that he's done something similar with me. I'm the imaginary, perfect love that he can go to as a touchstone. Over the years, our ideas of each other have floated away from the actual people we've become.

Theoretically, I could fly to Australia to sort out my feelings. That would end it all, I'm sure. Confronted with the real person, all the intense emotions would go away. I would know that he was just a guy, someone for whom I might feel, at most, friendly affection. The solid mass of longing would dissolve, and then I could get on with my life.

It's not all that often that I simultaneously have a week to spare and a few thousand bucks, but that's not really what stops me. I'm proud and stubborn, and I believe that since I went there and found him, it's the least he can do to come to me.

There's probably something else at play too: I'm not really sure I want to give up my want.

❋ ❋ ❋

I begin to wonder how different "real" love is from my imaginary affair. In any relationship there's both reality and the perception of reality. As long as I see the other person as smart or sexy or handsome or good, and as long as I can hang on to the feeling of loving and being loved, then it's real. But somehow we're able to hang on to those feelings and beliefs even when objective reality diverges. Actions don't necessarily alter beliefs, and beliefs matter more.

Before you fall in love, you begin to imagine the other person. You create your lover, extrapolating on reality, dusting him or her with gold. You embellish to the point of perfection, and then fall hard for the image you've made. With all my traveling, I may have spent more time imagining than others. But a huge amount of *all* love takes place in the head. In the middle of any relationship we can spend more time, hour for hour, thinking about the other person than we spend in his presence. And after any breakup, there's no telling how long we might pine for someone. Love itself is in the mind's eye.

❀ ❀ ❀

In the middle of my cold, broke, miserable winter, I get a letter. A valentine. I take it up to my fifth-floor window. Outside, the snow looks like a great white silk duvet, and I remember the word *doona*, an Australianism for quilt. Even the elevated train is muffled tonight. Somehow the years since I've seen Justin have piled up to seven.

The letter is longing and romantic; he says he loves me. He says he looks in the mirror and knows he made a mistake. I was the one who got away. He says that he wants to see me and that he's ready to really do it. No more talk. Oh, and he's getting a divorce. This will become our pattern: When our real-world relationships are starting to slide, one of us reaches out.

I wonder, wishfully, if I played a tiny role in the divorce. Of course, there must have been all kinds of big, real-life things, about sex and money, hypothetical kids, dishes in the sink. Mundane things I never got to have with him. We never got to break up over ordinary disputes, because our love is perfectly preserved. But maybe I represented some little seed of doubt about his marriage. Maybe there was an escape clause in his head, and I was its face.

When I get the valentine, saying things I would have longed to hear even just the summer before, I don't feel the usual excitement. I feel sick. I have a real-life boyfriend, and I believe he's the only rope out of a crevasse. Dominic is not some fantasy of meeting in a tropical paradise, but a potential, realistic future. I knew Justin for two months, that's all, a brevity I find astonishing for all the time I've spent thinking about him since.

I leave the letter on my desk and revisit it a couple of times the next day. I move it to my bedside, then to my dresser drawer. I feel like I need time to think, to fit the letter somehow into the context of my present life. Dominic and I are planning our move to Washington. Justin is half illusion; he can disappear from view. I think of how he failed to tell me about his marriage, and the times he said he'd come to me and didn't. *Now it's too late*, I think with frustrated regret. I'm getting my life together. Dominic is my man. He's been there for me, from the breakup through the blizzards, and now he's invited me to follow him.

A few more days go by, and I realize I've decided what to do. I ignore Justin's valentine. I don't call or write back. I can't bring myself to throw it out, so I put it in its own unmarked file, wedged between manila folders of freelance contracts and credit card bills.

❀ ❀ ❀

Transplants from New York to Washington always have a hard time. The trick is to not wish that Washington is New York, to not even compare them. Like I really shouldn't compare Dominic to the Englishman. If you accept Washington on its own terms—a swampy, suburban, Southern company town—it has its charms.

I take to it more easily than Dominic does. I'm apprehensive about leaving New York, but I'm not as attached. My life went haywire there, and I feel a little like I would about a romantic rejection: Oh yeah? I'll reject you right back. Dominic didn't care for the job he had while waiting on the State Department, but he has deeper friendships in New York than I do. And after ten years, his love for the dense buzz of the place, and the neighborhood that made him feel on the cutting edge, is still intact.

I miss the way the buildings in New York swaddled me up.

Washington is horizontal rather than vertical, with broad avenues and low-rise apartments slightly too far apart. But in Washington I spend less and have fewer distractions, so I can write more. Our apartment has hardwood floors, big windows, and a view of Meridian Hill Park. We go to Bed, Bath and Beyond and buy a shower curtain and rugs. We hire a cleaning lady.

Dominic and I get up together every day. He rides to work on his motorcycle and I settle down at my stainless steel desk. I meet his entering class, which is full of people with boyfriends or girlfriends trying to decide whether to stay together. The foreign posting looms ahead of each pair, and Dominic and I talk about it too.

Shortly after we move, I get coveted assignments from two different publications. And I've begun to write about lobbyists, so it's really a good thing that I'm in DC. It seems like I've made the right move. I'm still in a hole, but I feel like I'm finally digging out. I've gripped the rung I was flailing for, and there's no way I'm letting go, even if I have to live in Burkina Faso. Especially if I have to live in Burkina Faso, which would fulfill my desire for the strange and make me exotically saleable as a writer. Maybe this will work out after all. I can travel the world and still have a home base, not in the form of a place but of a person.

We grow closer. It's not that there's no conflict: We gripe over what to buy for the apartment, and whether to eat out or in. But it's real. I don't feel the intense, irrefutable desire that I've felt in the past, but I think that's a good thing. I don't feel like I need to get away from him, either, like I did from Stu and Seattle. It's a happy medium, where I can be calm and stable and not get crushed. We're a good fit, deeply interested in one another's work. We call each other multiple times a day. On weekends we ride around new neighborhoods on his motorcycle, with me navigating from the back. We make a good team.

I'm starting to achieve a delicate balance. There's no reason to rock the boat.

❀ ❀ ❀

I haven't thought about Justin all that much, not since I ignored his letter. The spell is finally broken. How else would I have been able to resist his plea? Now I'm clear-eyed and realistic. I see that nothing was ever going to happen there.

I get an email one morning when I sit down at my desk. It's six months after the valentine. Justin says he misses me and that he wants to talk, and signs off "your love." This raises my hackles. Now I see him as an interloper, wanting to intrude on my domestic tranquility. He went and got married on me, back when we were making promises that still seemed true. Now I've found what I want. Or at least what I need. I email back with carefully platonic words, and tell him that I'm living with my boyfriend. No "love," no x's and o's. He emails me back, but this time I don't reply.

How dare he, I think. He's been nothing to me in real life. I desperately need this harmony I've found, and I was never going to get it from him. Saved from drowning in New York, I'm just regaining emotional and financial stability, and those are the most important things. I feel like I finally have a little breathing room, to figure out what's next. I have some more of the mental space I need to write, and I'm grateful to Dominic for helping me get it.

And yet . . . I'm a little bit bored. Dominic is high-functioning in bed, always up for it, but robotic and silent. I sometimes feel like I could be anyone. I know that just-okay-in-bed is supposed to be okay, that that's how you stay in a relationship. I count my blessings—my clean, calm apartment; my nice, calm boyfriend; and my time to write.

I lie in bed that night and think of Justin. It's harmless to think;

we're all allowed the privacy of our own minds. I think about when he became feverish under our mosquito net on the Sepik River and started saying delusional things. I think about Justin's hair, and how Dominic never lets me muss his. But I know that Justin is just a symbol. He represents a carefree time in my life, that's all. Now I have a few more cares; I've had more successes and failures. I may think my life is dull, but that's just because I'm a freak for escape. *Was* a freak for escape. I'm getting over all that now.

I keep thinking about Justin in bed.

I decide I'll just email him back, and do so the next morning. He replies right away. *Fourteen hours ahead,* I think. *What's he even doing up?* He says he wants to talk to me. I think about that, and decide to acquiesce. I give him the home phone number, and I tell him when to call: not before 9:00 AM my time the next morning, which happens to be when Dominic goes to work.

I don't think there's really anything wrong with this; after all, why can't I talk to an old friend? But my judgment is blurred because that thing is happening again. The faster heartbeat, the sense of anticipation. For what? It never comes to anything. But anticipation of pleasure is a kind of pleasure itself.

I sit down at my desk the next morning while Dominic is getting ready to go to work. I open my email and there's one from Justin: He says he can't wait to hear the sound of my voice. Dominic glances over my shoulder, or maybe it's more than a glance.

❋ ❋ ❋

Dominic has never been very trusting, not just of me but of the world in general. I know he has a jealous streak even though he's subdued and ever-reasonable on the surface. It's already forced me into weird contortions.

Several months into our relationship he asked how many people I'd slept with. I was dumbfounded. I didn't think anyone asked that question beyond the age of twenty-three. We were in our early thirties. Who cared? How many people you'd been in love with—now *that* was an interesting question. But sex could mean anything. The person you fucked could have been forgettable or life-changing. Counting lovers was as inane as ticking off countries, when what mattered was what had made an impact.

We were walking down Avenue A toward a Mexican diner, and I stopped and turned to him and asked if he was kidding. But I saw on his face that he wasn't. We resumed walking, and I suddenly thought much less of him. A month earlier in our relationship his question would have been a deal-breaker, a sign of an anxious, visceral sort of sexism that I wanted nothing to do with. By the time we had the conversation, though, I was already sliding into dependence. I remembered a friend, years earlier, warning me to always, always, always make my number less than the guy's. I'd scoffed at her for insisting I carry on such an absurd double standard. But now I hesitated and decided to play it safe. As I did so, my old self dropped her jaw at what I'd become.

I thought back—put on the spot, I wasn't sure of the precise figure. I tried to think of what I'd told Dominic about past relationships, the major boyfriends, and then added a handful so that my number wouldn't seem implausibly low. I thought rapidly, knowing that my hesitancy looked bad. I had a premonition that we were introducing a new poison into our relationship and felt a flash of hatred. I hated him for doing this to me, showing a part of himself that forced me to lie. I hated myself, because I knew I was going to stay with him anyway—that I was lying in order to do so.

"Fourteen," I finally said, low-balling it, hoping it would be a little less than his number. Unfortunately it was a few more. His pale skin reddened. "I haven't gone out with anyone who'd slept with that many people," he said. "As far as you know," I shot back. I felt knocked off kilter, not quite believing that we were having this conversation.

Dominic stowed the figure away as a resentment, to be trotted out every now and then under the guise of another gripe, specifically that I'd "done more" than him in life. He'd say I'd been to more countries, or had more adventures, which wasn't really true. But his overarching pathology was that he'd missed out, and the idea that I was more sexually experienced played right into his fear.

Maybe this was one of the very things that drew me to him. Someone who's jealous, suspicious, watching like a hawk, gives me one of the things I've always craved: something from which to escape. And Justin was the escape hatch I'd held on to, polished to a shine, for any time I thought I needed another life. Justin and I had served each other well over the years. I thought we'd both started to know what we were really doing. We must have known that we were never going to meet. That would have made our relationship real and therefore imperfect. We were just on call to provide relief. We were each other's safety valve from the pressures of normal life.

🌸 🌸 🌸

I don't know if Dominic just accidentally glances at the computer, or if he's peering over my shoulder, trying to confirm his worst fears. But he sees the words "I can't wait to hear the sound of your voice." He'll claim later that at first he thought it must be from my mother. But he looks more closely, and sees that it's a guy's name I've never mentioned.

And now the placid surface explodes like I never knew it could. "What. The. Fuck?" he shouts. I'm stunned into immobility. He demands to see the rest of the email chain, and I don't want to show him because I know the one thing he'll catch, my only incriminating words, in which I tell Justin specifically to call after 9:00 AM, Dominic is enraged. He walks back and forth, roaring. He's saying "fuck" and "goddamn," and then he picks up a heavy boot and hurls it at the wall. I've never seen him like this.

I feel panicked, like my lifeboat is sinking. I've screwed this up in a totally unnecessary way. Through stupid little acts, from emailing Justin back in the first place, to opening my browser before Dominic had gone to work, I've threatened my whole life. And I was so good when I ignored the valentine! Now I might have destroyed what I've made.

When we've calmed down, I plead my case. I haven't seen Justin in more than seven years. It was dumb and wrong of me to flirt with him online, but the whole thing is imaginary. He lives in Australia, for God's sake. He means nothing to me, I insist. This is a lie, he obviously means something, but even if I were to admit it, I wouldn't be able to explain just what. It's in my head. How can he rail against something that's in my head? How can he even know it's there? Well, in Dominic's world, maybe you can know. When he went out for another government job, he had to take a lie detector test. But it's true that I haven't seen Justin in years. This is the irrefutable fact. And if I haven't seen someone in this long, how could he possibly mean anything to me? How could this be a real thing? Lie detector tests, I remember Dominic telling me, pick up the physical symptoms of lying—the sweat and the higher pulse. And even though, in the scale of infidelity, I know that what I've done is minimal, I also know that I'd flunk a lie detector test. I'm not lying about what happened, but I'm lying about the way I feel. Justin makes me sweat and pulse.

Dominic says that he overreacted; he shouldn't have thrown the boot. But he's infuriated and deeply hurt. When he leaves for work, I think our relationship might be mortally wounded. Justin, who should not exist as a part of my real world, has had an all-too-real impact, like a dream that makes you sleepwalk off a bridge.

All I can think is that I have to save my relationship with Dominic. Without him I know that I'll flail. I'll be back in Queens with the snow and the debt, or I'll have to retreat somewhere else, maybe all the way back to Vancouver. I'll do anything to hold on to my life. I must become meticulous. Tonight I'll start to mend fences; I'll plead and declare my love. Eventually this will work, if with a lingering scar of distrust. But right now I have to clamp down on all risk. The first thing I do is block Justin's email address. The next is to open my filing cabinet. I thumb the manila folders until I find it: the letter he sent last winter. I look at his rounded cursive and the smudged ink. I must have smudged it myself. Had I cried? I'm crying now. I take it and leave the apartment, walk two blocks down Sixteenth, and choose a public garbage can. I know I'm acting irrational, but I look around as though Dominic could be watching. I tear the letter into pieces and throw them in the can, tears streaming down my face. There, that should do it. That was the only physical artifact I had of him, the only thing he'd touched. Now he'll cease to exist.

ON LIVING A BEAUTIFUL LIFE

chapter thirty-one

*W*e're stunned when Dominic is assigned to Paris for his first tour. Our realistic expectation was somewhere like Tunisia or Paraguay, some developing country off the beaten path. To me Paris is unimaginative. I see it as elegant and stodgy, like someone's well-dressed great-aunt. As we enter the whirlwind of preparation, supervising movers and packing bags, a little part of me wants to dig in my heels. I ask myself why: I'm a free-lance writer; I should be able to work anywhere. I know how to move; it's been my life's MO. I know how to settle in, find the nearest grocery store, meet new people. I speak French, solidly if not expertly, from the French immersion school I attended until the ninth grade. In the first, second, and third grades, I was banned from speaking English in class, which left me with a lasting confidence.

I know that my life sounds enviable, not least to my twenty-one-year-old self. Choosing has never been my strong suit, but if I'd had to, this might have been the exact life I envisioned for myself back then. I'm countryless and frictionless, moving on to another place. I have qualms, but there are many reasons I've decided to go ahead and go. For one I can't leave Dominic. I've been telling myself that a person can be a home base just as well as a place. Whether he's up to it or not, I'm fashioning him into my rock. The disruption that leaving him would cause in my life seems greater than the disruption of moving to Paris.

For another, my self-image is as a person who would go. I'm the kind of person who would do this, and therefore I have to. Even if I don't love the reality, I love the story of following my diplomat boyfriend to Paris, and of being a writer there. I want to have the enviable life just because it's enviable.

And, of course, it's a new place. You build up momentum and it's hard to slow down.

❀ ❀ ❀

Our apartment in Paris, which is provided by the embassy, has twelve-foot-high ceilings, parquet floors, and French doors in every room, which open onto little wrought-iron balconies. There are two bedrooms and two bathrooms, plus two rooms meant for living or dining. The fireplace is marble and there's wainscoting throughout. We have not only a garage off the courtyard, but down under the building, in a low-ceilinged warren with hard-packed dirt floors and numbered wooden doors, our very own *cave,* a cool damp room meant for storing wine.

Gerard Depardieu's daughter lives in our building, so we occasionally spot him hulking in the driveway. The Plaza Athénée, where a single cocktail in the lobby bar can cost twenty-four euro, or around thirty dollars, is at the other end of Avenue Montaigne from our apartment. It decorates its balconies with flowers and bunting, as though the majestic facade weren't pretty enough. One day on our street we see a yellow Lamborghini with license plates from Qatar; on another a flock of paparazzi case the Chanel boutique across the road. We have regular celebrity sightings—major and minor movie stars plus the fashion designer Karl Lagerfeld. He looks exactly like he does in the magazines, and Dominic says that being him must be like being a superhero, having to put on the same outfit every day.

In short, we've stumbled into some absurd American fantasy of Paris come to life, and neither of us can quite get over it all. In fact Dominic, who's been broke on and off since childhood, plunges into sullen silence when we first move in. He struggles to express why, and my interpretation is that his conception of himself—as an unlucky boy grown into an edgy man—is crashing violently into our new reality. I have a more minor identity crisis: I think I'm tough and adventurous, and now this? But mostly I find it comical. We're living in a Disneyland for rich people who are too dull to think of anything else.

As we get to know the area, we like it less and less. We're just off the retail end of the Champs Élysées, which is lined with monster stores selling music and electronics, and the middle-of-the-road chains that dot every city in Europe. The smaller residential streets between our apartment and the Seine become prettier the farther you get from the Champs Élysées, but I wonder where all the people are. I wonder if they're all in their country homes, or if their apartments are so big they can spend most of their time inside. There are at least a dozen plastic surgery clinics in the immediate vicinity of our place, identified with discreet brass plaques. The customers roam the sidewalks like zombies in the aftermath of their procedures, skin stretched taut and lips plumped, alike and unnatural. Their off-kilter, double-take looks seem like the work of a B-moviemaker. The faceliftees scare me, because becoming them is one possible outcome of a life spent trading on sex appeal, and I know that I've dabbled that way. It's just so hard not to walk through that door. I remember Mark, in Australia, joking that I was "living on pure charisma." Even now I sometimes wonder about myself. I have great affection for Dominic; we're attached, we're very much companions. We say we love each other and we mean it; how different, after all, is *wanting* to love from loving? And yet there's a current flowing underground, our personal *cave*. I know that if I hadn't so desperately wanted to get back on my feet, we might not be together. I don't—and didn't—have the crazed passion I did for Justin or the Englishman. I know those passions were unstable, but I still think of them as pure. The fact that I couldn't resist makes them somehow more honest. In my head, a trade lurks in my relationship with Dominic, sullying the waters.

❀ ❀ ❀

I don't hate Paris. I find friends. It turns out that a college friend of Kristin's, Nicole, lives here with her boyfriend, Toby. She's a Vancouverite who ended up in Paris by way of Singapore and San Francisco. I look her up and immediately understand why she drew Kristin in. She and Toby are warm and smart and some of the best cooks I've ever met, and I accept every invitation they extend. Through them I meet others, German and English and French, and they help me feel at home. We have Dominic's colleagues too, but I like being able to step outside of the embassy circle.

It's hard to find an unbeautiful place. While so many American cities have urban blight at their centers, Paris has reversed the equation. The poor have been banished to dystopian apartment blocks on the outer fringe. The well-to-do live in the center, in certain *arrondissements* more than others. The architecture is splendid, from the stone Haussmannian facades of our neighborhood, to Gothic cathedrals, to the narrow medieval streets of the Marais. These last are my favorite. The Marais—the "swamp"—is the only part of the city that wasn't overhauled in the nineteenth century, in the name of sanitation and modernization. I love the way that, on the narrowest streets, the buildings are so close they seem to almost meet overhead.

Beauty seems to be municipal policy. Window displays are detailed dioramas. The garbage men and women wear matching bright green uniforms. It's considered rude to go around in sloppy clothes. At first I think it's tiresome to have to dress up to run out for a coffee, and be looked at askance for walking around with a coffee in the first place. I start to appreciate the obsession with aesthetics, though, because I get to enjoy it too. It pleases me to see a man in a fur coat and fedora, or a slim middle-aged woman walking her dog in the early morning mist, in lavender suede high heels. The philosophy is that things should be nice to look at, and they are.

❋ ❋ ❋

Dominic has an ear for languages. He speaks Arabic better than I ever will, from the military's hardcore language training and the semester he spent in Tunisia. The State Department rates Arabic a three on its language scale, the most difficult category, whereas French is a breezy one. But Dominic started studying French just months before departure, and his natural reserve compounds his fear of making mistakes. He resents what he sees as my superior skill, and this becomes the basis of one of our recurring fights. He sinks into despondency one night because I crack a simple joke at a dinner party, and people laugh. We leave right away, and I try to console him as we walk home, through the Place de la Concorde, past its great Egyptian obelisk. Dominic wraps my French-speaking into his notion that I've had more experience than him. As our fight proceeds through its usual steps, he points out that I've been to more countries than he has, which while technically true is misleading as far as life experience goes: He served in the Army; rode an Internet start-up to highs and lows during the first dot-com boom; spent time in Tunisia, Yemen, Kuwait, and Iraq. But he still talks about the country count, the way he talked about the sex count, and sometimes brings them both up in the same conversation. He says he'll be unhappy until he has more experience too, and I think he's telling me that he wants to do things without me before he can really be with me, like travel alone and fuck other women. This makes me unhappy and insecure, and I constantly find myself playing down my past to reassure him and convince him that we should be together. As I try to twist my life into something he'll find more palatable, I'm becoming a person I don't like. Inside the cavern of our relationship, I begin to see my past as negative. All this experience I've sought, all the places I've been, count against me.

❀ ❀ ❀

We don't own any wine worth storing in *a cave,* and our belongings don't begin to fill the apartment. The embassy provides a few pieces of loaner furniture to tide us over until our shipment arrives: a love seat, a small table, and a few chairs made of cheap pine. We hang on to it all even after we get our own stuff. I take over one room as my office, and Dominic takes over another, where he keeps his computers and guitars. He wants to use the little pine table to store his record collection, but I insist that we make it a dining table. Dominic would almost always rather eat out than in, even if it's just at the pizza place around the corner. But I cook and encourage meals at home. When we're not eating, the table becomes a repository for all kinds of things—paperwork and books and stereo parts—so it feels makeshift. I want us to buy a real dining room table, which I think will make this feel like a real home, and us like people at the center of one. I think back: I've never had a dining room table of my very own. Even with Stu we only had a little kitchen table that usually ended up piled with tools, though I never objected back then. I fixate on the idea of getting a table. But when we go out to buy furniture, we end up getting a matching love seat and armchair. They're spectacular in a certain way, very of-the-moment. The designer Philippe Starck, who's tricked out restaurants and hotels around Paris, also has a furniture line. Our new pieces have Lucite legs and bright white upholstery and are wildly out of our price range. They are more square than soft, and completely impractical. We live in fear that one of us will spill food or wine on them, and friends with children make us nervous. Our home looks better than it feels.

Dominic and I are close and companionable. Together in a new place, we spend almost all of our nonworking hours together. We walk the length of the city together. When we go out motorcycling, looking for new neighborhoods, we find places where the streets are narrower and we can sprawl in grassy parks. We walk up and down the Canal St.-Martin and over its little bridges. We try speaking only French to each other for hours at a time. We have favorite restaurants and museums—not anything as staid as the Louvre, but we love the Palais de Tokyo, which is walking distance from our apartment, and rotates through exhibits of Takashi Murakami and Vanessa Beecroft. Like all couples, we have dozens of little pacts, spoken and unspoken, that let us function, from closet space—he needs more than I do for his bespoke suits—to the iron-clad understanding that I will never again do anything like I did when I emailed Justin.

As with all couples, our internal workings are a mystery to outsiders. We repeat the same fights but still call each other five times a day. For a while we're each other's sole confidants. Dominic tells me the minutiae of his job, and says that I could walk into his office and do it better. I have him read all my first drafts, and wonder if he might be the more talented writer. We're intertwined in our own bubble, capable of spending days on end, one-on-one. Dominic doesn't have the hobnobbing sociability of many of his colleagues, but he has a natural tendency to make peace. I still vividly remember my chaos from before I met him, and how I almost torpedoed our partnership with my imaginary lover, and so I embrace our placid life.

It's completely different from my life in Seattle. In objective, physical terms, our Paris apartment is the most beautiful place either of us has ever lived or—as we've already accepted—will live, whereas Seattle was the opposite. Now, among diplomats and journalists and expats, I feel like I'm with peers, while in Seattle I didn't. Now I'm guarded, evaluating every word for possible consequence, whereas back then I expressed every other thought and whim. Stu loved me in a way that Dominic never will.

And yet some things are the same. I look around and wonder how I got here. Every morning I wake up with the same question on my mind: Why does my situation, of living in a beautiful apartment with my boyfriend, spending my days writing, feel like a prison sentence? Why has the old desire to escape—that I felt in my parents' home in high school, and later living with Stu in Seattle, and later still as I tried to imagine a future with Paul, come back to me? It's different this time: Now I'm afraid of throwing grenades into the middle of a calm life, whereas before I did so without a second thought. My peace with Dominic is fragile, but I need it. I think of Houdini again, and his back-and-forth between self-entrapment and escape. This time I've compressed the two together, so that I want both things at once. My wanderlust hovers, repressed, under the surface, while I both desire and fear its potential consequences.

ON PRESSURE
chapter thirty-two

O *nce again, I'm living a* subterranean life. I think of Raphael, from Peru, and wonder if he's living in Paris. I haven't dared try to find out, though I've run through scenarios of what would happen if I ran into him in the Metro. Aside from the fact that I don't really trust myself, Dominic's wariness over any ex-lover/friend would be too much of a hassle. Once, though, I'm listening to RFI, Radio France Internationale, at my desk, and I hear a deep-voiced dispatch from the Middle East. At the end, the Paris news anchor says the reporter's name: "That was Raphael Denon reporting from Gaza." I'm electrified, thinking of Peru, but I don't do anything; I don't try to reach out.

Instead, I do the thing that most predictably lets me know I'm unhappy. I start calling Justin again. He now has a girlfriend, a Russian emigrée, a businesswoman-turned-painter whom he obviously admires. Mostly he listens and counsels me like a friend, and it's a huge relief to talk to him. It's like getting in touch with an earlier self, someone blithe and heedless and not worried about the future. There's not much romance in the things we say. He seems to know that I just need a voice on the other end of the phone, one that flirts a little and praises safely from a distance, making me feel desired without upsetting the status quo. Dominic desires me, or at least we fuck two or three times a week, but it's somehow not enough to make me feel wanted. There's an additional kick to my conversations with Justin: As I delete the previous-caller list from the phone, there's the frisson of getting caught. Some people like physical risk. I court the possibility of blowing everything up.

I know that I'm just thinking about other men because they symbolize escape. But even now that I've identified my pathology, I'm not sure what to do. I'm not sure if I should fight it or give in. If I stay, am I just trying for something that's not going to work anyway? If I leave, am I doing the right thing, making a strike for healthy independence—or am I just doing what I've always done?

I try to dismiss my unhappiness in Paris as merely an external problem. I tell myself that it's the dullness of the city, the Sunday closures, the insufferable correctness of the place, anything but me. Surely I can be loyal to Dominic, and my mood will perk up when we hit a more challenging post. But I feel that old restless desire for travel and change, and it's tied up intimately with sex. One night I sit on the edge of our bed and let myself think about lifetime fidelity, a subject that, in one-day-at-a-time-alcoholic style, I usually avoid dwelling on. The lamp on my side of the bed is on, the light splashing across the parquet of the walk-in closet. Dominic is in there hanging his clothes, reviewing his silk ties for the next day. I hope, as I always do, that he'll choose one of the ones I gave him. But simultaneous with that cozy loyal wish is something else. I imagine having sex with this one man for the rest of my life. And suddenly I have tears in my eyes. It would be like banning myself from ever seeing another country.

In movies about male infidelity—take, say, Woody Allen's oeuvre—I always find myself sympathizing with the male protagonist. Lee Simon, the character played by Kenneth Branaugh in

Celebrity, is mocked as a silly screw-up as he follows his libido and thereby messes up his and everyone else's life. And yet I understand how you might want desperately to throw over safety and security, and let yourself be consumed by new love. Female cinematic adulterers are harder to identify with, because they tend to get punished severely. (Thelma and Louise drive off a cliff; Emily in *A Perfect Murder* sees her husband and her lover die; Connie in *Unfaithful* sees her lover die; et cetera.) But there are other reasons I side with the cheaters. For one, unlike women of an earlier era, I wasn't raised to subordinate my desires to the needs of others. Being an adulterer means selfishly putting one's own desires first, and maybe this is the real sin women are committing when they stray. For another, I have sympathy for Lee Simon and the others because I know that the desire to escape isn't simple or trite. It comes out of a profound and painful confusion over life's most important question: What will make me happy?

Sitting there on the bed, I know for certain that I can't do it. By which I don't mean to suggest that Dominic could be forever committed and faithful—that's never been clear. In fact, his continued ambivalence is probably one of the things that's kept me with him this long, since it never threatened to ensnare me in the way of true love.

Now, though, I have to admit that his ambivalence is neither here nor there. I can't do this thing I'm pretending to do, this tranquil domesticity, this fidelity. At least not with him. But my tears are because I don't know if I can do it with anyone.

ON EPIPHANIES
chapter thirty-three

*W*e *drive from Rome up to* the rolling Umbrian countryside, and at the end of a long driveway, off a narrow rural road, find the two-story house with patios and a terra-cotta roof. There are barley fields beyond the swimming pool and the neatly mowed lawn, making the place just rustic enough to earn the label "farmhouse" without the presence of actual mud or manure. Friends from New York, who are more Dominic's friends than mine, have invited us and others to share it for a week.

There's not much to do right here at the house. You could go running along the rural roads through sunflower and lavender fields, or play tennis a couple of miles away. It's a ten-minute drive to the town of Todi, where the steep, cobblestoned streets are scattered with salumerias, gelaterias, and restaurants. But really this vacation was conceived of as a big, amicable hang-out. There's a pool table in the den, and a big kitchen for group cooking. We're supposed to enjoy talking to our friends, relaxing by the pool with a book, or taking group excursions to hilltop towns like Spoleto. We're five couples. I know and like the couple who organized the rental, Natalie and Gil, and I've hung out with Dominic's best friend, Jack, and his girlfriend, Melinda, but the others I've never met.

I like the idea of a big group. I like to talk and cook, and I've brought books that I've been meaning to read. Natalie leads dinner preparation most days, and I help, and we all sit down to eat together at a long wooden table.

It should be charming and delightful, but it's not. I try to figure out why we're failing to bond. One woman is ill with some kind of food poisoning, so we don't see much of her. I find one of the men abrasive. But mostly we lack group chemistry. I think it's because we're all couples in the early stages of coupledom, ranging from Natalie and Gil, who've been married for five years, to Ben and Paola, who met a few months ago in Brazil and can only see each other now and then because she can't get a visa to visit him in New York. Paola seems more anxious about this than Ben. With the possible exception of Natalie and Gil, we're couples who are still clinging to each other, a little ill at ease. No one can flirt. We can't gossip about ourselves. Positive news about one's relationship is safe to share with the group, but I'm not close enough to anyone here to talk about what's getting me down. We can't declaim drunkenly on the nature of love, or the general nature of humanity, because that too could veer into the relationship-impacting zone. Our shared intellectual interests seem to be few. That leaves careers and pop culture, and several of our housemates have dull-sounding jobs that they're no more interested in talking about than I am in listening to them talk about. It's not much to get through a week. One night the women are all at the wrought-iron patio table, and Melinda tells us about how wonderfully things are going between her and Jack, how his mother loves her, and how she expects a marriage proposal soon. This makes both Paola and I depressed, for different reasons.

Jack and Melinda are excited about the midweek excursion they've planned to Florence, which is a few hours away by car. Amid the city's masterpieces, the Uffizi Gallery is supposed to be so mesmerizing that it made the French writer Stendhal fall to his knees and nearly pass out. An Italian psychiatrist later coined the term "Stendhal Syndrome" to describe the condition afflicting those overwhelmed by Florentine beauty. The city is a can't-miss, as the guidebooks would say. Not only that, but Jack and Melinda have arranged for a special guide, an art historian, to take them around. Neither Dominic nor I have ever been to Florence, and they invite us to come along.

We don't want to go. I know that if there's one crucible of Western art I should see—that I should want to see—it's this. But it's not even an internal debate. We can't muster the slightest interest.

My reaction to the prospect of Florence gives me stark evidence that something has changed. Once I would have hauled myself five hours across the desert to see a historically significant pile of rock. Even when I lost some of my interest in sightseeing per se, of the need to check off sanctioned destinations, I still loved new cities and art museums. In high school I took a class called Western Civilization, where we studied all the great works of the Renaissance, and I would have given anything to fly to Florence right then. I've even had Stendhal Syndrome in other cities. As a teenager in the east wing of Washington's National Gallery of Art, walking among the Picassos and Pollocks for the first time, I kept feeling weak in the knees and finally had to sit down in the ladies' room. After visiting the Topkapi Palace in Istanbul I couldn't talk.

Travel is life-changing. That's the promise made by a thousand websites and magazines, by philosophers and writers down the ages. Mark Twain said it was fatal to prejudice, and Thomas Jefferson said it made you wise. Anais Nin observed that "we travel, some of us forever, to seek other states, other lives, other souls." It's all true. Self-transformation is what I sought and what I found.

You go out into the world a sponge, and everything blows you away—the first palm tree, the first laundry line strung over desert-yellow dust. Now, though, I've absorbed too much. I know that Florence won't have any impact. Zip. I know this because nothing does anymore. Not the Tuileries, not the cathedral at Chartres. They're admirable and beautiful, but they slide right out of my consciousness, and I start wondering what to have for dinner. Dominic, I think, feels something similar. Of course he does—we live in Paris. And we've both lived in New York, and I've lived in Egypt and Pakistan and Australia, and he's been in Iraq and Yemen and Tennessee. And the list goes on. We're afflicted by Stendhal Syndrome in reverse. Stendhal was overwhelmed, but nothing can do that to us.

We just want to go to the beach. On the day the others go to Florence, we decide to drive to Rimini. It takes hours to get there on the squiggly roads, and we get stuck in bumper-to-bumper traffic. Rimini is nothing special. Umbrellas and lounge chairs are available for rent on the beach, packed closely together to accommodate the crowds. The sea is opaque in the glare of the sun. The groups of children, parents, and potato-shaped grandparents remind me of the beach in Moraira.

Dominic dubs Rimini the Jersey Shore of Italy. We eat mozzarella and tomatoes in a beachside restaurant and rent an umbrella of our own. We lie down with our towels and books, and take turns going into the water. There are no epiphanies here, but there are no epiphanies anywhere anymore. Except for this: When traveling stops changing you, it's time to go home.

ON GOING HOME
chapter thirty-four

*D*ominic *and I are sitting at* our flimsy pine table, the one I'd wanted to replace with something more substantial. I've made a wintery, slow-cooked beef stew that he likes. Christmas is approaching, and we've booked separate vacations, an idea that was my suggestion. In the past we visited our respective families together.

Since returning from Umbria we've grown more peaceful. It's as though we've had all the arguments we could think of, and now, knowing how each one will end, we don't need to have them anymore. Who has more life experience, and when we're going to get a dining room table, no longer matter. He's set on continuing his State Department track, moving from country to country every couple of years, and I know that following him would be hard even if everything else was just fine. Which it isn't. I got together with Dominic in a moment of emotional crisis, but since then I've struggled toward something lasting with him—something that in retrospect may have never had a chance, but that we wanted to try for nonetheless. At some point I recovered: recovered from the Englishman, and from my sense of despair. I don't know exactly when it happened, but Dominic healed me. Now, though, I'm ready to give up the struggle and let the current take me away.

"I'm not coming back," I say. We look at each other, both surprised, me with tears in my eyes and him turning red. He stands
up and walks in a circle, then sits back down. There are no shouts;
nothing is thrown across the room. After some time, he whispers,
"I've kept you for too long."

Later I'll think about that phrase again and again. On the one
hand it sounds too lighthearted for the end of a two-and-a-half-year
relationship. It's something you say when someone drops by for a
minute, en route to somewhere else, and you ramble on for half an
hour. But it also says that maybe this relationship was always just
a way station for both of us, and that maybe we both knew that.
We were on trajectories that would inevitably take us apart—like
meeting someone in a Peruvian nightclub or on an Australian beach.
Maybe we've overstayed our welcome with one another, but that's
the only serious mistake. Dominic's phrase suggests that just because
you know a thing is going to end, doesn't mean that you shouldn't do
it. I'll come to believe he's right.

In the next few days, we alternate between falling into our old
patterns and looking at each other like strangers. We don't know
how to behave. Does he help me pack? Do we sleep side by side in
bed? We rattle around the apartment, wondering what's next.

I have no stable job. I don't know where to live. I haven't cultivated people or places, so there's no one here for me but myself.
There's no desire—no man, goal, experience, place—to compel me.
Earlier in the year I covered marches against a change in French
employment law. The students at the barricades said they wouldn't
stand for "*précarité*," or precariousness. I thought it was dubious
grounds for protest, since how could you banish uncertainty? But
now I wish I had a little less precariousness in my life. I wish I could
demand that it be banned. I want to go home, but I don't have one.

I've booked my ticket so that I leave Paris a few days after Dominic. The apartment is empty when it's time to go. Early on a Friday morning, as the Christmas lights fade into the mist, my friend Toby stops by on his way to work and helps me bring my four suitcases downstairs.

❋ ❋ ❋

When I was a kid, and into early adulthood, I loved being on planes. I loved the sense that time was suspended, that I was in between, and that I would land somewhere and find everything strange— roads and faucets reconceived, language a jumble of sounds, the time of day out of whack. Then flying became tedious, and all too often I had a pretty good idea of what things would be like where I landed.

On the flight from Paris, though, maybe because I haven't got a clue about the future, I feel some of that old happy suspension. The clouds seem symbolic again, signs that good things might lie ahead. The fear of precariousness has been replaced. I remember that feeling of being open to the world, ready for anything to happen. I've created perfect freedom, which is scary but also exciting.

You could say that I forgot to make a life. Forgot to get a steady job, or belongings, or a family of my own. I forgot to choose somewhere to be. My friends in New York are getting married two by two, and Kristin, in Vancouver, is a banker with leisurely weekends, and about to buy a five-bedroom house. I forgot to do the things that, despite decades of feminism, I still feel the niggling weight of, in a way that I imagine men don't. My parents wonder what will become of me, because the way I've chosen to live fits no pattern they understand. My father had the same job for thirty-five years.

But I created *my* life. If you choose one path you can't choose another. I'll never wonder what it would be like to sail across an ocean or move to Europe or just take a year off to chill out. I'll never doubt myself in a strange land, never be scared of languages or funky rooms. America's foreign wars won't seem quite as alien as they might have, because of the places I hitchhiked when I was barely grown. I won't be cynical about human nature, because strangers have helped me so many times. My ripped suitcase, as it tumbles onto the carousel, is bursting with life.

I followed my wanderlust. It bruised me sometimes, and took me to all kinds of highs. Now that my thirst is slaked, I get to start anew.

ABOUT THE AUTHOR

© TREVOR BUTTERWORTH

*E*lisabeth Eaves is the author of *Bare: The Naked Truth About Stripping,* and her travel essays have been anthologized in *The Best American Travel Writing, The Best Women's Travel Writing,* and *A Moveable Feast: Life-Changing Food Adventures from Around the World.* Her writing has also appeared in numerous publications, including *Forbes, Harper's, The New York Times, Slate,* and the *Wall Street Journal,* and she holds a master's degree in international affairs from Columbia University. Born and raised in Vancouver, she lives in New York City.

ACKNOWLEDGMENTS

For their support and wise advice, I'd like to thank: Ruthie Ackerman, Jim Benning at World Hum, Trevor Butterworth, David Farley and the regulars at the Restless Legs Reading Series, Betsy Lerner, Merrik Bush-Pirkle, Jessie Sholl, Melissa Silverstein, June Thomas at Slate, Brooke Warner, and Elizabeth Weinstein.